Barbara Fox is the daughter of Gwenda Gofton, with whom she also wrote the memoir *Bedpans and Bobby Socks*. She is the author of *Is the Vicar in, Pet?* and co-author with Emma Gray of *One Girl and Her Dogs*. She grew up in Ashington, Northumberland, and Newcastle upon Tyne and lives with her family in West Sussex.

Gwenda Gofton was born in Newcastle and has lived in the North East all her life apart from the wartime years she spent in the Lake District and four years as a nurse in London and the USA. She has four children and nine grandchildren. She is still a regular visitor to Bampton.

BY BARBARA FOX

Bedpans and Bobby Socks
Is the Vicar in, Pet?
When the War is Over

with Emma Gray
One Girl and Her Dogs

When the War Is Over

Far from home, far from family, safe from the war – a true story of two Second World War evacuees

BARBARA FOX
AND GWENDA GOFTON

sphere

SPHERE

First published in Great Britain in 2016 by Sphere

1 3 5 7 9 10 8 6 4 2

A CIP catalogue record for this book
is available from the British Library.

ISBN 978-0-7515-6139-5

Typeset in Bembo by M Rules
Printed and bound in Great Britain by
Clays Ltd, St Ives PLC

Papers used by Sphere are from well-managed forests
and other responsible sources.

MIX
Paper from
responsible sources
FSC
www.fsc.org   FSC® C104740

Sphere
An imprint of
Little, Brown Book Group
Carmelite House
50 Victoria Embankment
London EC4Y 0DY

An Hachette UK Company
www.hachette.co.uk

www.littlebrown.co.uk

To Sue Adamson and Sue Fox, a very special book group.
Also in memory of Campbell Gofton and all
the others who didn't come home.

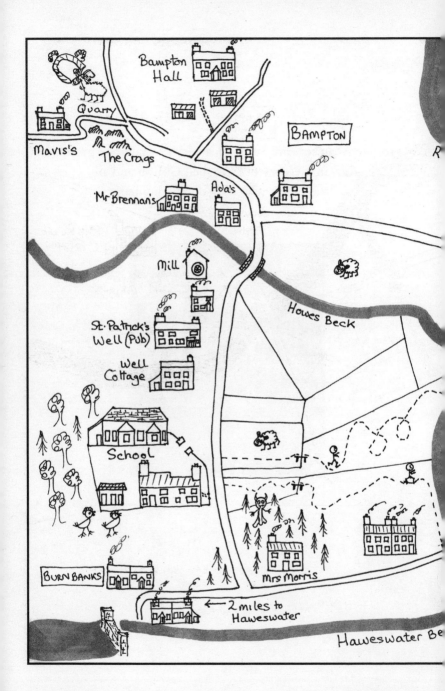

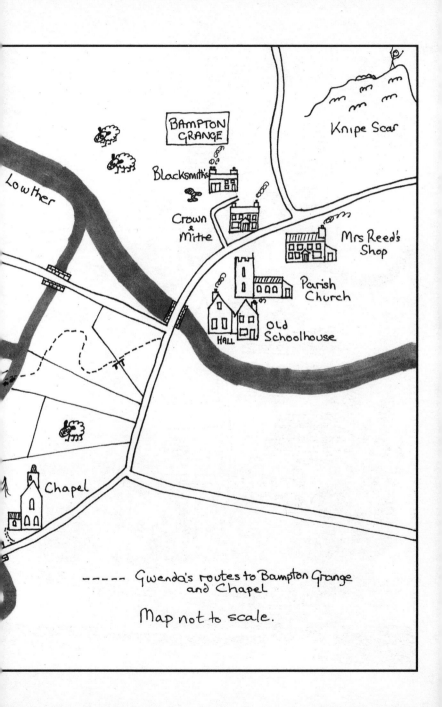

Lowther

BAMPTON GRANGE

Knipe Scar

Blacksmith's

Crown & Mitre

Mrs Reed's Shop

Parish Church

HALL

Old Schoolhouse

Chapel

----- Gwenda's routes to Bampton Grange and Chapel

Map not to scale.

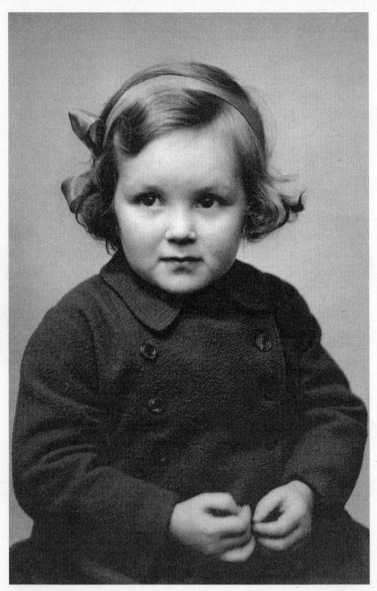

Gwenda, aged three

Chapter one

I can't remember when I first became aware of the war because it feels as if it was always there. I was born in 1933, six years before the Second World War began, and by the time I was old enough to half-understand adults' conversations it was already part of them. It was in the queue at the butcher's, it was on the wireless – which my parents always listened to in respectful silence – and it was what Mam and Dad's tennis crowd spoke about at tea after a match, not always bothering to check if my brother Douglas and I were listening.

I was five years old – very nearly six – when it finally started in September 1939 and Doug was about to turn nine. We lived in a semi-detached house in High Heaton in the east end of Newcastle. We knew everyone in our road and they all knew us. My best friend, Barbie, lived a few minutes' walk away and Nona and Marion were round the corner. My world was

the streets around us and the parks where we played. It was a
modern world, steeped in its past. At the top of the road ran an
old wagonway along which horse-drawn carts had once trans-
ported coal from a long defunct colliery down to the River
Tyne. From nearby streets, buses and trams took workers and
shoppers in and out of Newcastle, and if you walked a bit
further, you could catch a bus to Whitley Bay or Tynemouth.
The buses to the coast were always packed at weekends and
holidays, whatever the weather.

We rarely caught buses as a family because my father,
Arthur Brady, had a car, but he was one of the few. In fact, you
were more likely to see a horse and cart in our road than a car.
Milk, eggs, fish, tea – they were all delivered that way. Mam,
whose name was Gwendoline though she was always known
as Gwen, was particular about whom she bought what from,
but she was quick to shoo Doug out of the house with a bucket
and spade if one of the horses left a pile of muck outside. She
and Dad loved their neat suburban garden and Dad would
mix the muck with straw to make manure for the vegetables
and flowers. I was never far behind Doug in those days, so I
would follow him into the street, issuing instructions, while
he would tell me I could do it myself if I was such an expert.
I knew what trick he would play on me when he was finished as I skipped ahead of him down the garden path – stick
the bucket as close to my face as he dared without actually
rubbing my nose in the stuff. But, being Doug, he lulled me
into a false sense of security every time, stopping to tie up a
shoelace or pointing at something to divert my attention, and
every time I fell for it. And every time I shrieked and said
how disgusting it was. And every time Mam said, 'That'll be

your job when you're older, madam, so don't turn your nose up like that.'

I might have been a city girl but there were fields and farmland all around us. Sometimes, walking back from Jesmond Dene along Freeman Road, you might see the cows being herded at milking time, swishing their long tails and depositing far more disgusting-looking business than the horses ever did. Dad knew a lot of farmers through his job at the Cattle Market branch of Barclays Bank and sometimes took Doug and me when he went to visit them. I liked it best when I was allowed to play in the hay or bottlefeed baby lambs, rather than the endless hours we sat round kitchen tables where I soon got bored of the adults' conversation and slipped off to find a cat to stroke or another room to explore.

We played in the road – tying one end of our skipping rope round a lamp post when we didn't have two people to turn, chalking a wicket onto someone's wall for cricket – but I had another playground: Jesmond Dene. The steep-sided valley of the Ouseburn, a small river that flows into the Tyne, boasted crags and waterfalls and thick vegetation that made it hard to believe we were just yards from the main road. Adjoining it was my other paradise, a park called Paddy Freeman's, with a playground and a field and a lake where the old men sailed their boats and where Doug and I liked to skate in winter. Doug and I treated Paddy's – as everyone called it – and the Dene as if they were our own back garden; in fact, we spent so much time in them that we knew the park keepers by name and they knew us.

My favourite person in the Dene was a man called Mr Winter, but who everyone knew as 'the Birdman'. He was

Doug and
Gwenda with
their parents,
Arthur and
Gwen

neat and tidy and his shoes were polished, he had a wife and a home, so I'm not sure how or why he spent his days feeding the birds there; I'm not sure if anyone knew. But he was our friend and I couldn't remember a time when he hadn't been there. We would usually find him on one of the paths, standing with his arms stretched out in front of him, elbows bent and palms facing upwards, rather like a beggar might ask for money, but offering chopped nuts and pieces of cheese to the birds. They landed on him or clustered round his feet to feed. He had names for many of them.

One afternoon Barbie and I spent hours sitting on a bench watching him and trying to remember what the most frequent visitors were called, but we only ever got two or three of them right.

'How can you tell that's Fred and not Percy?' I asked him, frustrated by my lack of success.

'Ah,' he'd say, 'when you get to know them you see the differences. It's not just their appearance, it's their personality. They're like people, you see. We all have our little quirks, don't we?'

If we stood quietly beside him, the birds would land on us as well.

Some people were wary of the Birdman, but anyone who made the effort to talk to him ended up liking him. And he was interested in other people too, always asking Doug and me what we were up to or how our parents were keeping.

It's hard to believe that all these things that were so familiar to me would become so distant and feel strange and alien when I eventually came back to them.

*

We might have gone to Australia, and then I wonder how different our lives would have been! It sounds almost cruel today, but hundreds of British children were evacuated to countries of the Commonwealth during the Second World War. However, the only reason my mother considered it for Doug and me was because she had family there – her brother Walter, who had emigrated at the age of twenty-two and lived in a town called Port Pirie in the state of South Australia with his wife and children. I found out about her idea by accident. I wasn't supposed to be listening, but I was good at listening to things I wasn't supposed to hear and adults in those days often spoke as if children weren't there or were too young to understand. Sometimes my mother would lower her voice or look to see if I was paying attention before she began something not intended for my ears, but I knew to keep my head down in my book or to talk even louder to my dolls and pretend that the words of the grown-ups were washing over me. That way you got to know things but kept out of trouble.

That afternoon Mam was trying to engage Dad in conversation, which was never the easiest thing to do.

'They'd be safe with Walter,' she was saying.

My ears pricked up. Though I had never met Walter, letters were exchanged regularly and my grandmother spoke about her eldest son as if he had just popped down the road and would be back any second, which was probably what she was hoping.

'Hmmm,' said my father, who was more intent on reading his paper.

'Did you hear me, Arthur? If war does break out we could

send the children to Walter's. It's worth thinking about. They'd be safe there. We wouldn't need to worry about them.'

My father seemed to realise all of a sudden that this was a serious matter and lowered his newspaper.

'To Walter's? To Australia? It's a bit drastic, isn't it? We might never see them again!'

My mother tutted and shook her head, as if she had expected a response like that from him.

'Don't be daft. They'd be with family and not some stranger, like the Government is talking about. I'm not sure I like the idea of them going to any old so-and-so's.'

'That's true enough. But Australia! Strewth! Still, if you think it's the right thing to do . . . '

'Well, I'm just saying he's offered to have them.'

I ran to find Doug and blurted out that we were going to live with the cousins and aunt and uncle we had never met on the other side of the world. I thought it sounded like a great adventure and couldn't understand why the colour drained from his face – which always happened when he was upset – as he rushed to tell Mam and Dad he didn't want to go. Later I was told off for eavesdropping and the matter was never mentioned again.

My family had a nice life in those days and none of us wanted it to change. On Saturday mornings Mam went to meet Kitty, a longtime friend, for coffee in Newcastle. They had both been milliners and always looked very smart in their outfits with matching hats, gloves and handbags, but then so did most of the ladies you saw in town. Saturday evenings were spent with Kitty and her husband Jack at our house or theirs, and while our parents chatted or went to the pub, I played with their daughter Kathleen. In the bed we shared on those nights, I devised a game, tapping out a tune on the wooden bed-head and seeing if Kathleen could identify it. She was younger than me, and rarely guessed correctly. 'For goodness' sake, Kathleen,' I would exclaim. 'That was "God Save the King"! Don't you know it?' Sundays were reserved for solo whist with friends Nan and Arnold, another couple we saw a lot of. In the summer my parents played tennis at the club beside Paddy's or picnicked with the same crowd at Druridge Bay, a huge sandy beach a few miles north of the coal-mining town of Ashington.

Family was important, too. We regularly visited my maternal grandmother and aunt and uncle in Whitley Bay. Aunty Edith, Mam's sister, was the only person we knew who had a fridge as Uncle Eddie, a veteran of the First World War, worked in the gas company showroom. They had one child, my cousin Beryl, and we were good friends. My father had been the youngest of twelve children (his parents had died before I was born) so there were dozens of relatives on his side of the family though the only ones we saw regularly were Aunty Nell, the sister he was closest to in age, and her husband and daughter.

There was no television then, but the wireless and gramophone provided entertainment and Dad showed cartoons on his cinematograph for family get-togethers.

We weren't a wealthy family by any means, but somehow our finances stretched to having a maid. It wasn't that uncommon then for people like us to have one. I suppose today she would be called a live-in help or an au pair, as the word 'maid' suggests a rather grander set-up than our suburban semi. Our maid was called Ivy and it was her job to look after me and Doug; to keep us looking presentable, to feed us, to bath us and to keep us out of mischief. She wore a navy dress in the morning and changed in the afternoon to a fawn one with a pretty pinny. Ivy combed my hair and tied a ribbon in it that matched whatever I was wearing that day. These ribbons were washed and ironed and kept in a special tin. But, in spite of Ivy's efforts my hair would quickly become tatty and my ribbon lopsided, my clothes grubby, yet, somehow, Doug managed to remain as fresh and clean as when he had dressed that morning, his blond, silky hair always staying in place. I think Mam would have preferred it if I'd had the fair hair and Doug the unruly brown hair and the rosy cheeks that went with it.

I adored Ivy. She had the small bedroom at the top of the stairs and on her afternoons off she would lie on her bed and sing the latest popular songs to herself. She knew all the words as she used to buy the sheet music and read from it as she sang. I would slip into her room, though I wasn't supposed to, and lie beside her, watching and listening. If my mother had known I was there she would have told me to scram and leave Ivy in peace, but Ivy didn't mind. And I was careful not to make a nuisance of myself.

Ivy called me in to have my bath at six o'clock every evening. This was insisted on by my mother and thought highly unusual by my friends, who sometimes came to watch this ritual. One evening, when Barbie, Nona and Marion were squashed in the bathroom beside us, Marion picked up my ribbon tin from the shelf, took out the ribbons and threw them into the bath. I don't know who was more shocked by this act – me, the others, or even Marion herself, who looked surprised at her own daring. She stood there sheepishly as we watched the ribbons unfurling in the water.

'I can get them out,' she offered, looking at Ivy and me in turn.

Ivy didn't even raise her voice. 'I think it's time for you to go home, Marion,' was all she said.

And Marion ran.

Doug was three years older than me and I always wanted to do whatever he did. When he began to read, I wanted to read too. I watched enviously as he laid out his school books on the dining-room table to do his homework. I turned the pages, longing to enter the worlds they contained. Doug told me I was too young to read, but it wasn't long before I was pestering Ivy to teach me and, with her help and frequent trips to the library, I learnt to read long before I started school.

When Doug was learning to tie his shoelaces, I wanted to do the same. As he was struggling and getting tearful – and Mam was telling him that now he was a big boy he really ought to be able to do up his own – I was crying, 'I'll help, I'll help!' and getting ready to pounce.

But my mother raised her finger in warning. 'He has to do them himself. Don't meddle!'

I was too young that first time, but later I practised and practised – again with Ivy's help – and as soon as I had acquired my new skill I wanted to tie everyone's laces for them, whether they were wearing their shoes or not.

'Mam! Gwenda's done it again!' was a cry often heard from

Gwenda and Doug, aged two and five

Doug as he found his laces already tied when he went to put on his shoes.

I was the bane of his life, never more so than when I wet my knickers when he was looking after me and it was his job to deal with it.

I was overjoyed when I was finally old enough to join Doug at Cragside School, at the bottom of our road. Barbie was in the same class. When my teacher discovered that I could read already she sent me into one of the older classes to read the children a story. I felt extremely proud as I took my seat in front of them, clutching my book.

'This little girl can read better than a lot of you can and she's only five years old,' their teacher told them.

I could sense even then that this introduction was not going to endear me to these older pupils. The atmosphere in the room changed from curious to hostile. I realised at that moment that there might be times when it was best to keep my talents to myself.

But life as we knew it was ending and perhaps I had my first jolt of what was about to come the day I asked for the ice skates. Barbie had told me one afternoon at Paddy's that she was getting ice skates for Christmas so that we could skate properly when the pond froze again. It was the summer of 1939, Christmas was several months away, but with my birthday being in October I decided it was a good time to ask for a pair too. If there was a reason why Mam and Dad couldn't buy them for me as a birthday present, I could offer to be patient and wait until Christmas. If cost was a reason, I might even say they could be for both occasions. I waited until what I thought was a good time to ask – I was helping Mam as she wound a hank of wool into a ball and I hadn't complained once as I stood there, the wool looped around my outstretched arms.

'Mam, can I have a pair of ice skates for my birthday, please?'

I thought she might take some time to reply. I expected some 'Hmmm's and 'We'll have to see's and talk about my behaviour, but to my surprise she answered immediately, as if she had been waiting for the question.

'When the war is over,' she said briskly, continuing with her task.

The war? I may have been only five years old but I knew that the war hadn't even started yet. When I had got over my indignation, I spluttered that fact in reply.

Mam was unmoved. 'It's going to happen sooner or later and we're all going to have to make do with less, like it or not.' She took the wool from me. 'Thank you. Now go and comb your hair and get ready for tea, you scallywag. You look a fright.'

I knew there was nothing more to be said on the matter. I stomped away, furious with the war, or not-war, and with all those people on the wireless for talking about it all the time. I couldn't see what it had to do with ice skates, either. I hoped that it would start quickly so that we could get it over with. Then perhaps I would get the skates for Christmas after all.

Chapter two

I knew what the war meant – it meant that nasty Germans would try to kill us with bombs or gas and so we were going to have to leave our homes and go to live in the country where they wouldn't be able to find us. In the months leading up to our evacuation on the first day of September 1939, two days before Britain declared war on Germany, we had regular practices for air raids and gas attacks at school; a teacher would blow a whistle and we would see how quickly we could file out to the shelters in the playground, trying not to seem too pleased about missing some of our lessons whenever these drills took place. We had all been issued with a gas mask, which came in a cardboard box with a strap for carrying it (Aunty Nell, who liked the nice things in life, bought a leather case for hers), and we practised wearing them. The rubbery smell and tightness on my face made me feel sick as well as claustrophobic, but I was prepared to love this ugly thing that I was convinced was going to save my life. It even sat on the corner of my bed, though my mother insisted it stay in its box in case it gave me nightmares.

We now had our own Anderson shelter at home, shared with our next-door neighbours Mr and Mrs Young, in whose garden it was situated. Doug and I often sat inside it, breathing in its cool earthy smell and longing for the day we could use it for real because – despite the fear – war was somehow exciting too.

Australia had been forgotten and my parents had agreed that Doug and I should be evacuated with our school. Newcastle – with its busy river lined with shipyards and armaments factories – was considered to be at high risk of aerial attacks and its proximity to the city made High Heaton one of the priority areas for evacuation. Not all parents were choosing to send their children away but, looking back on it now, I can see that my parents were doing what they felt was in the best interests of me and Doug rather than what they truly wanted for themselves. So Doug and I prepared to relocate with Cragside School to Morpeth, about fifteen miles north of Newcastle. To my disappointment, Barbie wasn't coming – she was going to stay with an aunt and uncle in Ponteland, just a few miles outside the city – and nor were Marion and Nona as they attended different schools. But I was still looking forward to going.

Doug – who was almost nine – didn't seem to share my enthusiasm. He was a sensitive boy, though not always as angelic in his behaviour as his looks suggested. He would turn so white if he thought he was about to be smacked for a

misdemeanour that my parents often relented and spared him
the punishment. I wasn't quite so lucky. As the departure day
drew nearer and I chattered away about what we might get
up to in our new home, Doug had little to say on the subject.
I found it hard to understand, though of course I can see now
that it was me whose reaction was unusual: our home life was
settled and contented; we weren't spoilt – my parents had quite
strict Victorian values inherited from their own parents – but
we wanted for nothing; we went on days out and had a holiday
every summer; we received small though carefully chosen gifts
at birthdays and Christmas. Why would my brother wish this
way of life to come to an end?

There were to be two big departures: Friday 1 September
for all unaccompanied children and the following day for
mothers with very young infants, pregnant women and other
vulnerable people. As I had Doug, three years my senior, to
look after me, there was never any question of my not being
old enough to go without my mother and, besides, Mam was
keen to volunteer for the war effort herself and certainly not
keen to live in the house of a stranger.

My mother and Ivy went through the check list and packed
everything we would need in two small rucksacks. We weren't
allowed to take very much but my mother, who made most of
my clothes, packed a new dress she had made me from some
material Aunty Kitty had given her.

The night before our departure, Ivy scrubbed me more
vigorously than I had been scrubbed in my life.

'Ivy, you're hurting me!' I cried out.

But she carried on. 'You don't want your reception family
to think that city children are all dirty, do you? Mind you

don't forget behind your ears and the back of your neck when you're away.'

As she helped to dry me she kept trying to catch my eye. She looked more serious than usual. It didn't occur to me that our lives together were coming to an end. I smiled at her and she gave a funny little shake of her head that I didn't understand and planted a kiss on top of my head before I went to tell Doug it was his turn. She was just a teenager herself, though she seemed so grown up to me.

The next morning Dad said goodbye to us before he caught the bus to work. He would be home for his dinner at midday – which would be waiting for him on the table as he had to catch the bus back to the Cattle Market half an hour later – but we would be gone before he returned today. He kissed us both and ruffled our hair and told us we were going to have a lovely time away from the city and that he wished he was coming with us. I thought his eyes looked damp when he turned round in the street to give us a last wave, but decided it must be my imagination as I didn't think fathers ever cried.

The sun was shining and it still felt like summer. It really did look like a perfect day for a trip to the countryside. The morning dragged by. Doug was sitting quietly in the bedroom and didn't want to play and Mam told me to get away from under her feet. I ended up in the garden looking for worms until Ivy hauled me inside and told me it wasn't a day to go getting dirty. She gave us an early lunch. Everyone seemed quieter than usual, Mam and Ivy talking in strange clipped sentences. I was surprised that no one else appeared to share my excitement. The butterflies I had woken up with in my

Doug and Gwenda with Ivy

stomach had grown in number and were now flapping their wings trying to get out.

As soon as we had finished lunch my mother and Ivy walked with us to school from where buses were taking us to the station. Doug and I had our gas masks round our necks and a label saying who we were pinned to our coats. No one could part me from my gas mask. I knew that nothing bad could ever happen to me as long as I had it with me.

I had been skipping ahead of the others in my hurry to get there so I was shocked at the scene that greeted us in the playground. Women were weeping openly as they said goodbye to their children, some of whom were also crying. I wondered if the mothers were upset because they wanted to go to Morpeth too. Others just looked sad or serious. One of the teachers ticked off our names on a clipboard and told us which bus to board. Mam told me to stay with Doug, whatever happened, and marched us to the open-backed double-decker. As we said goodbye, Ivy began to sob and Mam was talking more quickly than she usually did and telling us to be good, and to wash the backs of our necks, and to always be polite, and to get on the bus quickly so that we could sit together. I couldn't see how we would ever get on the bus when she wouldn't stop talking and was relieved when she gave us both a final kiss and we could board.

Doug let me sit beside the window and I watched, not properly understanding, as Mam and Ivy wiped their eyes and blew their noses. I waved and they waved back, but less enthusiastically. I wondered what Ivy was going to do now without me and Doug to look after and could have kicked myself for not asking her that before. I was about to ask Doug if he knew

but just then the engine was switched on and a teacher who
wasn't coming with us went to shoo a couple of mothers off
the rear platform so that we could leave. As the bus began to
pull away, Ivy left my mother's side and walked along beside
it, waving with one hand and holding her hanky to her mouth
with the other until the bus was travelling too quickly and we
left her behind.

I was puzzled. We were going away to stay safe and to have
fun – that's what all the adults had been telling us –so why
were so many people upset? I put that question to Doug. He
was wearing his pale face, apart from a blotchy red patch in the
centre of each cheek. He shook his head in reply and hugged
his gas mask to himself, refusing to speak to me for the rest
of the journey.

It is hard to believe it now! I had never spent a night away
from my parents before and didn't even like playing in my
friends' houses; whenever I went to Barbie's I would ask if 'the
big girls' – her older sisters – were at home before I would go
inside, and her mother had grown used to leaving the front
door open for me so that I could make a quick getaway if I
wanted to. Yet here I was, happily leaving everything I knew
behind me.

It felt like a long walk from Morpeth station into town, but at
least it was downhill. A warm breeze blew on our faces. We
were wearing our heaviest clothes and the strap on my gas mask
was rubbing a patch at the side of my neck. I kept hoisting it
round, but it always fell back to the same position. A red Morris
Eight tootled past us and the driver waved out of the window
and shouted, 'Welcome to Morpeth!' I was hot and tired and

barely had the enthusiasm to wave back. We arrived at a large hall in the town centre where lots of people were waiting. A woman with a loud voice and a list in her hand was telling everyone what to do, the adults as well as the children. Not everyone looked happy about it. Another woman, who spoke more softly, was being kept just as busy rushing between us all, smoothing things over. We were told to stand on one side of the hall while the waiting adults stood on the other. Then the bossy lady called out the name of a local family and the name of a Cragside child or children, and the two parties stepped forward to meet each other. I don't think that everyone liked what they saw, but most of them departed together without protest. Doug and I were quickly assigned to an elderly couple, whose names we couldn't catch, who drove us back, very sedately, to a house on an estate hidden behind a pub.

In the tiny hallway the man took off his hat and hung it with his gas mask on a peg. He was a slight man, with thinning hair that he kept running his hand over, as if to check it was still there. His wife was taller and what Mam would have called 'big boned', with a long face.

'You're in the front bedroom,' she said to me and Doug, as if we had been there before, 'but you can put your coats on the right-hand peg before you go up.'

I let Doug lead the way upstairs. Our room felt stuffy and had an unpleasant smell, like eggs but with a hint of a woman's perfume. Doug opened the window. We sat on the edge of our beds, not knowing what to do. Being evacuated didn't seem quite so appealing now.

'Shall we unpack?' I asked Doug. He still looked pale, though the red blotches had gone.

'I suppose so.'

As I started to remove the items from my rucksack, I remembered my concern of earlier.

'Doug, what's Ivy going to do now?'

'She's going to be a nurse, didn't you know?'

I brightened at the thought. I liked the idea of Ivy in a nurse's uniform. Sometimes we had played hospitals together, though she had usually been the patient and invented injuries or illnesses for me to deal with. I hoped she would still let me be the nurse when we next played.

'Oh! I wish she could have come too, though.'

Doug grunted in reply.

'What sort of things do children eat?' the lady had asked us on the short ride home. We thought it was a peculiar question as in our house children and adults ate the same things, but without giving us time to reply she had answered it herself. 'I suppose you must like tomatoes. My husband grows them on his allotment and they're the best tomatoes in the whole town. Probably in the whole of Northumberland.'

She looked at him as she said this. It sounded more like an accusation than a boast. He just kept his eyes on the road and didn't react.

Tea was a plate full of fried tomatoes sitting in puddles of grease, with bread and butter on the side. I was almost hungry enough to eat anything, but as I bit into them, the overriding taste was the fat they had been cooked in. I had never been aware before of how much eating there was to do on a tomato – skin, then flesh, then seeds, each part taking forever to chew and swallow. I struggled to keep going. I thought

I was going to be eating that plateful all night. Doug was watching me. It was hard to know what he was thinking. I thought he might be struggling too but as if he knew what I was thinking he began to eat more vigorously.

The couple didn't sit down with us. The man had gone out and his wife was smoking a cigarette and talking to a neighbour on the doorstep. When I felt I couldn't eat another mouthful I put down my knife and fork neatly in the centre of my plate. I was starting to feel queasy. At home I would have had to eat everything, but at home I rarely had a problem in doing so.

'Good job my husband's not here,' said the woman when she came back into the kitchen. 'He lavishes more care on them tomatoes than he does on anything. Not your cup of tea, then?'

She took my plate away. I had eaten about three quarters of my helping but felt as guilty as if I had barely touched them. I wanted to tell her that I liked tomatoes really, I just wasn't used to having a whole meal of them, but speaking felt like too much of an effort. I gave a timid nod that I hoped conveyed both that I was sorry and that the tomatoes had actually been very nice. I hoped she wouldn't tell her husband, or Mam and Dad. We had only just got here and I was already letting everyone down.

An hour later, playing in the back yard, my stomach tightened and I felt the colour drain from my face. I looked desperately at Doug and sicked up a tomatoey mess all over the paving slabs.

The couple were kind enough, but unsure what to do with us. After that episode they sent us to play in the streets instead.

We ran wild all weekend, only returning for meals, staying out until late and enjoying the lack of supervision. On the Sunday morning, as we were making our way back for dinner, we noticed lots of people talking over their garden walls. Doug knew instantly what had happened. 'It's the war,' he said. 'It's started.' And sure enough, when we got inside the lady said to us, 'Mr Chamberlain's been on the wireless. We're at war with Germany. Now go and wash your hands.'

When Monday came we assembled in a local hall. Although I had agreed with Doug that it would be great if we could spend the rest of the war as freely as we had done those previous two days, I secretly felt pleased at the prospect of seeing my friends and starting lessons again. The hall was packed and teachers were attempting to split us into classes and to work out how we could all be accommodated. But when my name was ticked off, instead of going to join the others of my age I was whisked into what looked like a storage room. Our headmistress, Miss Nattress, was in there, piling up boxes to make some room for herself, and Doug was standing against the wall, looking worried.

'Ah, there you are, Gwenda.' Miss Nattress straightened up and brushed the dust from her hands. 'I'm afraid I've had some disturbing news.'

I felt those butterflies again, but this time they came from anxiety. Doug looked as if he was about to cry.

Her expression softened. 'No, no, don't worry. You've done nothing wrong, neither of you, but we're going to have to move you.'

She told us that one of the teachers would take us back to the house where we had been staying and that we must collect all of our things. I didn't dare look at Doug. I knew that this was my fault and I hoped that he wouldn't be too angry with me. It must have been because of the tomatoes, though the lady had been quite nice about it and had helped me to get changed into clean clothes, even admiring my new dress and telling me that I must have a very clever mother if she could sew like that. I was relieved when I discovered that the reason had nothing to do with me. A friend of our father had seen us on Saturday night playing outside at eleven o'clock and had felt it his duty to inform him. Dad had been furious. He had spoken to the billeting officer that morning and threatened to come and take us home there and then, but had been promised that another, more suitable family, would be found.

'And you're very lucky that we've found one for you,' said Miss Nattress. 'Some of Saturday's arrivals are sleeping in the ballroom of the hotel waiting for somewhere to go. There are poor women there with babies. But your new host only wants school-age children. I'm told she's very respectable and that your parents will be quite happy.'

A woman answered the door in a maid's uniform – a proper uniform with a starched cap and frilly blouse, far more formal than the outfit Ivy had worn – and showed us to our room. Though the house didn't appear particularly big from the outside, inside the space seemed to run away ahead of us, disappearing along corridors lined with closed doors, and up staircases. I don't think I ever went into more than three or four rooms in all the time we were there.

Our new hosts were called Mr and Mrs Appleton. We learnt from Freda, the maid, that Mr Appleton was an affluent man in Morpeth and ran his own business, but we would see very little of him and his wife. Freda told us that if we wanted to stay on the right side of the Appletons we mustn't make a noise. 'It's better,' she said, 'that they forget you are here.' I looked at Doug in alarm. I knew that some adults preferred children to be seen and not heard, but not to be seen either seemed like quite a tall order. Freda asked us what our routine was at home and to Doug's disgust I told her about our daily bath.

'Idiot,' he said later. 'She wouldn't have known any better if we'd said we had a bath once a week.'

At six o'clock on the dot Freda called me into the bathroom, where the water was already run. She helped me to wash, then popped out to call Doug as I was drying myself. A few minutes later Doug appeared, carefully got undressed, then stepped very quickly into the bath wearing his swimming costume. I was surprised, but knew better than to say anything.

Freda glanced across at him as she helped me to put on my nightdress.

'Do you always wear that for your bath?' she asked. She might have been suppressing a smile, but it was hard to tell.

Doug nodded, but turned a little pink. He hated telling lies.

After that Freda left us to bath alone.

It was impossible for everyone to be taught in the hall at the same time, so lessons took place either in the morning or the afternoon, according to a rota. The rest of the time we played with our friends in the woods close to the house. We had to be home at five o'clock, when Freda would serve us tea in a small dark room containing only a table and two chairs. Sometimes Mrs Appleton would appear from the parlour – her name for one of the fancy rooms we were not allowed to enter – to ask us if we had had a pleasant day. One day she had been playing cards with a group of ladies and brought them to have a look at us. They asked us questions about school and where we lived before we came to Morpeth, and I heard one of them say on the way out, 'They do look clean and they're very polite. I think you've been very lucky, Enid.'

Mam wrote to us every few days. 'Are you remembering to wash your hair and behind your neck and ears?' she reminded us in one letter. Realising we'd forgotten all about our hair, Doug helped me to wash mine using an enamel jug he could barely lift.

'Ow! Ivy never does it like this,' I protested, as he scrubbed my scalp vigorously with the tips of his fingers.

'Mam'll kill me if you get nits,' said Doug. He used my flannel to rub the suds from the shampoo into the back of my neck and behind my ears. I yelped again.

'Shhh,' he warned me and started tickling me instead. Once I started laughing I couldn't stop. Doug laughed as well and looked the happiest I had seen him since our arrival.

One day I fell over and hurt my knee when we were playing and was sobbing to myself as the two of us walked back for tea.

'I want to go home,' I wailed to Doug. 'Not this home, but Mam and Dad home. I want to see Ivy again.'

Doug stopped walking and turned to face me. 'Remember what the adults say,' he told me sternly. 'If you don't cry for home then our parents won't worry about us and our soldiers will fight better and win the war quicker.' He handed me his handkerchief. 'Wipe your eyes quickly and don't let Freda see you like this.'

*

Our stay in Morpeth was an adventure, but it would not be a long one. We played in the woods with both our Cragside friends and local children, some of whom my mother would have forbidden us from having anything to do with if she had seen them. Two of our new playmates were the evacuees from a few doors away, wild, skinny brothers whose clothes had holes in them and who seemed unable to stay still. Even their eyes were constantly darting around in their heads.

I overheard the maid from their house talking to Freda in the front garden one day.

'I don't know what their mother was playing at, but neither of them has a suitable coat or decent shoes or boots. What does she think they're going to do when the winter comes? Mrs Ridley says it's not her job to buy them new clothes as well, but I can hardly send them out in the cold with what they've got on now, can I? In fact I doubt their clothes will even last that long!'

'You do wonder at some folk,' said Freda. 'You need to go and see Mr Slassor in the town hall. He'll be able to help you. Mind, count yourself lucky, my mother's friend in the next street has got a lady and two little ones staying and the lady just sits there expecting to be waited on. She's had to tell her she's not running a hotel.'

One night, a few weeks into our stay, I woke up feeling hot and feverish. Freda noticed that I wasn't my usual self the next morning, but not wanting to stay in the house by myself without Doug, I insisted I was well enough for school. That night I noticed some spots on my tummy and arms when I was having my bath. I felt a bit better the next day, but there were more spots, including some on my face. When Freda caught me scratching myself she had a proper look at me and gasped. She told me I had chickenpox and that I couldn't go to school like that. Later that day Mrs Appleton came to inspect me, shaking her head and exchanging looks with Freda. I heard the two of them talking in low voices on the landing.

The next morning Freda came into the bedroom at the usual time. As she opened the curtains and lifted the blind she announced that our father was coming to collect us. She said it matter of factly, but when she turned round she shrugged and looked a little sad. I think she had grown fond of us in her own way. This time there was no doubt that our departure was due to me. I wondered what Doug would think and was relieved to see that as soon as Freda had left the room he waved his arms in the air and gave a silent cheer. I was glad to have done something right for once.

Chapter three

'Well, trust you,' said Mam as she opened the front door, though she squeezed us both so hard I had to wriggle to get free. As soon as I had taken off my coat she was lifting my skirt and pulling up my blouse to look for my spots.

'You're a sight for sore eyes, madam.'

'I'm so itchy,' I said. 'Even my head's itchy.'

'Didn't they put anything on those spots?' Mam tutted. 'You'd think they'd have heard of calamine lotion in Morpeth.'

A few minutes later I was sitting on the edge of the bath, enjoying the feeling of the cool lotion being smoothed onto my face, limbs and tummy.

'Have there been lots of bombs?' asked Doug, as he watched the operation from the doorway.

'Have you used the shelter?' I asked, before Mam had time to answer Doug. 'Can we sleep in it tonight?'

I glanced at Doug. We had planned what we would take into the shelter with us – books and board games and sticks of liquorice – and imagined what fun it would be to spend a whole night inside it.

'Please!' we both said in unison.

'Nothing's happened, and no you can't. You'd hardly know there's a war on,' said Mam. 'All that fuss getting you ready. Tschh! Still, better safe than sorry. But it wouldn't surprise me if the rest of your school came back any day now. In fact I hope they do because I don't know where you two are going to go.'

Dad had told us in the car on the way home that he had a job as an air-raid warden. He still went to work in the bank every morning, but three nights a week, after having his tea, he put on his uniform and metal helmet and set off on his duties. (My father was one of the world's most law-abiding men, so this job must have suited him perfectly. As an old man, his greatest fear was that he would die before he had settled up his milk and paper bills.) Up until now his job had consisted mainly of patrolling the streets, checking that everyone was adhering to the blackout regulations and carrying their gas masks wherever they went. He told us that he had had to have words with one couple whose blinds flapped and let out slivers of light when their windows were open. 'You just need one person to be careless,' he said, leaving the implication hanging. He added that in the event of an air raid he would be responsible for getting people to safety, sealing off dangerous areas, maybe even rescuing anyone who was trapped if he was on the scene before the emergency services. Doug said he wanted to go out with him on patrol, and I said that if Doug did then I was going too, but Dad made it quite clear that neither of us were doing any such thing.

Our bedroom looked clean and undisturbed. My dolls Neville Chamberlain Brady – who had been patriotically christened by Doug – and the more prosaically named Patricia and Brian, were sitting on my bed. Neville was a large china doll with moveable arms and legs, while Patricia and Brian were small and had cloth bodies and rubber limbs. Ivy always sat them up like that, resting against my pillow, and the thought of Ivy sent me rushing into her bedroom. The room was bare apart from the furniture. The little pots and bottles on her dressing table that she sometimes allowed me to sniff or dab my finger into, the cardigan that was usually on the back of the chair, the music sheets and women's magazines on the bookshelf – all of them had gone. Even the bed was stripped and the counterpane folded up at the bottom of it.

'Mam! Mam! Where's Ivy's stuff?'

My mother followed me in and surveyed the room, looking for just a second as if she was wondering the same thing herself. 'Well, she's gone to train as a nurse. You didn't think she would come running back just because you're home again, did you?'

In truth I didn't know what I had thought, except that Ivy would still be living with us, whatever she was doing. I bit my lip and tried not to cry.

Mam said more kindly, 'I'm sure she'll come back to see us and let us know how she's getting on. Now, come on, I'm making mince and dumplings for dinner. I bet you didn't have that in Morpeth. Are you coming to help?'

As if finally able to succumb to my illness, I spent the rest of that day and much of the next in bed. Odd words of people's conversations drifted up the stairs and slipped into my dreams. Once, I heard Mam's voice just a few feet away saying, 'Douglas even had to wash Gwenda's hair, would you believe it!' followed by the sound of sympathetic tutting, and I opened my eyes for just long enough to see Mam and Mrs Young from next door tiptoeing out of the room. I slept again and dreamt that Doug and I were running from the house in Morpeth into a bomb shelter, but the person at the entrance wouldn't let us inside because of my spots.

On the third day I was desperate to get up. When I suggested to Doug that we play a board game he jumped at the chance, which was a pleasant surprise as I usually had to beg him to play with me. He was finding it quiet with none of his friends around and he still had no school to go to. On top of that there was no Ivy, who had always had time for us both, and my father was hardly ever at home. Mam remarked that the war might not be such a bad thing if it meant we played so nicely together.

There was, however, one special person who I felt sure would be in his usual place. As soon as I was deemed no longer infectious, Doug and I wandered through Paddy Freeman's and into Jesmond Dene to find the Birdman. I started to run when I saw him but Doug grabbed my hand and held me back. I stopped in my tracks, hardly daring to breathe. The birds were coming out of the trees and flying towards him. Dozens of them. The bravest ones landing on his arms, one perching on his head, the others scrapping at his feet for the seeds that he had scattered there.

'Haway, Bobby. I've got a nice bit of cheese for you. That's it, don't snatch ... Hello, young'un, you've not been here before, have you? No need to be scared. Now now, Georgie, there's plenty for you all.'

He saw us watching and indicated that we should come over. Most of the birds flew away as we approached, but one little robin stayed on his shoulder, tipped its head to one side and looked at us as if it was waiting to hear what we had to say.

'Are you having a go?' asked the Birdman, as if he had just seen us yesterday. Then he added, 'I didn't expect you back so soon. How was Morpeth?'

'It was all right. We could do what we wanted. But Gwenda got chickenpox.'

'I've still got some spots,' I said, pointing to my face. 'And I sicked up my tomatoes.'

'Mr Winter doesn't want to know about that,' scolded Doug. 'Look, you've scared the robin away now.'

I folded my arms, wondering why it was always my fault.

'Oh, he'll be back,' said the Birdman. He gave me a quizzical look. 'It's not like you to be ill, is it? I hope they were looking after you properly.'

He turned his gaze to Doug, who shrugged. 'Well, I'm pleased to see you both. It's quiet without all you kiddies around.'

By keeping very still and copying the Birdman, some of the birds began to return and land on us as well.

'That's Bernie on your hand, Doug. You've done well to get him. He normally takes his time getting to know people.'

Doug beamed. (Years later – to prove his superiority in these matters – he would read from the diary he kept occasionally as a child: 'I had fifteen birds land on me today, but Gwenda only had eleven.')

'Now, how are your mam and dad?' asked the Birdman. 'And what about Ivy? You'll tell them I'm asking after them, won't you?'

We told him that we would, but in truth we didn't always pass on his greetings. Though she was polite whenever she saw him, Mam didn't share our fondness for our friend and had vetoed my request to invite him for tea. On the way home Doug brushed a feather from the back of my coat and told me to remember to wash my hands as soon as we got in.

I returned from Morpeth a bed-wetter and I would remain so intermittently for the next few years. I am not sure if anyone made the connection at the time between that and the upheaval I had gone through – I was certainly happy enough on the surface.

Mam found schools for us both in Jesmond on the other side of the Dene. Doug was going to Jesmond Towers, a prep school for boys, and I was going to the convent of La Sagesse, the Catholic school which my friend Marion attended. I had to wear a uniform which included a big velour hat. I tried it on in front of the mirror in Mam and Dad's bedroom. I quite liked myself in it, even though I couldn't stop it from falling down over my eyes.

The day began in the school hall, where we sat in silence, waiting for something to happen. I had never seen a nun before, nor did I know what they were or what they did, apart from some brief details imparted by my mother – to whom they were probably just as mysterious – so the sight of Mother Superior when I saw her for the first time was terrifying. She arrived like an apparition from the Middle Ages in her

habit and wimple – clothes that appeared to have swallowed
her and looked as if they might do the same to us. Just the
smallest oval of her face was visible, reminding us that there
was indeed a person inside those ghostly garments, but I don't
think I ever truly thought of her as human. A heavy silver
cross hung round her neck. When she reached her place at the
lectern we all rose. '*Bonjour, bonne mère,*' we chanted. It was
a few weeks before I understood what everyone was saying
and dared do more than mouth an approximation of it. She
replied in French. '*Bonjour, mes filles. Asseyez-vous.*' To which
we answered, '*Je m'assieds,*' and sat down again. After a Bible
story and some prayers we filed into our classrooms. Our
teachers were all nuns and I soon learnt that they had fiery
dispositions and that it was best to sit quietly, do as I was told
and try not to be noticed.

I walked to and from school with Marion and a girl called
Monique, who had a French mother, Doug keeping a decent
distance behind us. Monique laughingly corrected my mis-
heard words. One of the park keepers would meet us at the
entrance to the Dene in the morning and escort us through – it
was slightly sinister at that early hour, not the family haven that
it was in the daytime. At the other end it was just a short walk
to the school along a road busy with traffic and pedestrians.

In October I had my sixth birthday and there were no ice
skates. I had thought that maybe, just maybe, because the war
didn't seem to be a proper war, I might receive them after all,
but I could see straight away that the parcel that was handed
to me did not contain skates and did my best to hide my
disappointment.

Two days after my birthday, as we were having our

afternoon lessons, we heard the up-and-down wail of the siren. We grabbed our gas masks and filed into the shelter, nervous and excited. We listened for planes and bombs, expecting at any moment to hear explosions, but it remained eerily silent, as if we were the only people left in the world. The sisters kept us entertained and amused by organising games and singing songs, displaying a more human side than we were used to seeing. After an hour and a half we received the all-clear. I could hardly wait to tell Mam and Dad about my first air-raid warning and ran all the way home.

As Christmas approached the nuns taught us carols in French. '*Il est né, le divin enfant*,' I warbled to Mam in my sweetest singing voice, rocking the imaginary baby Jesus in my arms and making her go all misty-eyed. I had to make up the words I'd forgotten but as neither of us understood what I was singing anyway, it didn't matter.

We made our parents a card in which we thanked them for looking after us. I was proud of the tree I had drawn, with an angel sitting at the top. Sister Madeleine wrote our greetings for us and signed them in her beautiful italic script. Mine read, 'From your loving Wenda'. I was still terrified of the nuns and didn't dare tell Sister that my name was wrong, but one of my friends cried out, 'She's called Gwenda, not Wenda!' Sister Madeleine paid no attention. Mam gave me a queer look when she read it but laughed when I told her what had happened.

Christmas Day arrived and Grandma, Aunty Edith, Uncle Eddie and Beryl all came to us, as was our usual custom. My favourite present was my Venus pencil case from Santa Claus, a wooden green box with special compartments for the crayons and different grades of pencil. I spent a long time just taking

Gwenda and Doug at the beach with their mother (left), and friends Nan and Arnold

everything out of the box, rearranging it all, and putting everything back in again.

In the new year rationing of bacon, butter and sugar began, though other foodstuffs were also getting scarce.

'We'll know where to go if we ever run out of anything,' said my mother to my father one evening after tea as she carried a shovelful of hot coals from the kitchen fire to the hearth in what she always called the drawing room, where they liked to sit. That day she had discovered the shelves in her local greengrocer's empty of fruit and later witnessed two women in the grocer's shop fighting over the last tin of peaches. We all knew that she was talking about one of Dad's sisters, who had recently announced that she was buying bars of soap by the dozen as they would soon be in short supply. Mam had retorted that if everyone did that then there were bound to be shortages but my aunt had just shrugged and said that it was every man or woman for themselves from now on.

Petrol had been rationed since the start of the war, which meant the end of the excursions Doug and I had enjoyed with Dad. We had both inherited his love of cars and used to urge him to go faster when we were out together. He even let me drive the car sometimes on a quiet lane close to where we lived; I would sit on his lap and hold the wheel, following his instructions to keep the mascot lined up with the white line in the middle of the road. But now Dad saved his petrol allowance for essential journeys and the odd run out to the coast or country as a treat.

January of 1940 was one of the coldest and snowiest in living memory, causing havoc to transport and industry. Even the sea froze in some places. I could hardly wait for school to end each day so that I could go sledging at Paddy Freeman's. I had so much fun slipping and sliding on the frozen lake in my shoes that I almost forgot about the ice skates I might have had if it wasn't for the war. I wasn't even sure if the war was still going on. Grown-ups were calling it the 'Phoney War' as nothing much seemed to be happening in Western Europe. Some people had stopped taking their gas masks with them when they went out, even though it could deny them entry to cinemas and cafes as well as earn them a reprimand from the warden. Others were moaning about the rationing and wondering why we all had to suffer. Evacuees were coming home to their families. One day in the early spring-time my school came back from Morpeth and I could return to Cragside, and one Saturday morning Barbie and Nona appeared with Marion on the doorstep, grinning and asking if I was coming out to play.

But as spring turned into summer it all began to change. One of the boys at school regaled us with a gory tale about a German soldier being washed up on the beach in Whitley Bay, and though Mam told me not to repeat it, she didn't deny that it had happened. A little while later the same boy told us that an enemy aircraft had been shot down in Cresswell Bay, not far from the beach my parents had so often frequented with the tennis crowd. It felt as if the war was getting closer. One day a barrage balloon – great whales in the sky that gave me the creeps whenever I saw them – broke loose from its tethers and damaged some houses when it crash landed.

But by far the worst thing to happen was the cancellation of the Hoppings, part of Newcastle's Race Week festivities. That trip to the fair on the Town Moor was an annual treat for the whole family. Dad would have a go at rifle shooting – he was a good shot – and Mam, taking after her own mother, liked the boxing and the wrestling. Doug and I were given pennies to spend on the hoopla, but I was just as happy eating candyfloss and watching the showmen calling everyone to their rides. It was a big, glorious, colourful festival – and probably a raucous one after dark – and to be told that we wouldn't be going this year was a bitter blow. Doug asked Dad why we weren't allowed to have fun any more and Dad tried to explain that no one was trying to stop anyone's fun, but that many of the showmen had gone away to fight, and then there were all the practical restrictions on hosting the fair to think about, like the blackout.

Mam and Dad listened to the news as intently as ever. When Germany invaded the Low Countries in May, the Phoney War was over. On the same day, Mr Chamberlain resigned and the King appointed Winston Churchill as our new prime minister. Mam and Dad seemed to think this was a good thing. Hitler had now conquered most of Europe but he hadn't counted on Mr Churchill, who asked us all to stand up to Hitler so that all of Europe could be free.

After one news broadcast, I absent-mindedly began to sing 'London's Burning' as I skipped around the kitchen with my dolls.

'You wicked girl,' said Mam. 'I don't want to hear you sing that ever again.'

I was so surprised by her reaction that after a defiant stare I started singing it again, thinking she might start to see the joke. This time she sent me to my room until I could behave myself. As I sat, seething, on my bed, I told Neville, Brian and Patricia that I hoped I would be evacuated again soon, a very long way away, with some nice people who could be my new mother and father.

Memories of those who stayed:
'Cheers on the Tyne for HMS *Kelly*'

I was a fifteen-year-old schoolboy, living at the seafront in Cullercoats near the mouth of the River Tyne. On Monday 13 May 1940, I noticed a trio of warships approaching the river very slowly. I got on my bicycle and cycled to North Shields, to the bottom of Howard Street, where there was a vantage point looking down at the river and the Fish Quay. I arrived in time to see three destroyers proceeding very sedately up the river. Two of them seemed undamaged but the third was almost sinking, with a severe list to starboard. As they went past me I heard the faint sound of cheers coming from men working on the banks of the Tyne at the Fish Quay, the ferry landing and in the shipyards.

I learnt subsequently that the destroyer was HMS *Kelly*, commanded by Lord Louis Mountbatten. She had been torpedoed off the coast of Norway and managed to limp back across the North Sea.

Lord Mountbatten wrote of the incident later:

' . . . when this perilous journey began, my Navigator asked me where we should make for – and without a second's hesitation I replied: Hebburn. I knew the ship's birthplace was where she should return . . . '

HMS *Kelly* went back to the shipyards of Hawthorn Leslie, where she was repaired and returned to service in October. In May 1941 she was sunk in the Mediterranean, with the loss of one hundred and thirty men. These men are commemorated, along with the twenty-seven seamen who perished in May 1940, in Hebburn Cemetery.

David Cawthorne, Newcastle, May 2015, aged ninety

David is the husband of Gwenda's friend Barbie, one of the characters in the book.

Chapter four

In July 1940 we were evacuated again. I was six and Doug was nine. This time the danger felt more real. A few days before our departure, just after 5.30 pm, in broad daylight, the first bombs fell in Newcastle. I'm sure the windows trembled as Doug and I sat finishing our tea at the dining-room table. One of the bombs hit the Spillers flour mill on the Tyne, another on the engineering works of Hawthorn Leslie and two more landed in the river nearby. Half an hour later three high explosive bombs, aimed at the shipyards in Jarrow, landed in a residential area and caused many casualties.

In truth, I don't think it occurred to us to be worried. Strange though it may sound, to my six-year-old mind there was something exciting about a bomb dropping and we had our Anderson shelter and gas masks to keep us safe. We even had our own secret weapon right behind our house – a searchlight station that sent its huge shafts of light into the sky. Doug told me it would scare any German planes well away from High Heaton and I believed him. I told Mam my thoughts and she agreed with me; luckily I didn't understand what she meant when I heard her say to Aunty Edith that we were 'a sitting target'.

When she had learnt that the oldest children from Cragside School were going to the village of Bampton and the younger ones to Tebay, both in the county of Westmorland, Mam had insisted that Doug and I should not be separated and that I should go to Bampton with my brother. Miss Dixon, the teacher who was to accompany the Bampton evacuees, promised she would do her best to see that we were housed together, though explained that she might have little influence over matters once we were there.

Dad looked on the map to see where Bampton was, and said, 'Strewth! You really are in the country this time.' He knew the area from his days as a young man when he got his thrills driving his motorbike up and down the mountain roads of Northumberland and the Lake District. 'There's a nice pub there, I seem to remember,' he added. 'I had a very welcome pint there one day.'

Mam put us in our smart red blazers on the day of our departure so that we would be able to spot each other at Newcastle Central Station as I was going by bus and Doug's class was walking. Parents had been asked to say goodbye to their children at school as the station was going to be very busy. If I felt a little more anxiety this time, I don't really remember. I kissed Mam and quickly got onto the bus before she could start talking about washing necks and behind ears.

Gwen and Arthur Brady on their wedding day, 1929

I gave her a wave before sitting down beside a friend. I didn't know then that I would never go to school with any of these children again.

The bus pulled up in front of the station. As I stood in the aisle, waiting to file off, I felt someone tug my blazer. I looked down to see Philip Orde, a pleasant boy whom I sometimes played with.

'Gwenda,' he said quietly from his seat. 'Gwenda, can I ask you something?'

I nodded, and he indicated that I should move in closer so that he could speak without being overheard. But before Philip had chance to say anything I heard the teacher calling my name. 'Gwenda Brady, don't dilly dally. You're holding everyone up.'

A gap had opened up between me and the child in front and I could only smile at Philip apologetically and hurry along down the bus. We lined up on the pavement where a teacher ticked off our names and checked that we were all still wearing the labels which gave our name, age and the name of our school. When this was done Philip sidled up to me.

'Gwenda,' he said again, and this time there was an urgency in his words. He looked as if he might cry. Then he hissed in my ear, 'Gwenda, will you marry me when the war is over in case they try to make me marry someone I don't know?'

At six years old, I hadn't given much thought to marriage other than that I might like to marry a farmer one day. I wondered briefly who these people were who were going to make Philip marry against his will. Surely that wouldn't happen. But he looked so sad and sincere that I could only nod my head fiercely.

'Oh, thank you, Gwenda,' he said, brightening immediately.

We filed into the grand station entrance to wait while one of the teachers went inside to find out which platform our train was leaving from. It was colder in here than it was outside, with a vigorous breeze blowing through the arches. A wave of sound rolled out of the cathedral-like interior – of noisy children, teachers trying to keep order, guards and railway staff shouting instructions. A group of young soldiers walked quickly past us, bags over their shoulders, talking and laughing as they went, as if they were on their way to a party and not to war.

I couldn't see how I was going to find Doug. Mam had made it sound easy: 'Just look for each other's blazers.' But I could hear how busy the station was and I was frightened to leave my own party, who at least were catching the same train as me, even if we had different final destinations. If I went inside and got lost, I might end up being evacuated with the wrong people, with strangers! I put a hand on my gas mask to reassure myself of its presence and another on one of my rucksack straps. My rucksack contained little more than a couple of changes of clothes, my sponge bag, a comic for the journey and a packed lunch. Mam had given us a banana each, something we wouldn't see again until the end of the war. Despite my protestations, she hadn't let me take any of my dolls but said that maybe, if I was good, she and Dad would bring them one day when they came to visit.

I heard a steam engine shrieking as it came into the station. One of the boys in my class was shouting, 'I bet that's our train! I wonder how many carriages it's got.' And one of the girls was saying to her friend, 'Haven't you been on a train before? I thought everyone had.'

I began to worry that I might never see Doug again. When the teacher looked my way I cautiously put up my hand. 'I need to find my brother. I'm going to Bampton with him.'

The teacher frowned, as if suddenly foreseeing that I might cause her some problems, but before she could say anything in reply the teacher who had gone to check on our platform came back and she was pointing and smiling at something over our heads. I turned round to see a group of children marching towards us, flushed and breathless from their long walk, Miss Dixon leading the way. At the front of them was a boy from Doug's class and a few places behind him I saw that shock of almost-white hair and a flash of red.

'We were singing on the way,' said Doug, as I took his hand and held it tightly, surprised that he didn't protest. 'And people were waving to us. It was like being a soldier. I hope this war lasts until I'm old enough to join up.'

On the train we were ordered to sit on our bags or cases and to keep our gas masks round our necks. It wasn't very comfortable sitting on my rucksack. I kept moving it around so that the hard parts didn't poke me. Several children ran to the train window as we crossed the River Tyne, eager to see if there was any evidence of the recent bombings, but a teacher ordered them back to their seats. We chugged along slowly. The land rose steeply on the left of the train where I was sitting and I wondered what it must be like to live in the terraced houses that tumbled down the hill and if their floors sloped down to the valley too. When I looked out the other side, all I could see were factories and warehouses and occasional glimpses of the shiny grey river. After a while the view became more rural. Seeing it made me feel more contented. And I was with Doug, so everything would be all right. Mam had packed us enough food to last all day and, realising how hungry I was, I retrieved my sandwiches – now rather squashed – from my rucksack. Doug looked at his watch, then did the same. I wondered how Philip was, and thought about telling Doug what he had said to me, but decided to wait. If I told him now he might laugh about it with his friends who were sitting near us.

Later that afternoon we arrived in Penrith from where a fleet of buses took us to our destinations. With the warm sun coming through the window, I closed my eyes. It felt like only a few minutes later that we had stopped and everyone was getting out of their seats. We were outside a small stone-built hall, where a group of ladies – important-looking with their clipboards – were waiting for us. As we entered the building, a few people who were sitting inside looked up with interest. Some of them whispered to each other and pointed. There was a mixture of men and women and a lot of the men looked like farmers.

'Come along, up to the front where everyone can see you all,' said one of the ladies, who appeared to be in charge.

There weren't enough seats for us all and I sat on the floor. Even though we had been sitting down for most of the day, my legs felt tired. I kept my gas mask round my neck but took off my rucksack and hugged it to me. Two ladies offered us all a cold drink and a biscuit and one of them told us not to look so worried.

'We're going to find some nice homes for you all,' she said. 'You don't know how lucky you are coming here.'

Another one said something in agreement, but in such a strong accent I only caught a couple of words.

More people began to arrive and soon the hall was packed. It was hot and noisy and I longed to be outside. When we had finished our drinks the lady in charge asked us to stand up and face everyone, the tallest ones at the back. I grabbed Doug's hand and held it tightly. Once again, he didn't try to shake me off like he sometimes did, in fact it felt as if he was gripping my hand just as firmly.

'A'll 'ave that big strong lad,' cried a hefty, red-faced man, pointing at Doug. He had a large prominent tooth that rested on his lower lip when he wasn't talking. I wished someone else had picked him. I knew this man might be very nice but it would be hard not to stare at that tooth all the time. I gripped Doug's hand even tighter and looked up at him to see if he was going to tell the man that I had to come too. But Doug was showing no reaction and that's when I realised that the man had pointed at the tall, well-built boy standing behind us, who looked three years older than his nine years.

Just then another man cried out, 'Hey, no one said we'd started yet. I might want 'im too!'

The lady in charge glared at both the men. 'We shall do this properly. These are children, not animals.'

The man with the tooth looked embarrassed, but the other one just folded his arms and muttered something under his breath.

I had been to an auction with Dad at the Cattle Market and what happened next was similar to one, despite the good intentions of the lady in charge. The tall, strong-looking boys and girls were chosen first, just like the healthiest cattle were. Nobody seemed interested in Doug and me. Doug was a gangly boy, much taller than I was but skinny, and that pale hair gave him a delicate look that belied the fact he was as healthy as the next lad. As for me, I was the smallest and youngest child there and not on anyone's shopping list.

I did hope, though, that a farmer might choose us. Ivy and I had borrowed *Rebecca of Sunnybrook Farm* from the library and she had read it to me before I was able to read it myself. I wanted to belong to a Sunnybrook Farm as well and looked on wistfully at the girls who were trooping off to become Rebeccas instead of me.

Twenty minutes later there were only four of us left.

A lady who reminded me of my grandmother was staring at me and I beamed at her. She said something to her husband but he shook his head. 'We didn't come here for a little one,' I heard him say. The lady smiled at me weakly before looking quickly away.

'And the lad doesn't look as if he could lift a shovelful of shit,' her husband added. They settled on the two other children who remained.

Miss Dixon gave our arms a quick squeeze. 'Now don't you worry, everything will turn out just fine.'

I hadn't felt worried before, but began to feel anxious.

'I'll be happy to take the boy – and another boy if there is one,' said a lady who had just arrived, coming up to the front of the hall to stand beside us. She gave me an apologetic smile accompanied by a small shrug. I had dropped Doug's hand but took it again now.

'Oh hello, Mrs Thornton. I'm afraid there are only these two left now,' said the lady in charge, adding, as Miss Dixon said something in her ear, 'They're a brother and sister, Douglas and Gwenda Brady, and it's their mother's wish that they stay together.'

The lady nodded her head at this information but didn't say anything. I thought she had a kind face. I hoped she might smile at me again but she was looking at Doug, a slightly curious, amused look, as if she knew something about him already.

'So no more boys?' she said after a long silence.

'As you can see, Mrs Thornton, I've just got this pair left.'

The hall was almost empty now. A few people were talking by the door and comparing notes on the children they had chosen. One of the clipboard ladies was sweeping the floor and pretending to sweep one of the men out of the door with her broom. The man doffed his cap at her then did the same thing in our direction before he headed off with his young evacuee, steering him outside with a friendly hand on his shoulder.

The lady in charge sighed. 'Mrs Thornton, might you consider taking them both? I know you wanted . . . ' She tailed off and looked down at her list in despair.

Mrs Thornton appeared to be thinking. 'I just don't know anything about girls,' she said finally, in a voice that sounded as kind as her face. 'With having two boys of my own, you see.'

Miss Dixon asked if she might speak to her in confidence and the two women moved out of earshot. The kind-faced lady looked once or twice at me and Doug as Miss Dixon was talking to her. I kept smiling back at her until my smile felt frozen and I had to let it go, but Doug looked at his shoes and seemed disheartened by the whole process.

Finally the lady nodded and smiled, a slightly worried smile. 'Oh, look at you both! I can hardly leave you here, can I? I don't know what my husband will say but we'll just have to win him over, all three of us!'

A few minutes later we followed Mrs Thornton out into the late afternoon sunshine.

Chapter five

We were in a tiny village in the heart of the country. It smelt of the country for a start – that smell of grass and things growing, and that animal smell that could be unpleasant when you came across it in the city but that felt as if it belonged in the air here. The sounds were different from the sounds at home – the most persistent being the baaing of sheep, birdsong and the surprisingly loud droning of insects from the hedgerows. Whichever way we looked there were fields and hills.

Mrs Thornton said it was just a short walk home, but insisted on carrying my rucksack as she said I looked tired out. We headed out of the village, leaving behind an old church, next door to the hall, and a road lined with cottages, and came to a bridge. I leaned over the edge and looked at the wide river. It was running quite quickly but looked shallow enough at the edges to be able to paddle in and fish for tiddlers or sticklebacks, like we sometimes did on days out with Mam and Dad. I glanced at Mrs Thornton. She was smiling to herself, as if she couldn't quite believe what she had done.

A man met us in the middle of the bridge with his sheepdog.

'Mrs Thornton, I must be seeing things! I could swear you wanted boys.'

'They're a brother and sister and want to stay together,' she replied, as if that was all the explaining that was necessary. 'Now, can you guess the boy's name?'

The man looked at Doug. 'Now, how am I meant to do that?' His dog sniffed Doug's legs and Doug was glad to have an excuse to bend down and pat it. 'There's not much meat on him so perhaps he's Slim Jim,' he offered, winking at me.

Mrs Thornton laughed. 'Would you believe it, he's called Douglas!'

'Well, I never. Mr Thornton will be tickled pink at that,' said the man. He wished us well and carried on.

At the other side of the bridge we turned right along a country lane, but Mrs Thornton stopped us for a moment and pointed straight ahead. 'That's our chapel,' she said. Doug and I saw a building standing by itself in the middle of the fields, about half a mile away, but neither of us could think of anything to say in reply.

I was too short to see over the dry-stone walls into the fields that bordered the lane, but on the right rose a steep hill, cut through with layers of rock. When we came to a raised ledge that ran alongside the path, it felt as if it had been made for me to walk on so that I could have a better view.

From my vantage point I couldn't see any houses in the direction we were headed. The afternoon sun seemed to hold the whole valley in a shimmering ball. I wondered where we were going and how long it was going to take to get there. I cheered up when I finally saw other buildings ahead, but then Mrs Thornton pointed to a house across the fields to our left, which appeared to be miles away, telling us that that was our destination, and my heart sank.

'We're now in Bampton. The place we were in before was Bampton Grange,' she explained as we arrived in the new village.

A lady coming towards us with a face as round as a teacake stopped and put her hands on her hips. 'Mrs Thornton, I can't believe my eyes! Did you not say to me just the other day in chapel that you wanted boys and that you knew nothing about little girls? And look at that little thing beside you! She can't be older than five or six.'

Mrs Thornton looked at me thoughtfully. 'Hmm,' she said. Then she added more brightly, 'But we were both girls once, Mrs Heatherside. There can't be too much to learn.'

'Oh my, that was a long time ago! But I suppose you and Mr Thornton are used to having children around, Mr Thornton in particular.'

Mrs Thornton said that was true, then asked the lady to guess Doug's name. I wondered why she didn't ask her to guess my name as well, though I knew mine was probably too difficult to guess as people sometimes remarked that it was unusual.

The lady said Doug might be called George, after the king, and as she was talking another lady came along and joined in the game, after first complimenting Doug on his beautiful blond hair. I started to feel that I must be invisible.

After both ladies had agreed that the name Douglas meant

that my brother and the Thorntons were made for each other, we said goodbye to them and walked across another bridge, under which a narrower river ran. We passed more houses and a pub, and then we were leaving the village behind and the house that Mrs Thornton had pointed out earlier was nowhere in sight. My legs ached and I was too hot in my blazer. I wondered how many miles we had walked and if we would ever arrive.

As if reading my thoughts, Mrs Thornton said, 'Nearly there now! Look, that's the school!'

Now I saw that there was indeed a large building cradled in the woodland ahead, though I was more interested in seeing our new home. But to my surprise, when we reached it Mrs Thornton opened the gate and led the way up a path to the front door.

'Here we are, home at last!' she said cheerily, and added with a laugh, 'At least you'll never be late for school.'

I glanced at Doug. I didn't want to live in a school and I wondered if he did. He looked worried too.

We entered via a large porch which was crammed with fishing rods, walking sticks and several pairs of boots. That, at least, felt like part of a normal house. A door led from there into a long corridor. Mrs Thornton gave an exaggerated sigh. 'Ahh! Let's leave our bags here and have a cup of tea. You must be exhausted, you poor things.'

I was even glad to slip off my gas mask, which had started to rub on my neck again.

A door on the left led to the kitchen, a large square room with a flagstone floor. There was a dresser to the left of the door and a wooden table in the middle of the room, surrounded by several chairs. At the far end was a big range and an open fire.

'Sit yourselves down,' said the lady, pulling out two of the chairs. She fetched me a cushion. 'It's a while since I've had anyone as little as you in here. How old did you say you were?'

She went through a door to another room where I heard her fill the kettle, then came back and put it on a trivet that swung out over the fire. I almost forgot my tiredness and felt a growing eagerness to start exploring.

Doug and I looked at each other across the table. It wasn't home, but there was something homelike about this room and though we both felt a little nervous, we were happier than we had been at any point since our departure. There was a rocking chair on either side of the range, one of which had a pile of knitting on it, while a table in front of one of the windows was covered in books and papers and all sorts of other interesting-looking bits and pieces. The lady hummed to herself as she made the tea and stirred something in a large pot.

'My husband will be here in a minute. He's the headmaster, you see, so he's going to be very busy getting ready for all you new arrivals. School's next door.' She pointed behind us. 'But I think you're having a day off tomorrow.'

The headmaster! That was worrying. And I remembered that this man might not even want us here – or at least, might not want me. After all, the lady had said that she wanted two boys. I hoped that her husband wouldn't be angry with her for bringing me back. I didn't want to be sent away. I liked this nice lady.

Mrs Thornton continued to chatter. 'You'll have to tell me

more about yourselves. And about your parents. You must get a letter off to them tomorrow to tell them that you've arrived safely. They'll be quite worried about you. You're such little things to be away from them! I can't imagine parting from my boys when they were that age.'

'Where are your boys?' asked Doug, and she told us that they were older than us and that neither of them were at home.

'Hugh is in the RAF now and John is at boarding school. I do miss them both. But you'll see John soon – it's nearly time for the summer holidays. How old are you, Douglas? I think John is probably just a couple of years older than you. Oh, what fun you're all going to have together!'

I could see that Doug's interest had been piqued by the mention of the RAF, but before he had the chance to ask any more questions we heard footsteps in the corridor and a man entered. The man was smaller than his wife and almost bald. He wore funny trousers that stopped at his knees and a tweed jacket. For a few seconds he seemed to stare at us and we at him and nobody spoke. During those seconds, which felt much longer, his expression turned from stern to surprised and finally to friendly.

'Well, well, well, so what have we got here?' he asked, though I don't think he expected us to answer. He shook our hands vigorously.

'This is my husband, Mr Thornton,' his wife told us. 'They're a brother and sister, and just wait till you hear what their names are!'

We both looked at him and then each other, unsure who was supposed to speak next.

'Well, you do have tongues, don't you?' he said briskly.

'I'm Gwenda,' I said, hoping that my name might be special after all.

'Gwenda,' he repeated, and he appeared to be mulling it over as if he might have a story to tell about a Gwenda, but then he just nodded and looked at Doug.

'And I'm Douglas,' said Doug, slightly cautiously after the fuss of earlier.

Mrs Thornton beamed. 'Isn't that a coincidence? They were the only two left when I got there, but the boy has got your name. I think they must have been meant for us.'

'Well fancy that!' Mr Thornton smiled at us, then at his wife. 'You've done well there, Eveline. Is Douglas your father's name as well?'

'He's called Arthur,' I said. 'And our mam is called Gwendoline.'

'Their teacher told me their father is a bank manager,' said Mrs Thornton, putting the teapot on the table. She looked at us both when she said, 'They're from a good family.'

I had a feeling Mam would be pleased to hear her say that. I sat up straighter, as someone from a good family should.

Mr and Mrs Thornton sat down beside us and asked us questions about Newcastle and our parents. Though sometimes Mr Thornton looked serious – and it was easy to see that he was a headmaster – he had twinkly eyes and he made us both laugh by producing a coin out of his ear. After a while Mrs Thornton said she would show us to our room, but Mr Thornton held up his hand to stop her and said, 'Before we do anything else, we need to think what you children are going to call us. They can hardly call us Mr and Mrs Thornton all the time, can they, Eveline? I'll think I'm in the classroom if they do.'

'What do you think, children?' asked his wife. 'What would you like to call us?'

Before Doug had a chance to say anything, I piped up, 'I want to call you Aunty and Uncle.'

Mr and Mrs Thornton looked at each other and Mr Thornton nodded at his wife. 'Well, Aunty and Uncle it shall be,' he said. Then he got up quickly and told his wife that he had a man coming to see him soon who needed some help with a letter he was writing and that he would be in his study. She said we would have tea a little later, when the caller had gone and Doug and I were settled.

Our bedroom looked out from the left-hand side of the house onto the garden and part of the wood. It had two single beds, each with a bedside table, a wardrobe, a chest of drawers and a large bookcase which I was drawn to immediately. Disappointingly, most of the books were for boys or they were serious-looking tomes by Charles Dickens or the legends of someone called Prester John. I hoped there were some girls' books somewhere in the house. I had asked Mam if she could send me my favourite comic, *Enid Blyton's Sunny Stories*, from time to time, but she told me that it wasn't being produced during the war, and nor were *Beano* or *Knockout*, Doug's favourites.

I didn't need to ask Doug what he thought of our hosts because I could tell he liked them. He didn't have the pale worried look he had worn on our arrival in Morpeth almost a year ago.

I stuck my head out of the window and thought I could hear hens clucking not very far away and nice Mrs Thornton singing in the kitchen directly below us.

'Doug, why does—' I paused, and tried out the word, slightly self-consciously, 'Uncle ... why does Uncle wear funny trousers?'

'They're called plus-fours,' said Doug.

'But why does he wear them?' I began to unpack my few belongings and lay them out on my bed. I wanted to see how they looked in their new home.

'Some men do,' he replied, and I would have asked him more but had noticed a strong smell coming from my rucksack and something sticky on my fingers. The banana my mother had packed for my lunch had split and oozed out over my bag and some of its contents.

'Why didn't you eat it?' scolded Doug when he saw the mess.

'I forgot. It's the teacher's fault. She made us sit on our bags, remember.'

'You'll have to clean it out. It stinks.'

I sniffed cautiously. 'It's a nice smell.'

'Not when it's been cooking all day under your bottom.'

I giggled. Just then Mrs Thornton called out to us that she was going to feed the hens and did we want to help her. I left the rucksack to deal with another time as we both ran to join her.

We sat at the kitchen table and watched as Aunty ladled soup into our bowls.

'And who is going to say grace tonight?' asked Uncle, when we were all served.

I caught Doug's eye across the table. We had never said grace at home, though I was familiar with the ritual from the months when I had attended La Sagesse.

Douglas and Eveline Thornton outside the schoolhouse

Neither of us spoke. Uncle looked at us both in turn. He had a look on his face that I expected he might use at school, a firm look that required an answer. 'Do you know how to say grace?' he asked.

Doug shook his head, then opened his mouth as if to change his mind, but Uncle had started speaking again.

'Well, it's the way we do things here. We always thank the Lord for what he gives us.'

'I can say grace,' I said suddenly. It had been a while ago, but I was sure that as soon as I said the first line I would remember the rest. Uncle nodded his approval and he and Aunty bowed their heads. Doug quickly did the same.

'*Béni soit le Seigneur pour le moment de ce repas,*' I began. '*Pour la joie d'être ensemble à partager le même pain. Rendons grâce à Dieu.*'

I stumbled once, and I knew my pronunciation wasn't good, but we had said it so many times when I was a pupil at the convent that it was almost as familiar and easy to recall as an old nursery rhyme.

Nobody spoke. Nobody said 'amen'. Aunty and Uncle were looking at each other across the table. I think Aunty's lips twitched slightly, but she seemed to be taking her cue from her husband.

'Amen,' I said loudly, in case they didn't know it was finished.

'Amen!' said Aunty, quite loudly too. 'Gracious, Gwenda, was that French?'

'And where did you learn it?' Uncle asked, picking up his spoon. It was hard to tell from his voice what he thought of my effort.

'At school, well not my normal school but one I went to when my school was away in Morpeth. It had nuns.'

'It was a convent,' said Doug.

'Are you a Catholic family?' Aunty asked, looking at Doug for an answer.

Doug shook his head. 'No. I don't think so.' Then he said more firmly, 'No, we're Church of England.'

Uncle smiled. 'I am glad you are from a Christian family. We are Methodists. Do you know what that means?' He didn't wait for an answer. 'We like to share the good news as we go about our daily lives.'

In truth, my parents – while they would certainly have classed themselves as Christians – were not keen on any outward signs of religion, finding it offputting and even embarrassing.

'Oh, Douglas, there's plenty of time for that,' said Aunty to her husband. 'Start your soup before it gets cold. Gwenda, you might need to blow on it first. Sorry, dear, as I've told you, I'm not used to little ones any more.'

'Yes, Eveline, but it's important they understand,' said Uncle. 'We may not do things the way they're used to, but if they are living here they will need to learn to do things our way.'

This man seemed to change from the twinkly-eyed one we had seen earlier to a rather forbidding one very quickly. I decided to stay quiet. I still wasn't sure if I had done anything wrong.

Doug asked them about their sons and Aunty was happy to chatter about them both. 'Of course we worry about Hugh, being in the RAF, just as we worry about all our young men who have gone to war. We can only pray that the Lord will take care of them all.'

'It's not to us to question His ways, Eveline,' said Uncle. Then, sounding slightly less serious, he asked us both if we were enjoying our soup and told us we were lucky to be here as Aunty was an excellent cook.

To finish there was junket. As I had the last spoonfuls I saw a little speck at the bottom of my bowl which on closer examination turned out to be part of the pattern. Then another appeared, and another. I think there were five of them, like seeds, painted onto the otherwise plain white china. There was something satisfying about revealing them. I felt as if I had eaten up everything properly.

I looked to see if Doug had them too, but his bowl was plain.

Aunty was watching me. 'What is it, Gwenda?'

'I've got spots,' I said, pointing.

'Someone hasn't eaten all her junket,' said Uncle, but his eyes were twinkling again. 'Look, my dish is clean and so is your brother's.'

'They're on the dish,' I said. I prodded them with my spoon to prove it.

'Don't tease her,' said Aunty. 'Well, you were the lucky one today, Gwenda. That's my magic dish and I didn't know where it had got to.'

'Why is it magic?' I asked.

'Ah, that's for you to find out,' said Uncle.

Doug yawned and I found myself doing the same.

'I think some people are ready for their beds,' said Uncle. 'Aunty will run a bath for you and I'll bid you goodnight and see you both tomorrow.'

After our bath Aunty came into the bedroom and found us both already in bed.

'Have you said your prayers?' she asked.

We had to admit that we hadn't.

'Perhaps tonight you can say them in bed,' she said, but Doug was already clambering out of his so I thought it best to do the same. We knelt at the side of them.

'What shall we say?' I asked, looking at Doug.

Aunty answered for him. 'That's up to you, but you should pray for the people you care about, especially anyone who might be in danger. And it's very important that you pray for your parents while you're here.'

Doug cleared his voice then began. 'Dear God, please bless Mam and Dad and keep them alive until the war is over.'

For the next three years we would begin our prayers the same way every night. I always finished with an extra silent one of my own: 'And please, God, don't let me wet the bed.'

Chapter six

I woke up once in the night, remembering I was somewhere new from the feel and smell of the bedclothes and something different about the air in the room. With the blackout curtains at the window I wasn't sure if it was morning yet, but after dozing again I woke to the sound of the hens and a door closing somewhere in the house. A little later still Aunty was tapping on the bedroom door, wondering if we were going to sleep all day and telling us that if we got up soon we could feed the hens with her and collect eggs for breakfast.

The hens lived in a paddock at the side of the house and had access to the small wood behind it. I was surprised to find myself a little nervous of these creatures – they were bigger and bolder than the birds we fed in the Dene and their little beaks looked mean and snappy. I thought there would be a dish to put the food into but Aunty told us to scatter the grain so that the hens had to scratch around for it in the dirt. She said it would make their beaks stronger and the shells of the eggs firmer. I didn't like the way one of the hens kept being chased away from the food by the bossiest one so I made sure that I gave her a special helping of her own.

We found warm brown eggs in the henhouse and put them in the basket. Then Aunty went looking for one of the hens who she told us was probably hiding in the wood, wanting to hatch her eggs into baby chickens. My face must have lit up at the thought of chickens as Aunty said straight away that there would be no eggs for breakfast if we allowed her to do that.

Doug and I spent the morning exploring. As well as the paddock and wood there was a garden with vegetables, fruit bushes and flowers, a garage where Uncle kept his car and motorbike, and some sheds and other outbuildings. The school was attached to the schoolhouse and could be accessed from the interior as well as the outside, and there was also a separate wooden building behind it in the right-hand corner of the plot. Uncle had already told me that I would be attending lessons in this annexe with the younger pupils. There was a playground between the two buildings, and when we realised that it was ours to play in whenever we wanted, it began to dawn on us that living in a schoolhouse might be quite a good thing after all.

Beyond the wood and on either side of the house, and over the road and as far as the eye could see, there were fields and farmland. Bampton Grange, the village we had come from yesterday, was straight across the fields, and we could see the chapel that Aunty had pointed out to us further down the lane through yet more fields. As we weren't sure if we were allowed to leave the schoolhouse grounds we decided to look round the house next. It was big compared to our home in Newcastle, but it was clear that most things took place in the kitchen, where Aunty was busy cooking what she called a 'mash' for the hens. The sitting room had a still, formal look about it, as if it was used only for special occasions, while the dining room was also Uncle's study and full of books and papers that had been tidied into piles. Upstairs we discovered a small bedroom above the front door that must have belonged to one of the Thornton boys, another that might have been for guests, and Aunty and Uncle's, though we only peeped very quickly round the door.

Back in the kitchen I saw my rucksack on the draining board through the open scullery door and remembered guiltily how I had left it in my room without saying anything. Aunty caught me looking.

'I think I'll be smelling bananas all day long,' she said, shaking her head and pretending to be cross. 'I've had to wash some of your clothes. How on earth did you manage to make such a mess?'

'The teachers made us sit on our bags,' said Doug protectively.

'Did they really? Well, what a waste, and when bananas are getting so scarce in the shops. I don't think I've seen one for a few weeks, but perhaps it's different in Newcastle.'

Just then Uncle came into the kitchen and Aunty told us it was time to wash our hands for dinner, so the subject of bananas was dropped. Uncle said grace and Aunty served up rabbit pie and new potatoes.

'I do hope all the evacuees are settling in well,' said Aunty, as we ate. 'It's a big change for them, being away from home for the first time.'

'We were evacuated before, as well,' said Doug, and we told Aunty and Uncle about our time in Morpeth. When Aunty heard about my chickenpox she said, 'Oh you poor little thing,' and Uncle said that they couldn't have been good Christian people to send me home because of a few spots, then he winked and asked me if I had counted them all.

After dinner we looked round Bampton. We were surprised to see that it was so small we had walked through most of it on our way to the schoolhouse from the church hall the day before.

'That must be the pub Dad told us about,' said Doug as we passed the St Patrick's Well Inn, and the thought of our father turning up there on his motorbike made us both smile.

There was a mill beside the stream and just over the hump-back bridge a young woman was cleaning the windows of a house which was also the post office. She must have seen us reflected in the glass as she turned round suddenly. She was slim with dark hair that was set in neat waves around her head.

'You must be Douglas and Gwenda!' she said with a wide smile. 'Billy's told me about you, but I don't think you've met him yet. Mr Preston, the teacher? He's been with Mr Thornton this morning. It's a busy time for them. I'm his wife, but you can call me Ada if you like. My mother is a friend of Mrs Thornton so you'll probably meet her soon as well.' Then she added, 'Sorry, so many new names for you!'

A woman went into the post office so Ada excused herself and said she hoped she would see us again soon. We heard the voices of children close by and saw that two boys were playing inside the mill wheel. We watched them as they started walking and made the wheel turn slowly round until a man came out of the mill house and chased them away.

A road led out of the village up a steep slope that was covered in rocks and boulders. Doug saw one of his school friends, a boy called Peter, sitting on one of the rocks and we went to join him.

'What's it like where you are?' Peter asked us.

Doug shrugged. 'It's OK.'

'It's the school,' I said.

'The school? You poor buggers! I thought I had it bad.'

'It's nice,' I said, looking at Doug for affirmation.

Instead he said, 'At least the Germans will never find us here.'

'Pfff. I wish they would. It might liven things up,' said Peter.

He picked at a scab on his knee. 'I've got to go to the lavvy outside. And there's no bath. No bathroom! I'm not staying here. I'm going to write to me mam and tell her I'm coming home. She didn't want me to come anyway.'

'But what about the bombs?' asked Doug.

'I'm not scared of bombs. Mam always said she'd rather we all died together, anyhow. I'll probably die of the plague or something if I stay here.'

'We're not scared of bombs either,' I said.

Doug asked where he was living and Peter pointed up the hill and said he was staying in a cottage 'bloody miles away' and that the elderly couple he was living with wanted him to chop some wood for them later. 'They said it'll be nice to have some *young blood* around, but if they think I'm their slave they've got another think coming.' Then he stood up suddenly and said he had to get back for his tea. 'At least the food is good. We had meat for dinner. Loads of it as well!'

When he had gone, Doug and I were silent for a while.

'I think we were lucky being picked at the end,' Doug said at last, almost reluctantly.

'Yeah, lucky no one wanted a skinny boy with no muscles!'

'You mean lucky no one wanted a girl who wets her knickers all the time.'

'I don't any more.'

'Well, just make sure you don't start again.'

'I bet you can't jump onto that rock in one go,' I said, standing up and leaping for the next boulder. I managed to crash into the side of it instead and banged my knee.

'Ow!' I sat down on the grass and rubbed it. 'That really hurt.'

'You're not going to cry, are you?'

'Of course not.' But I did wish that Aunty was here so that she could see how brave I was being. 'I like Aunty,' I said, as I got up to try again. 'She's going to teach me to knit.'

'Uncle's going to take me fishing,' said Doug, standing victoriously on the boulder after his jump.

'When did he say that?'

'When you weren't there.'

'Can I come too?'

'I doubt it. You'll be too busy knitting. Come on, I'll give you a head start. Last one back to the schoolhouse is a squashed banana.'

When we got back we went straight upstairs to get washed and to comb our hair before tea. Doug helped me to re-tie my ribbon.

Aunty looked at us as we entered the kitchen.

'I tried to do Gwenda's hair,' said Doug, misinterpreting her expression. 'But I'm not very good at it.'

'What a kind brother you are!' said Aunty. She wiped her hands and came towards me. 'I'm not very good with ribbons myself, but it looks as if you've done a good job, Douglas. Do you think your mother can give me some lessons in looking after little girls when she comes to visit?'

Doug smiled and shrugged. 'She sometimes says Gwenda is twice as much trouble as I am.'

'Oh, I'm sure that can't be true,' said Uncle, winking at me from one of the rocking chairs.

At teatime Aunty wanted to know what we had seen of the village and I told her we liked the big wheel at the mill.

Aunty seemed to shudder slightly. 'You didn't go inside it, did you?'

We shook our heads, glad to be able to do so truthfully.

'Well I'm glad. And now I'll tell you a story about my son, John. He's a good boy, really, but boys will be boys from time to time. I'm sure you know that, Douglas. Well, one day John was playing in the wheel and the miller started it up, not knowing that he was inside it. Luckily he heard him shouting and turned it off quickly. But I don't care to think about what might have happened otherwise. John was bruised quite badly, but it could have been a lot worse.'

I listened, fascinated and appalled. I couldn't wait to go back and have another look.

After we had eaten our bread and jam and thick slices of fruit cake and the tea things had been cleared away, Aunty handed us sheets of paper and sat down beside us.

'We're going to write to your parents now,' she said. 'I know you won't have much to say yet, but you can write a longer letter at the end of the week.'

I couldn't think what to write. A fly made a noisy entrance from the scullery and buzzed around our heads for a few seconds until its buzzing became a frantic and continuous 'zzzzzzz'. I looked up and saw that it had become trapped on a sticky piece of paper hanging above the table. I asked Aunty what it was and she seemed surprised that we hadn't seen a flypaper before. She said that flies were a menace in the summer and that this was the best way to catch them. I was worried that its wingless body was going to break away and land on me and couldn't relax until the creature was totally still.

Doug was scribbling away and I wondered what he was writing. Yesterday already felt like a long time ago. Leaving home, the train journey, even the walk to the schoolhouse from Bampton Grange, all felt as distant as memories of last Christmas or my birthday.

'And when you're finished we can put the hens to bed,' said Aunty, seeing me gazing into the air.

I stabbed my pencil on the paper with more conviction. 'We are living in a school,' I wrote, and after thinking a bit more, added as an explanation, 'Uncle is the headmaster. He and Aunty are very nice. I fed the hens. They liked me. Please bring Neville and my Venus pencil case.'

Doug glanced across at what I'd written. He had covered most of one side of the paper. Now he turned it over and continued to write.

I covered my letter with my arm. 'Stop copying.'

Aunty made a gentle tutting noise. 'You've both done well. I'll post these tomorrow. Your parents are going to be thrilled.'

Eveline Hewetson, later Thornton, aged twenty-one

Aunty opened the door of the henhouse and Doug and I tried to coax the hens inside.

'You can give them a little treat now, but they won't get one every day,' said Aunty, giving us some kitchen scraps to feed them. 'Look, they're getting used to you already.'

I looked for the one who had been bullied earlier and recognised her from her brown and white mottled feathers.

'Judith!' I called. I'd been thinking of a name for her since this morning. 'Come on! I've got a treat for you and I'm going to give you extra food tomorrow as well.'

Aunty shook her head and waggled her finger at me. 'Best not to have favourites. A fat hen won't lay eggs.'

Memories of those who stayed:
'One to wipe and one to polish'

I lived with my parents and little brother Peter in Monkseaton, once a village in its own right but now absorbed into the town of Whitley Bay on the north-east coast. I was eight when the war started and Peter was just one. My father was a builder and he had kept one of a row of houses he had built in Allendale in the Northumberland countryside for the family, so it made sense for my mother, Peter and I to move there. I remember Campbell, one of my uncles, coming to visit us there one day. Cam, as he was known, was the youngest of my father's siblings and more like an older brother really as he was just a few years older than me. He found me and some of my cousins in one of the bedrooms and asked us if we would like him to draw Hitler in Po-land. Intrigued, we gathered round to watch him. He proceeded to draw a picture of Hitler sitting on a potty, which we all found highly amusing. Cam was always a joker. He worked as a joiner for Dad but was longing for the day he was old enough to join the RAF.

After a while my mother decided she would rather come home to face the bombs than share her living space with the numerous relatives who had joined us there and we returned to Monkseaton. I attended Tynemouth School as it had cellars which could be used as bomb shelters.

One morning, as shortages began to bite, our headmaster delivered the following advice about economising on lavatory paper: 'You are to use only two sheets – one to

wipe and one to polish'. This has gone down in school
folklore.

Alder Gofton, Ponteland, Newcastle upon Tyne,
July 2015, aged eighty-four

Gwenda met Alder through her cousin Beryl in the 1950s,
not long before setting off to work in America for three years.
They met again on her return and were married in 1961.

Chapter seven

Doug didn't need to leave the building to go to school; a door down the corridor, past the staircase, led to the classrooms where the older children were taught. Uncle took me into my classroom in the wooden building and introduced me to my teacher, Miss Williams. I was the first to arrive. Miss Williams sat me at a desk in the front row and chatted as we waited for the other pupils. I was the only newcomer in the class so attracted a lot of attention as they arrived and took their seats. One boy stopped in his tracks in front of me and said something that sounded like, 'Wh'istow?' I looked at him blankly, baffled as to what the question might have been.

'Hurry along, Johnny. I'll introduce Gwenda to you all in a minute,' said Miss Williams, to my relief.

'Gwenda-suspender,' a voice behind me sniggered, but I

decided to ignore it. I'd heard it too many times at Cragside
School to let it bother me.

When everyone was in their seats Miss Williams explained
to the class that I had been evacuated with my brother and over
thirty other children because of the bombing in Newcastle,
which produced a few gasps and some whispered exchanges
behind me.

'She's a very brave little girl,' she added, smiling at me, but
I didn't know what she was talking about as I really couldn't
think what I had ever been brave about.

As we began our lessons, it quickly became apparent that
many of my classmates were only just mastering the basics of
learning to read and write. The teacher wrote each letter of the
alphabet onto the blackboard and the children repeated them,
one at a time, before copying them into their books.

'And what begins with the letter H?' asked Miss Williams,
to which they chanted in unison, 'Tired mother says "Hah!"'
and sank back in their seats placing a weary hand on their
chests. For some reason, this made me want to laugh.

Miss Williams complimented me on how neat my writing
was. But I was bored. I was glad when this part of the lesson
was over and the children all took a book from their desks
to look at on their own. Miss Williams told me to choose
one from the shelves. I picked up a story about a lamb called
Snowball because I liked the cover, but read it so quickly I was
back within five minutes choosing another. I remembered my
experience at Cragside reading to the older pupils and how
hostile they had been. Perhaps I should force myself to read
more slowly so as not to draw attention to myself. But curi-
osity won in the end and I picked up part one of a children's

encyclopaedia and carried the vast volume back to my desk. The first chapter was about the aboriginal people of Australia. The man in the picture had very dark skin – almost black – and was wearing hardly any clothes. I stared at him for a while then, as the teacher was walking up my row and I didn't want her to catch me looking at a rude picture, I quickly turned the page to the next chapter, 'Africa', and began to read. Miss Williams made no comment when she passed me.

The bell rang for playtime but before we went outside we each had a bottle of milk to drink that had started to go warm. My new classmates took me into the schoolyard. Some asked questions, while others just stood and stared. They had funny accents, but I could understand most of them if I concentrated.

'My dad says Newcastle's a dirty place,' declared Johnny, the boy who had asked me something earlier. 'He said when you blow your nose there it comes out black.'

'Eugghh!' A couple of girls giggled and looked at me even more closely.

'No it's not,' I said, not wanting to get into an argument but at the same time feeling that I should defend my hometown. I had never heard anyone say this about Newcastle before and I was sure we wouldn't have lived there if it was true as my mother had an aversion to dirt.

'Maybe it's your dad what's dirty,' said a girl to Johnny. She had been sitting beside me in class and her name was Mavis. She had told me that she lived on a farm 'oop on t' crags'.

I smiled at her gratefully.

The children were fascinated to learn that I was living with the headmaster and his wife.

'My brother's in Mr Thornton's class and he says everyone's

scared of him,' said one girl, adding helpfully, 'You'll be all right if you mind your Ps and Qs.'

'He's great at cricket,' said one of the boys. 'He can bowl anyone out!' He bowled an imaginary ball at his friend.

'My mam says it's thanks to Mr Thornton that my brother got into the grammar school,' said someone else.

'Have you really had lots of bombs?' asked Johnny.

Everyone looked at me closely. I told them about the big ones on the Tyne just a few days earlier, and about the afternoon I had spent in the air-raid shelter when I was at La Sagesse. It didn't seem very much to report but most of the gathered crowd appeared to be impressed.

'Have you seen any blown-up houses?' he persisted.

I had to admit I hadn't.

'We've got shelters at Burnbanks,' said another boy importantly. 'My dad says if anywhere gets bombed round here it'll be us.' He stabbed his finger at his chest several times to prove his point.

'Why's that?' asked Mavis.

'Because of the dam,' he said scornfully. 'You don't think the Jerries are interested in you and your farm, do you?'

'How do you know? They might be.'

The boy snorted in reply.

A girl sitting on the wall beside me who had a big blue ribbon in her hair gave me a nudge. 'They flooded Mardale, you know, to build the dam. My mam was right upset. She and my dad got married in the church there.'

'Aye. And they had to dig up the bodies from the graveyard and bury them somewhere else,' said the important-sounding boy.

'I'll tell youse all what,' said one girl, moving in closer and lowering her voice. 'My uncle reckons you can still hear the church bells.' She looked at all our faces. 'He was passing by one night and they were chiming.'

Though I wasn't sure what they were talking about, I made a note to relay this tale to Doug as he was a lover of spooky stories.

At lunchtime Doug and I went back to the schoolhouse to eat with Aunty and Uncle. Most of the children went home, though some, who lived further away, brought their own lunches and ate them together in the main school building.

Uncle joined us just as Aunty was saying that perhaps we should start without him.

'There's thirty-five of them, Eveline, plus the young Stacey boy. The nurse is inspecting them all today. Hope you two have had a good wash!' He winked at me and Doug. 'I've put them with Miss Dixon, the Newcastle teacher, for now. Apart from young Gwenda, of course.' He smiled at me. 'She's with the little ones. How are you getting on there, Gwenda?'

I said very well thank you, as it would have been impolite not to.

Uncle had been right about Aunty. She was a good cook and we ate well again with a small piece of meat each and potatoes and spinach from the garden.

'Did they really flood a village?' Doug asked suddenly, after carefully placing his knife and fork on the edge of his plate. Mam hated cutlery being waggled around almost as much as she hated elbows on the table. He looked first at Aunty but then allowed his gaze to rest on Uncle.

'Ah, you've been talking to the Burnbanks boys and girls,' said Uncle. He put down his knife and fork too. 'We've seen a lot of change around here in the last few years, haven't we, Eveline. When they wanted to build a dam to turn Haweswater into a reservoir they needed somewhere for all the workers to live. That's what Burnbanks is. There are about sixty houses there, I think. Then we needed more classrooms for all the extra children, so the corporation built us the wooden building that you're in, Gwenda. They say that when the reservoir is full it will supply all the water for a huge part of north-west England. But building it meant losing the hamlet of Mardale.'

'A sad day,' said Aunty. 'It was a lovely little valley.'

'Progress, Eveline. It sometimes means tough decisions.'

Dams were what Dad and Doug constructed when we went for picnics by the river or at the seaside, with me obeying orders and collecting sand, stones and pebbles. I wondered if this was the same sort of dam.

'I'll take you both there one day,' said Uncle, and I caught Doug's eye over the table and grinned at him.

'Dennis has asked if I can play there one night after school,' said Doug, and Aunty looked at Uncle and said, 'We'll have to see. We don't know the Burnbanks people as well as our own.'

The afternoon was more interesting. My class joined the older class of seven- to nine-year-olds and went into one of the fields to do some drawing and learn about nature. But I was glad when the bell rang. I was going to help Aunty with the hens again. Judith seemed to know me now and this was the closest I had come to having a pet.

The schoolhouse (left) and the school, as seen from the road

Aunty was in the lane talking to a man beside a grocer's van, which had a Penrith address written on the side of it. She introduced me to him when I approached.

'Ah owp thou's garna be 'appy 'ere,' said the man. 'Wer'st thou frae?'

Once again, I could only stare at him in reply and wonder if he was speaking English.

Aunty looked at me sharply.

'Pardon?' I said.

The man repeated his question but it didn't really help. Aunty seemed to realise my problem. 'He's asking where you come from, Gwenda.'

'Newcastle,' the man repeated when I had told him. 'Ships and coal. She'll be glad to be here away from it all.'

'Her father's a bank manager,' said Aunty. She handed me a paper bag of groceries to take inside for her, and added, 'You can keep Miss Williams company in the kitchen while she waits for her bus.'

As I was going up the path I heard her say, 'You wouldn't believe the state of her bag – covered in squashed banana. I'm still scrubbing it now. What a waste of good fruit!'

'Aye, well, that's t' city for you. They most likely think bananas grow on trees.'

I was a little embarrassed to see my teacher sitting at Aunty's kitchen table drinking a cup of tea, but she smiled and patted the seat beside her.

'Don't mind me. I'm not your teacher once school's finished. Did Mrs Thornton tell you that I usually stop by before I catch the bus back to Penrith? It makes the time go by more quickly and she and I have a good old natter. She's very good to me. Did you enjoy yourself today?'

I said politely that I had done.

'You'll get a good education here, you know. Your parents don't need to worry about that. They've got a saying in this village: "They drove the plough in Latin." Has Mr Thornton told you that?'

I had no idea what she was talking about and was relieved that her attention was diverted to Doug, who had just come into the kitchen. He shook hands with Miss Williams and sat down beside us.

'I was just telling your sister, Douglas, that there's a saying here in Bampton: "They ploughed in Latin and swore in Greek." Oh, you look just as baffled!'

We both smiled at her apologetically.

'It always was a good school, you see. It used to be called Bampton Grammar – it turned out bishops, lawyers, you name it. But it didn't matter who you were – you all got the same classical education, the farmhands as well as those destined for loftier professions. So that's where the saying comes from.'

I nodded, still not quite sure what she meant. Doug said that he had always wanted to learn Latin, and Miss Williams said that Mr Thornton would be pleased to hear that as it was one of his favourite subjects. Doug looked as if he wished he had kept his mouth shut.

We wanted to play outside before bed but Aunty thought we looked tired and said that was what a lot of change did to you. She suggested that we sit quietly and read instead. I didn't fancy any of the boys' books in our bedroom but the book of Bible stories for children had nice illustrations so I chose that. Doug and I sat at the kitchen table while Aunty and Uncle sat on the rocking chairs on either side of the range, Aunty with her knitting and Uncle smoking his pipe and gazing thoughtfully into the distance. Aunty told us later that was how he looked when he was thinking about his next sermon, as he was a Methodist lay preacher and often went to preach at other chapels in the area. But tonight his thoughts were closer to home as he exclaimed out of the blue, making us all jump, 'Gwenda! Are you reading or just looking at the pictures?'

'Reading,' I said.

'Read it to me then, go on.'

I read a few sentences then looked across at him. He nodded to himself then tapped some of the ash from his pipe onto the fire. 'You must have been far too good for the little class today, young lady. I shall put you with the older ones tomorrow.'

'She writes nicely as well,' said Aunty. 'Fancy putting her with the babies, Douglas.'

'Well, Eveline, that was part of the reason for starting her off there, so that we could ascertain her level. And they're hardly babies. But it seems we've got ourselves a pair of clever ones here.' He gave a small chuckle. 'They'll be keeping us both in our places if we're not careful.'

Aunty put down her knitting and went out to the scullery. 'I'd forgotten I was going to give your bag another scrub, Gwenda. I'm still finding banana in it.'

'Banana?' asked Uncle. 'What's all that about?'

He shook his head as he heard the story. 'Well, what a waste. It's a while since I've had the good fortune to eat a banana.'

I wished my mother had never given me that banana and I silently cursed the teacher who told us to sit on our bags. I wondered when I was going to hear the last of it.

But then Uncle asked me if I had been trying to make a banana split and that made everyone laugh.

Chapter eight

The kitchen was the heart of the schoolhouse. The kettle hummed on its shelf over the fire and Aunty sang as she moved between the range and the table, the scullery and the garden. She was never very far away. Doug and I spent most of our time with her when we weren't at school or playing outdoors. Aunty was a very cheerful person; I rarely saw her down-hearted or without a smile ready to break out on her face. She was always doing something, whether it was preparing meals, making a mash for her hens, washing clothes, chopping wood for the fire or tending the schoolhouse garden. Most food preparation took place in the scullery, and dishes were washed there, but making bread and cakes and pastry was done at the kitchen table, where I liked to kneel on a chair to help.

Clothes were washed in a large poss tub, which was kept outside in the summer months. If I happened to be passing

I would give a hundred 'posses' with the stick. The tub was filled with clean water and everything got rinsed twice before going through the mangle, which drained into the scullery sink. Then the clothes were hung to dry in a secluded part of the garden.

There was a large sack on the floor of the scullery which I couldn't resist peering into. Aunty said they were Uncle's prunes. I didn't know why they belonged to Uncle as we all ate them for pudding two or three times a week, but that was how Aunty always referred to them.

By far the most interesting part of the kitchen was the table by the window, just as you entered, that was piled with all the things nobody knew what to do with. Leaflets, knitting patterns, hair grips, articles torn from newspapers, odd knitting needles and empty reels of cotton, bits of wood, things to do with fishing, and plenty of other items I couldn't even identify. Aunty said it was ripe for a good old tidy and I could help her to do it one of these days.

A door from the scullery took us into a narrow outdoor passage at the back of the house which faced an outbuilding with three doors. The right-hand door was for the coal house; the left-hand door led to a store room where meat was hung and tools were kept; the middle room had storage space down each side but also led to the garden and the wood and was known as the 'through-place'.

We quickly made ourselves at home in these new surroundings, though visitors to the house would express surprise when they saw us there. One of the regulars was John Dargue, Sunday School superintendent and Methodist preacher, who was rather deaf and disdained the use of bell or knocker, announcing his arrival by flinging open the front door and shouting, 'Anyone at home?' As I happened to be coming out of the kitchen as he made his grand entrance one day, I don't know which of us was more surprised to see the other. Another frequent visitor was Ada Preston's mother, Mrs Hutchinson, who was smart and attractive like her daughter.

'I don't know anything about girls but I'm learning fast,' Aunty explained to Mrs Hutchinson as I helped her to roll out pastry. 'I'm starting to wonder if it isn't so difficult after all.'

I was now in Miss Pickup's class with some slightly older boys and girls as well as a few of my age. She was very strict, and being new and still rather unsure of things, I sat quietly and found it easy to behave myself at first. I watched in horror when a naughty boy was called to the front of the class and struck on the knuckles with a ruler, but I would suffer that punishment myself before too long. It hurt but didn't leave a bruise. I made friends with Janet Sattherthwaite, who lived with her three sisters on the road to Butterwick, the next village to the north; Marjorie Scott, who was the daughter of the postman; and though we were no longer in the same class, I stayed friendly with Mavis Kirkup from the crags. My new friends thought my accent was funny; I thought theirs was funnier but was too outnumbered to bother arguing my case. From them I learnt to call the stream running through Bampton 'the beck' (the larger one we had to cross to get to Bampton Grange was the River Lowther), that the hills were called fells and that an apple core was a gowk. I asked them the name of the craggy mountain behind Bampton Grange, whose shape changed depending on where in the village you were when you looked at it, and they laughed and said that it wasn't a mountain, it was Knipe Scar. I thought they said Knife Scar, an appropriate name as the layers of rock that ran through it looked sharp.

I invited my new friends to come round after school but they seemed reluctant at first. Playing under the nose of the headmaster was clearly not very appealing. But when they realised that we had the whole playground to ourselves and that Uncle was far too busy to hover over us out of school hours, they came without any coaxing though I don't remember them ever stepping foot in the house, and I rarely, if ever, went into theirs.

One warm evening Marjorie and I forced open the window of Miss Williams's classroom and crawled inside. I don't think that either of us had been in an empty classroom before, certainly not when the rest of the building was deserted too. It was still and silent, the chairs standing on the tables, the blackboard wiped clean, the flowers someone had picked for Miss Williams on their way to school releasing a pleasing odour. We couldn't resist scribbling on the blackboard and pretending to be the teacher. I tried to re-enact Miss Williams's alphabet lesson.

'Now, what does tired mother say?' I asked Marjorie as I pointed to the letter H.

Marjorie, who was too old for the little class, couldn't remember, so I sat down beside her to demonstrate. 'Hah!' I said, as I flopped back in my chair.

'Hah!' said Marjorie, drawing out the sound for longer and flopping back even further.

I went further still, toppling sideways off my chair and onto the floor, making us both laugh.

We found a dressing-up box in the cupboard, pulled it out and rooted through the costumes. Folded neatly inside separate bags were outfits for something called a harlequin and something called a pierrot. I put on the chequered harlequin one, while Marjorie wore the baggy white top and trousers and skullcap of the pierrot. Marjorie said she thought they had once read a story about them in the younger class and acted it out.

'I think I've turned you into a witch,' I said, as I rubbed chalk onto Marjorie's face to make her look like the pierrot in the picture. 'Oh, you do look frightening!'

'There *is* a witch in Bampton,' said Marjorie, and she told me about Jinny, whose house you had to run past in case she came out and grabbed you.

'Have you seen her?'

'No, you never see her properly. But she stands behind the curtain and watches everyone go by.'

I hadn't realised that witches were real and wondered what Doug would say when I told him.

We clowned around in our costumes for a while. I would have liked to show Aunty what we looked like, but as we weren't supposed to be in the classroom anyway we reluctantly took the costumes off and put them tidily away, then slipped back through the window into the playground.

I was an imaginative child and happy to play on my own, too, when there was no one else around. I discovered a pile of broken crockery at the bottom of the wood, where it backed onto the schoolyard. I never did find out who threw their old china there, but it must have been accumulating for many years. I sat down to examine it all. Most of the pieces were just a couple of inches wide, remnants of broken cups and plates and saucers. I wondered if I could fit some of them together again, then gave up on that idea and began to make pretty patterns with them on the ground. Later I had a better idea. I didn't know if it would work, but I carefully began to balance the pieces within the branches of one of the bushes in the wood, one that was big enough for me to crawl inside. I took Aunty outside to show her the pretty mosaic house I had made. Eventually the wind blew the pieces down, but that didn't matter – I built another one. It was an occupation I would return to again and again, something I did with my friends – and Doug, if he was in the mood – but that I was just as happy to do by myself.

On Friday evening at the end of our first week there was a knock on the door and Doug's teacher, Miss Dixon, was standing there clutching a bag. Aunty must have been expecting her as she welcomed her inside and made her a cup of tea, while I was instructed to fetch the parkin from the larder. This was one of Aunty's specialities and was a bit like my mother's gingerbread, but denser and darker. Aunty said that Doug and I could have a piece too.

'It's delicious. Is it a local speciality?' asked Miss Dixon politely. She was a small woman with a precise way of talking. It was hard to imagine her as anything but a teacher.

Aunty said that she wasn't sure exactly where the recipe had come from, but that as far as she knew parkin originated in Yorkshire or Lancashire.

Miss Dixon, it turned out, was here to have a bath as the place where she was living – like Doug's friend Peter's new home – did not have a bathroom. It would be the start of a weekly ritual.

'Miss Household fills the tin bath in front of the fire, but I wouldn't feel comfortable doing that in someone else's home.' Miss Dixon dabbed some invisible crumbs from her lips with a handkerchief. 'It's very kind of you and the headmaster to allow me to use your facilities, Mrs Thornton.'

Aunty said that it was no problem at all and asked Doug to show Miss Dixon where the bathroom was when she had finished her tea. But seeing the embarrassment on Doug's face, she changed her mind and said that perhaps it was more appropriate for me to do so. The thought of his teacher coming here for such an intimate purpose was clearly too much for my sensitive brother.

The bathroom was next door to our bedroom. I pointed to the lavatory, which was just opposite, mumbling the word as quickly as possible and hoping she wouldn't ask me to repeat it. I knew that teachers must use the lavatory as well, but at the same time it seemed rather unlikely that Miss Dixon would ever sit on one.

'I've brought my own towel and toiletries,' said Miss Dixon, putting down her bag on a chair. 'I think Mr and Mrs Thornton have been kind enough already.'

I was about to leave her but she put a finger to her lips and pushed the door closed behind me. 'Are you both happy here, Gwenda?' she asked. 'You seem to be but I thought I should still ask you.'

I nodded fiercely.

'And Douglas?'

'Yes, he is as well. Uncle's taking us to see the dam soon.'

'Uncle? Your uncle's coming to see you?'

'No, not a proper uncle. This Uncle. Mr Thornton.'

'Oh, I see, so you call him uncle.' Miss Dixon looked at me closely. 'Well, I'm pleased it's working out so well for you both. I liked Mrs Thornton the minute I set eyes on her in St Patrick's Hall and I can tell you, Gwenda, she and Mr Thornton are very well thought of in the community. Some of the other boys and girls aren't as happy as you are but it's early days, isn't it. I don't think anyone should make any rash decisions yet. Now, thank you, Gwenda. I've been looking forward to this bath all week.'

When I got downstairs Doug was waiting for me. 'Let's get out of here until she's gone,' he said.

The word 'chapel' had come up on several occasions during the week so Doug and I had sensed that it was an important place in the lives of Aunty and Uncle. We had been warned that Sunday was a day for worship and rest, and not for playing, but it began much the same way as any day, with letting out the hens and collecting the eggs. If a hen was sitting on her eggs I left the collecting to Aunty as they would try to peck me when I felt around in the straw, something they didn't do to her. I continued to favour Judith and loved the way she was always so pleased to see me.

As the service wasn't until eleven, Aunty spent the morning preparing lunch. I helped to make the batter for the Yorkshire puddings, whisking the mixture until my hand ached, when Aunty gave it a final whisk before putting it in the larder to keep cool until our return. The milk and butter stayed here as well. Aunty scalded the milk jugs before she tipped the fresh milk from the farm into them every morning.

Doug and I put on the smartest clothes we had brought with us, though Aunty declared that looking clean and tidy was more important than fine clothes and that God would be quite happy to see us however we looked. She wore a pretty summer dress and hat, while Uncle looked dapper in his usual plus-fours and stockings with the addition of a trilby. I had been worried that they might turn into different people on Sunday, but Uncle still had the twinkle in his eye and Aunty was as smiley as ever.

The four of us set off down the lane away from Bampton before crossing into a field to continue our journey. There were two stiles to cross, and when we got to the first one I wanted to stand on it and see how far I could jump but Uncle frowned at me so I got down quickly. We came out onto a lane, crossed a bridge, and there was the chapel.

I couldn't remember ever being inside a church or chapel before so had no idea what to expect. Aunty and Uncle were very proud of their chapel, which had been built thanks to the contributions of its founder members – including several local farming families – sixty years earlier. Many of the descendants of these people were present today, their families having lived in this valley for generations. Though Uncle had been headmaster in Bampton since 1918, he came from Appleby and Aunty from Langwathby, near Penrith, so they were relative newcomers.

We sat on raised seats near the back so we could see everyone as they came in. I recognised the round-faced lady we had met on the day of our arrival a week ago, Mr Dargue and Mrs Hutchinson, who was sitting at the organ. Then Ada arrived with her teacher husband, Billy. There were very few children.

I did my best to sit still and occupied myself in the boring parts by finding everyone's hymn for them well in advance. Uncle sang very loudly and his voice was one of the clearest when we had to make responses.

I didn't understand a lot of the sermon and my mind kept wandering off to other places, but when the preacher said we should give God our most treasured possession, I sat up straight and listened. We must not value material goods too highly, he said, looking round at us all. If we had anything that we thought too much of, then it was best that we give it to God instead. And now I was sure he was looking right at me. It was as if he knew how much I valued my Venus pencil case, which I hoped Mam and Dad would be bringing with them when they came to visit us next weekend. I wasn't sure what God would be able to do with it, though. Would He use it himself or would it go with a large collection of everyone else's treasured possessions in a sort of heavenly museum? I wondered if Aunty had ever given anything to God and what it might be. Perhaps Uncle would give Him a pipe or some of his prunes. Sighing with the realisation of what I must do, I made up my mind to give my pencil case to God when I was reunited with it. The preacher didn't say how we were to do this, or perhaps I had missed that part, but I knew from my days at La Sagesse that God moved in mysterious ways and that it would happen somehow. I smiled with satisfaction at my plan. Aunty looked down at me and gave my hand a squeeze.

After the service the round-faced lady bounded up to Aunty. 'Mrs Thornton! How are you getting on with the children? I still can't believe you've got a little girl!'

'Oh, very well so far, Mrs Heatherside, though I'm sure I've still got a lot to learn.'

'And what did Mr Thornton think when he discovered that the boy's name was Douglas?'

'Oh, he was pleased about that, as you can imagine.'

'And what is your John going to say,' she continued, 'when he comes home and finds his house full of strange children?'

'I am sure he'll be delighted to have some playmates for the summer,' replied Aunty. 'Now, we really ought to get going or the dinner will be burning. Where is that uncle of yours, Gwenda?'

'Uncle!' exclaimed Mrs Heatherside. 'Well I never!'

Uncle was shaking lots of hands and talking to some of the men. Aunty gave a small nod in his direction and he said his goodbyes, as we did the same. I wanted to race Doug back across the fields until I remembered that there was no running allowed.

After dinner we moved to the sitting room. Apart from our peek round the door earlier in the week it was the first time we had been in this spacious room with its smart three-piece suite and large piano. Doug had borrowed a John Buchan book from upstairs and I was reading my *Sunny Stories* for the umpteenth time. The comic was getting tattered now. When I saw a pile of magazines on a table I went to fetch one, desperate for something new to read. They were the magazine of the Women's Institute, *Home and Country*, but before I had chance to start reading, Uncle, who often disappeared for a while after meals, came into the room and went straight to the piano.

'Do either of you play?' he asked us as he sat down on the stool.

We told him that we didn't.

'Come and sit up here and I'll teach you,' he said.

We squashed onto the stool, one on either side of him, as he played a tune with one finger and sang at the same time.

> *I will make you fishers of men*
> *Fishers of men*
> *Fishers of men*
> *I will make you fishers of men*
> *If you follow me*

He began to play it again. 'Come on, you can join in,' he said in his schoolmaster voice.

I started to sing. Doug mumbled along too, less enthusiastically.

'You can learn to play it, as well. It's a very simple tune. Just watch me, then you have a go.'

I did, and I started to get the hang of it. I could hardly believe that I was playing the piano. I vowed that I would learn the tune perfectly before next weekend when my parents were due to visit so that I could show them my new-found skill.

Doug and I had to go back to chapel for Sunday School before tea. We were split into groups according to our age and our names were marked in a register. I recognised Barbara Noble, who had been in my first class, as well as a couple of boys and girls from my new class. Barbara lived in Bampton Hall, the local farm, and delivered our milk every day with her older sister Muriel.

'On Whit Sunday we get books for good attendance,' Barbara whispered.

'When's that?' I asked her, the mention of books making me sit up straighter.

'Oh, not for ages. We had it a couple of months ago. You have to have Easter before you have Whitsun.'

That was a blow. Easter wasn't until next year. I couldn't wait that long for a new book.

Sunday School was more enjoyable than the service had been that morning. My teacher, a cheerful young woman, read us a Bible story, asked some questions about it, then led us in singing.

Doug and I walked back across the fields on our own, sheep scampering away from us if we got too close. I asked Doug when he thought the war would end.

'How should I know? Maybe next week. Maybe next year. Maybe not till we're grown up.'

'So do you think we'll still be here on Whit Sunday?'

'When's that?'

'It's not till next year. But you win books then if you go to Sunday School every week.'

'That's ages away. You must be able to find something to read before then.'

'All the books at home look so boring.'

Doug didn't comment on the fact that I'd called the school-house 'home'. The word had slipped out quite naturally.

'Have you read *Treasure Island*?'

'Isn't it for boys?'

'Well, it doesn't matter. You like boys' things, don't you, apart from those silly dolls. Come on, I'll race you to the next stile.'

Eveline and Dougie Thornton in the schoolhouse garden, early 1950s

'But we're not allowed to run!'

'They can't see us here unless they've got a telescope. Last one's a nincompoop.'

After tea Doug and I could hardly believe that we had to return to chapel yet again for the evening service. I could see from Doug's face and the way he kept trailing behind as we walked there that he didn't think much of the idea. There was a visiting preacher, whose long words and booming voice made me feel tired, and after the service he came back to the schoolhouse with us. Before we left I had helped Aunty to set the table in the dining room for two, and she served supper there to the preacher and Uncle while Doug and I had a glass of milk and some bread and cheese with her in the kitchen.

When we had said our prayers and Aunty had wished us goodnight, Doug said to me from his bed, 'Three times in one day! I hate Sundays. I hate chapel. I don't like God very much either.'

'Shhh! Aunty might hear.'

'I don't mind if she does.'

When I was sure she was back downstairs I said, 'I quite like God.' But wanting to stay on Doug's side, I added, 'But I've had enough of Him today. I thought that preacher man was never going to stop talking.'

'I've had enough of Him for a lifetime,' said Doug. 'I'm going to tell Mam and Dad next weekend I want to go home.'

Chapter nine

Hitler was going to invade Britain, though it was hard to imagine the Germans storming into Bampton. Would I wake up one morning to see them running down Knipe Scar waving their guns in the air or sailing on rafts up the River Lowther? It felt unlikely, but the boys could hardly wait for it to happen. As my friends and I skipped and played hopscotch in the sloping playground, one of their favourite playtime activities was telling each other what they would do to the Germans when they arrived. The Percy brothers from Burnbanks practised fighting every night with walking sticks and their mother's frying pans. Someone else claimed to know how to make Molotov cocktails out of lemonade or beer bottles. Marjorie and I thought they were a bloodthirsty lot.

If Uncle noticed that the boys' games or conversations were becoming a bit too gory, he would run into the playground himself, plus-fours billowing in the wind, and kick a football around with them. He was a great believer in allowing children – boys in particular – to 'let off steam'. He encouraged them to stay after lessons were over to play cricket or football on the school field on the other side of the road. Even the ones who had been punished by him that day forgot their grievances and brightened up when he joined in too.

One playtime before we broke up for the summer holidays the boys were singing, 'Run Adolf, run Adolf, run run run,' to the tune of 'Run Rabbit Run' and chasing Jez Percy, who was pretending to be Hitler. Jez stopped every now and then to give the Nazi salute before ducking and diving away from them. He was such a funny lad, even Marjorie, Janet and I joined in. I knew the original song as my parents had some Flanagan and Allen gramophone records, and this new version stayed in my head all day. I would have liked to sing it to Aunty and Uncle to make them laugh but something told me not to. Perhaps I would sing it to my parents when they came to visit at the weekend, but then, perhaps not. You could never tell what they would find funny, like that time Mam had got annoyed when I'd sung 'London's Burning'. But this time it was making fun of the enemy, so surely it was all right? Still, I had the nagging feeling we were being naughty when we sang it, so I held back.

The evening before I had sung one of the French carols I remembered for Aunty. Pleased with myself at the effect it had on her, I followed it with a song that Ivy had taught me, 'I'm gonna sit right down and write myself a letter'. I liked the part where we had sung together, 'Woh-oh' and wiggled our hips. It was hard to believe that it was almost a year now since I had said goodbye to Ivy when Doug and I had left for Morpeth in September 1939. I still thought about her sometimes.

'Oh, Gwenda, that's not a song for little girls,' said Aunty, shaking her head. 'Make sure Uncle doesn't hear you singing that.'

I stopped singing, disappointed but relieved. I was fond of Uncle and liked to please him. Everyone said how strict he was and though Doug and I had not been at the receiving end of his anger ourselves, we had witnessed how quickly his smiles could turn to disapproval.

On Saturday, the day before Mam and Dad's visit, Doug and I went with Aunty to Bampton Hall to collect the milk for the weekend. I wondered if I might see Muriel or Barbara, the farmer's daughters, but there was no one around. The milk was waiting for us in the scullery adjoining the farmhouse kitchen.

'Now that you know where to go, this can be your job from now on,' said Aunty, as she exchanged the empty can for the full one.

As we made our way back across the farmyard I heard the sound of yapping dogs and two or three – or was it even four – little white things shot out from one of the barns and came running towards us. I froze. Aunty bent down to pet them and they allowed her to, but they seemed to sense my fear and snapped around my ankles.

'They're quite harmless,' said Aunty. 'Look at the size of them compared to you. Just ignore them.'

It was hard to ignore them when they seemed intent on terrifying me. A man's voice called out to them and they eventually ran off.

Eveline and Dougie – in typical attire – with farmer's daughter Muriel Noble

I nudged Doug as we walked past the house where Jinny the Witch lived. Was it my imagination or did the curtain twitch as we went by? When Aunty was out of earshot I told Doug what I had seen. Doug said that Jinny was waiting for a girl of about my size to walk past on her own and that her bony fingers were so long they would shoot out through the window and grab me without her even needing to open the door. That night he got up to one of his old tricks and sneaked round to my bedside, ran his nails gently down my head and hissed, 'Jinny's come to say hello.' Even though I knew it was him I shrieked so loudly that Aunty came shooting back upstairs and I had to pretend I thought I had a spider in my bed so as not to get him into trouble.

Earlier in the day I had helped Aunty to make a cake and scones for Mam and Dad's visit. It felt funny to picture my parents sitting at Aunty's table. We had been apart for two weeks but I had been too busy to think about them much.

Aunty didn't need to use reconstituted eggs for her baking like Mam and Aunty Edith did. Here in Bampton we had everything we needed, or it felt as if we did to me. Perhaps I was just young and adaptable enough to accept everything we were given as normal, or perhaps Aunty was just very good at making a little go a long way, but I was barely aware of rationing when I was there, apart from missing the odd sweet or some of the more exotic fruits, like grapes and oranges. And Uncle was a keen country sportsman when he got the opportunity so there was often fish or rabbit on the table.

Our parents were due after dinner on Sunday so we were allowed to miss Sunday School that day. My face must have fallen at this news as Aunty asked me what was the matter. I told her that I needed to go to Sunday School every week or I wouldn't win a book at Whitsuntide. Aunty said that there would be plenty of time to make up for it and that she was sure that Mr Dargue would understand on this occasion. Doug, meanwhile, was shaking his head at me behind Aunty's back, terrified that Aunty was going to change her mind and make us go after all.

After Sunday dinner, and checking the kitchen clock every minute, Doug and I went into the village to wait for the car so that we could show our parents where the schoolhouse was. We knew that they would arrive dead on time because Dad always did. We heard his Vauxhall Ten before we saw it, and then there it was, coming over the little bridge, Mam sitting up very straight in the passenger seat.

Dad tooted a few times when he saw us and Doug looked around self-consciously, as if he was worried what passers-by might think, but there was no one around. The car pulled up beside us and we hopped into the back.

'Long time no see,' said Mam. 'Don't I get a kiss then?'

I felt slightly shy of them at first. I think I even felt a twinge of disloyalty, knowing that we were living quite happily without them and that I hadn't been as desperate for this moment as I had thought I would be, though now that it was here I couldn't stop smiling. Mam was wearing one of her own creations, a green flowered dress with a matching hat. Dad was in a suit and tie but had taken off his jacket and rolled up his sleeves for the journey.

'You've both grown since we last saw you,' said Dad, glancing at us in the rear-view mirror. 'The country air must be suiting you. By Jove, it's a terrific drive.'

'Your father thought he was Henry Segrave,' said Mam, as Doug pointed out the way to the school. 'He hasn't changed, even if you have.'

'So, how are you getting on?' asked Dad. 'Tell us all about it.'

I looked at Doug.

'It's good,' he said, seeming to have forgotten his outburst of the previous Sunday. 'Aunty and Uncle are very nice, aren't they, Gwenda?'

I nodded. 'Me and Aunty made you a cake for tea. Uncle's taking Doug fishing in the school holidays and Aunty's going to teach me to knit.'

'Aunty and I,' corrected Mam, before saying, 'They don't mind you calling them Aunty and Uncle?' Her voice suggested that she might mind, even if they didn't.

'No, they like it.'

'This is it, this big building,' said Doug. 'Go up the drive, past the house and you can park beside the garage.'

'I suppose we'll have to put on our airs and graces,' said Mam. 'Is this land all theirs?'

'Shall we get your cases out or go and say hello first?' asked Dad. But before anyone could answer anyone else, Aunty and Uncle were coming up the path to greet them.

As it was Sunday we were in the sitting room. Aunty brought in a tray of tea. Doug and I finished ours quickly and waited impatiently for the grown-ups to finish theirs and to stop talking so that we could show our parents the village and take them to the beck. We were also impatient to see what my mother had packed in the small suitcases she had brought for each of us, but Aunty had already said we should wait till later and that we should make the most of having our parents with us. I wondered if Mam had remembered to pack the Venus pencil case. I almost asked her, then decided to wait and let it be a surprise. I wondered if I would still want to give it to God when I had seen it again.

Uncle was telling Dad about his work on the parish council and some of its wartime responsibilities. 'I'm going to be getting the school involved with this as well,' he said, with a nod towards me and Doug. 'We're going to store waste paper, rags, rubber, metal – whatever might come in useful. It's good for the children to learn what we make things from, as well. A lot of them – and these are the ones I teach, the older ones – didn't know you could make paper from cloth. Then when the berry season starts I'm going to give the whole school the day off for fruit picking. Eveline is in the Women's Institute and they'll be taking charge of the jam-making, just like in the last war, if you're old enough to remember. Hah! That's made you two sit up and listen!'

Doug and I had perked up at the mention of a day off school. The adults chuckled.

'Very worthwhile,' said Mam politely. She took a sip of her tea and to fill the sudden silence began to tell them how she had started work serving tea to the troops as they passed through Newcastle Central Station at night. 'I can't believe how young some of them look,' she said sadly. 'Just boys, really.'

'Our eldest son is in the RAF,' said Aunty.

'What a worry for you,' said my mother, looking at Aunty with concern, then at my father to make sure that he looked sympathetic too.

'At least John, my youngest, is still at school. He's twelve now, boarding in Appleby. The children will meet him soon.'

'We're going fishing when he comes home,' said Doug. 'Me and John and Uncle.'

'You and your fishing! Well, I hope John doesn't mind you going along too,' said Mam.

'Oh, he's looking forward to meeting them both,' said Aunty. 'It will be company for him.'

There was a brief pause in the conversation while Mam and Dad finished their tea. Uncle made use of it to say he hoped they didn't mind if he excused himself to write a sermon, but he knew they would be in good hands.

'Don't forget to show your parents the chapel,' Aunty called after us as we left.

We walked towards the village. 'Ah, St Patrick's Well,' said Dad as we passed the whitewashed pub. 'I knew it had an unusual name. Mind, it's handy for Mr Thornton.'

Doug gave Dad a look that suggested he should already know what he was about to tell him. 'Dad, I don't think he goes there. He doesn't drink beer or anything like that.'

'What? Not at all?'

'I don't think so. He's a Methodist.'

'Ah,' said Dad, 'probably signed the pledge.'

'A pretty little place,' said Mam as we walked over the bridge and passed the post office.

We began to wander down the lane that led to Bampton Grange. When we were halfway there she stopped suddenly and looked all around her. 'You can see why artists and composers are inspired by nature, can't you? I always hoped one of you two would turn out to be musical like your grandfather, but I think that gene vanished when I married your father.'

The clouds that had been around earlier had vanished and the sun was shining fiercely. The sky looked very blue against the reddy brown slopes of the fells. It felt as if we were in our own little world in this peaceful valley and I think that Mam felt that too. 'Very quiet,' she added, 'but I suppose that's why you're here.'

We crossed the bridge into Bampton Grange and stood facing the church hall.

'This was where we all went when we arrived,' said Doug. 'Everyone came to inspect us and choose who they wanted. No one wanted Gwenda so we were stuck to the end.'

'Oh!' Mam pretended to be annoyed with him. 'And is that the chapel Mrs Thornton was talking about next door?'

'No! That's St Patrick's Church, not a chapel!' I said, astounded at their ignorance. I knew from Aunty that church and chapel were two very different things, as were the people who went to them. 'That's the chapel over the fields. See that building over there. We have to cross two stiles to get to it.'

Mam and Dad looked to where I was pointing, but didn't say anything. Back on the lane we crossed into a field and wandered down to the beck. Mam and Dad sat on the bank while Doug and I took off our shoes and socks and paddled.

'I wish I'd brought me paper,' said Dad. 'It's champion here. Imagine having a river on your doorstep.'

'It's not a river, it's a beck,' I said. 'The river's over there.'

'Phew, it's turning into a hot one!' said Mam.

There was such a lot I had wanted to tell my parents, but now they were here I couldn't remember what it was. And I

detected something I couldn't quite understand – something
that seemed like a lack of interest but perhaps, with hindsight,
was more a reluctant acceptance that this was our new life and
that, providing we were safe and happy, they would prefer not
to know too much about it. Mam did ask a few questions, like
what we had to eat and how often we had a bath. And Dad
asked if we had been in the Austin Seven he had spotted in the
garage – we hadn't; Uncle used his motorbike when he went to
council meetings in Appleby on Friday nights. But otherwise
they seemed happy to sit and watch us play.

'Aunty Edith and Beryl are asking after you, and Grandma,
of course. And Mr and Mrs Young, next door,' said Mam.

'Have you seen the Birdman?' I asked, though I wished as
soon as I had said it that I hadn't.

'I don't know how you think I've had time to go wandering
down to the Dene just for the fun of it, Gwenda! I'm on the
rota at the station three nights a week. By the time I've caught
up on my sleep I don't have much time for anything else. And
you know your father is enlisting.'

We didn't know, but she said it quite casually. Doug grasped
its meaning more quickly than I did. He had been trying to
make stones jump in the water, but he stopped what he was
doing and looked at Dad.

'Are you going to fight, Dad? Really?'

Dad nodded. 'Well, whatever they need me for. I might
be too much of an old boy for that. But I'm enlisting in the
Royal Engineers.'

'The Sappers!' said Doug.

'The Sappers!' I repeated.

'You know what he's like,' said Mam. 'Desperate to be in

the thick of it. Desperate to do his bit. He doesn't need to, but he is.'

'I wish I could see you in your uniform,' said Doug.

Dad chuckled and said that maybe he would one day. Then he got to his feet and said he was going to test the water. He took off his shoes and socks and rolled up his trousers. His shins were so white they gleamed in the sun.

'*They* don't get an airing very often,' laughed Mam. 'Mr and Mrs Thornton might think you're sending them messages in Morse code if they're looking out of their window.'

After a few gasps at how cold the water was, Dad said he was going to follow the beck to see if he could find a bit deep enough to swim in, and Doug and I paddled along beside him. We didn't see another person, only sheep in the fields on either side. When we came to a calm pool of slightly deeper water, Dad said, 'This looks champion,' and proceeded to strip off down to his underpants, folding his clothes and putting them neatly on the bank. I was horrified and so was Doug. Supposing someone should see him – see us! Suppose Aunty suddenly appeared! I felt certain that she and Uncle would be shocked by this behaviour. I looked at my father's shiny limbs and even whiter underwear and felt my cheeks go pink. How could he embarrass us like this?

After a great splash and some oohing and aahing, Dad was now lying on his back, his toes sticking up, keeping himself afloat in the not-very-deep water with his arms. He called at us to join him.

Doug didn't hesitate for long before taking off his shirt. I was sure he wouldn't take off his shorts, but there was some-thing about the sight of Dad there that made him shed his

usual inhibitions and he removed them too. I remained in the
shallows, trying to look disapproving but thinking at the same
time what fun it looked.

Dad and Doug were splashing each other now and laughing.
My mother came wandering along the bank, picking her way
carefully. She had taken off her stockings and was clutching
her shoes and Dad's, along with her handbag. 'Honestly!' she
said. 'I don't think I'm dressed for this.'

'Have you got a towel?' I asked her, looking at Dad and
Doug.

'Don't be silly. I didn't know we would need one. They'll
have to dry off in the sun.'

'Come on, Gwenda!' called Dad. 'It's lovely in here!'

I knew I wanted to join them and when I couldn't resist it
any longer Mam helped to pull my dress over my head and I
splashed in after them.

'Mind that pike, it's looking for a nice meal,' teased Dad,
and I looked around in a panic before realising he was joking.
The shock of the cold lasted for only a couple of seconds. The
water smelled brown and earthy, but pleasant too.

'You see, it's smashing once you're in. Lie on your back and
kick your legs,' said Dad. 'I'll hold you. You'll be swimming
before you know it.'

We were all shivering when we came out, despite the sun.

'But what about my wet knickers?' I said, dismayed that I
hadn't thought about this before. Dad said it was a hot day and
they wouldn't be wet for long.

We sat on the bank warming up. A sheep peered at us
from the other side. Mam produced a bag of Black Bullets
from her handbag, all sticking together inside the paper, and

I remembered pre-war days out to the beach or the country with family and friends, and the picnics we used to have. Most north-eastern beaches were fenced off with barbed wire now and some were littered with great concrete boulders to stop the Germans from coming ashore in their tanks. But here it was a perfect summer's afternoon with no hint of the turmoil that was going on around us.

As soon as we got back to the schoolhouse I ran upstairs to put dry knickers on. The sun might have been hot, but not hot enough to dry sodden cotton. Dad and Doug had discreetly removed their underpants at the side of the beck and put their trousers on without them. I just prayed that Aunty and Uncle wouldn't be able to tell. Aunty was in the kitchen buttering the scones and slicing her parkin. Mam asked if she could help but Aunty shooed us both away. She apologised that Uncle was still in his study, but said that he would be joining us very shortly. This was my chance to show my parents my new party piece. I had slipped into the sitting room to practise a few times during the week and was confident I could play the tune Uncle had taught me. Mam would see that I had inherited some of her father's musical talent after all!

'Watch me!' I said proudly, going up to the piano and sitting down. 'Are you going to join in, Doug?'

'No thank you. I'll watch.'

'All right. Now, are you all listening?'

Mam had taken out her knitting. Her knitting! She obviously didn't know that sewing and knitting were not allowed on a Sunday. I hoped she would put it away before Aunty and Uncle came back into the room.

'We're listening,' she said.

I stabbed the first key heavily with my finger, and began.

> *I will make you fishers of men*
> *Fishers of men*
> *Fishers of men*
> *I will make you fishers of men*
> *If you follow me*

I turned and looked triumphantly at my parents. Dad smiled and nodded. 'Champion,' he said.

Mam raised her eyes to the ceiling and said, 'Well, it didn't take you long to become a Holy Joe, did it?'

'Don't you think it's good?' I asked, feeling hurt. 'I only started learning it last Sunday.'

'It's very good,' said Dad. 'Do you know any show tunes?'

They were looking at each other in a way that suggested they disapproved of something, but that neither of them was going to say what it was.

'I only started learning a week ago,' I said grumpily. 'How could I have learnt anything else in that time?'

'I was only joking,' said Dad. 'It's smashing.'

'We went to chapel three times last Sunday,' said Doug, before thinking better of it and adding, 'but one time it was Sunday School and that doesn't count.'

'We didn't mind,' I added, suddenly fearful that we were going to be taken away from here and back to the war zone of Newcastle. One girl from Doug's class had returned home already after writing to tell her mother she was unhappy. But I didn't want to go home yet. There were so many things

I wanted to do here this summer – follow the beck with Marjorie, meet John when he came home from school, visit Mavis on her farm on the fells, perhaps even teach Judith some tricks.

'I should think not, you're very lucky to be here,' said Dad, to our relief. He gave a small chuckle. 'Remember those places in Morpeth? Tscchh! I don't know which was worse. Hadn't a clue about children, either of them. Still, I suppose there are worse things to worry about at the moment.'

Over tea Dad and Uncle talked about cricket and cars. Dad said he wouldn't be keeping the Vauxhall once he had gone into the Army.

'They go stale if they're not driven,' he said to Uncle. 'I'd rather replace it with something newer when I'm back for good.'

Doug and I were surprised to hear this. That Vauxhall was his pride and joy. But my father was always like that with his cars – making impulsive decisions, changing from one model to another according to his whims.

And then it was time for Mam and Dad to go.

'Can you come next Sunday?' I asked, thinking that it seemed like a perfect arrangement.

Mam said it would have to be later in the year, when Dad was home, but they didn't know when that would be yet.

After we had said goodbye, and Doug and I had chased the car into the village and waved until it had disappeared, I remembered that I hadn't introduced Mam to the hens. That would have to wait till next time.

'Fancy Dad being a soldier!' said Doug as we walked back to the schoolhouse, feeling a little sad. 'He'll show those Germans.'

Later Aunty helped us to unpack our cases. Mam had made me a new dress, at least I thought it was new until I realised she had simply added a lace trim to the bottom of one of my old ones to make it last longer. She had also taken away one of the dresses I had been wearing to make some alterations. She had sent some other clothes too, including some winter ones. There was also a compendium of stories for girls with the name 'Beryl Walton' written in the front – a cast-off from my cousin, but a very welcome one. Neville, my doll, was there, and so was my pencil case. I was pleased but felt a flicker of discomfort at the same time – now I would have to make a decision about what I was going to do. It had been a good day and I knew I had God to thank for that. But did I really want to give up such a prized possession? With a heavy heart I opened the lid, hoping that it wouldn't be as nice as I remembered. The crayons and pencils looked so perfect in their compartments, their sharpened points all the same length. I took them all out, looked at every item in turn and put two pencils and two crayons back into the case which I then put under my bed. Later, when we had said our prayers and Aunty had said goodnight and left the room, I reached down and put it on my bedside table. I knew that God would find a way to take it if He wanted it, and hoped I would fall asleep quickly as I didn't really want to be awake when He came.

Memories of those who stayed: 'Good old Hitler!'

We lived in Wallsend, just a few miles outside the centre of Newcastle, where my father and one of my uncles worked in the shipyards, a reserved occupation. My uncle was killed while working there and his wife took a job in the shipyards herself to make ends meet for her family. She was a hard worker and a thrifty woman. Everyone knew her as 'the widow' and gave her their cast-offs and she was known never to turn anything down. When she died many years later she had four layers of carpet in her house.

Early in the war I was evacuated to Ellington, a mining village on the coast about twenty miles north. I used to call the lady who looked after me 'Aunty'. One day Aunty saw something blue on the window ledge outside and went to get it, thinking it was the little blue bag we put in the rinse with the whites on wash day. To her surprise it was a budgie and he was very tame. He used to perch on the end of the table and to everyone's amusement say, 'Good old Hitler! Bad old Churchill!' Then one day he flew away.

We had no air-raid shelters and Aunty and I just sat beneath a very heavy mahogany dining table during the warnings.

I was evacuated again later in the war but the experience was not such a happy one. I stayed in four places where I wasn't wanted and ran away from two of them before being found in the bus shelter with no money. However I was happy in the fifth place.

Patricia Small (née Beadle), South Queensferry,
July 2015, aged eighty-four

Pat and Gwenda met when they began their nurses' training in Newcastle in 1952 and they have been friends ever since. Pat was Gwenda's companion when she set off to work and travel in the USA in 1957.

Chapter ten

When I woke up the first thing I did was look at my bedside cabinet but it was too dark to be able to make anything out. It wasn't until Aunty had come in and opened the blinds that I could see properly. The pencil case was still there! I closed my eyes and opened them again more slowly, as if to give it one last chance to disappear, but it remained in its place. I felt a mixture of regret and relief. God had not wanted it. He either did not need it or I was a better person than I thought and He had seen no need to deprive me of it. I decided to ask Aunty or Uncle about it later, as they would surely have an answer for me.

Down in the kitchen Aunty – who was a very early riser – was coming in from the garden where she had been picking raspberries. Doug and I had our usual boiled egg and soldiers before hurrying off to school. The term was coming to an end and Miss Pickup had relaxed a little and was turning a blind eye to some of our misdemeanours brought on by excitement. I was excited about something else as well, for I had just learnt that Ada was expecting a baby. Every time I saw her I tried not to stare. Some days I could hardly tell that she was pregnant and thought she must have already had the baby, but Aunty assured me that the baby was due in October and that we would all know when it had arrived. I could hardly wait for this child to be born, especially as Ada had already promised me that I could help her to look after it. I hadn't had much to do with babies before. Having a baby to take care of – whom I could love and who would love me back – might be even better than having Judith, my hen. When Mrs Hutchinson was round, she and Aunty would discuss whether Ada was doing too much in her condition and if it wouldn't be better for her to slow down. But Ada was tireless. She was up early in the morning to sort the mail, and whenever there was a telegram to deliver she insisted on doing this herself on her bicycle, regardless of how far she had to cycle.

'But thank heavens she's given up her motorbike now,' said Mrs Hutchinson. And Aunty agreed that we had to be grateful for small mercies.

If I idolised Ada, Doug was just as taken with her husband, Billy, who was now his teacher. I thought I would never hear the end of the day Mr Preston took them to the chapel and showed them how to draw things in perspective, or the Saturday when he gave up his day off to take Doug and some of the other Newcastle boys walking on the fells, pointing out the local landmarks and the wildlife.

Billy and
Ada Preston

Ada on her
brother's
motorbike

'That's High Street,' Doug told me, pointing to the range of hills that passed behind Bampton and headed off in the direction of Haweswater. We were walking back from the village after running an errand for Aunty. 'And do you know why it's called that? Have a guess.'

'Well, it's high, and—'

'It's the way the Romans marched, right over the top, two thousand years ago. So it was like their main road.'

I thought it was odd to build a road along the top of a mountain and said so.

'If they had been down here they might have been attacked by all the savages in the valley,' said Doug. And he pounced on me to prove his point.

A few days later school was over for the summer and John Thornton came home for the holidays. I had been looking forward to meeting him, but dubious too. I wondered how Aunty and Uncle would treat us now that their own son was around. They were delighted to see him and Aunty had been busy baking some of his favourite things. On his first evening home we all sat in the kitchen together, Aunty and Uncle in their rocking chairs – she with her knitting, he with his pipe – Doug, John and I at the table, while John talked about the last term at Appleby Grammar. He told us about sports day, about the eccentric geography master, about the boy who had been called from a lesson to the head's study who had said to his classmates before he left the room, 'It's about my father, I know it,' and it had been. He had gone home for the funeral but returned a few days later. It's a cruel war, Uncle said, and we all went quiet for a while.

John was three years older than Doug, so we were both slightly in awe of this clever, well-read boy. He had a thoughtful, sometimes serious expression but, like Aunty, he was quick to smile. If he was put out at coming home to find two evacuees in his house he didn't show it.

The next morning Doug and I followed him outside and sat like obedient dogs waiting for him as he rummaged around at the back of the garage where Uncle kept his car and motorbike. After some reorganisation had taken place, he carefully wheeled out a bicycle and propped it up against the side. He went back inside and came out with a can of oil and some rags. I was sent to fetch a pail of water and was allowed to clean the mudguards and the spokes of the wheels while Doug and John attended to the more serious jobs. John said he hadn't used the bike for several months, and was going to try it out.

'You can follow me if you like,' he called out, but he and Doug soon left me behind and I went back to the schoolhouse to wait for them. Doug looked pleased with himself when he got back, puffing and panting behind him, and even more pleased when John said that he could have a turn.

'If we use my mother's old bike we could cycle to Ullswater one day,' John said to him. 'You wouldn't mind cycling a woman's bike, would you?'

Doug was far too flattered by the invitation to say that he would.

When the boys had decided to move on to something else, I asked if I could have a turn.

'I think you're a bit small,' said John, not unkindly.

It was true. The bike had a high crossbar and I needed help to get onto it. But even once I was seated, my feet were

nowhere near the pedals. The only solution was to stand to
pedal. Doug and John accompanied me, one on either side, as
I wobbled around the schoolyard.

'There, you don't need us any more, do you?' said Doug
after a few minutes, making it more of a fact than a question.
'If you do the loop we did you don't even need to get off. We'll
see you when you're finished.'

'Just give us a shout when you want to stop,' said John
cheerfully, as they sent me on my way.

Helped by the slope of the schoolyard and a push from
the boys I managed the uphill part into Bampton without
any difficulty. I felt pleased with myself as I wobbled up and
over the little bridge and through the village before heading towards Bampton Grange, though I was relieved not to
see anyone I knew as I couldn't have lifted a hand to wave.
Instead of turning left into Bampton Grange I went right
and then right again towards Gate Foot, where a friend of
Aunty's lived in one of the handful of houses there. The lane
was empty of people and traffic, which was just as well as I
had little control over which side of the road I was on. From
Gate Foot it was downhill back to the schoolhouse. As I got
closer I looked out for Doug and John but there was no sign
of them and they didn't appear when I called out to them. As
I couldn't get off the bike myself, I had little choice but to do
the circuit all over again. By now my legs were starting to
ache and my whole body was tense from the effort of keeping
stable while not being able to sit down. As I approached the
schoolhouse the second time I looked in desperation for the
boys. Trust them to forget about me! I wondered how I was
ever going to get off this bike. To make it stop I was going

to have to deliberately fall and probably hurt myself in the process.

An elderly lady was walking towards me.

'Help!' I called out, without thinking what I was doing.

She gave a little jump when she saw me coming. She was very slight, with a grey bun, spectacles and a stick in one hand, rather like an old lady in a fairytale. Realising even as I was speaking that she was unlikely to be strong enough to stop me, I steered the bike towards the fence in desperation. The wheel hit a post and the bike stopped suddenly, tipped over and pinned me underneath it.

'Ow! Ow!' I pushed the bike up to free myself. I didn't want to cry in front of this stranger but I was close to it.

'Child!' said the old lady. 'Are you all right? Gracious me, you might have landed on that horrible wire.'

I stood up and brushed my grazed knees. I had rubbed some skin off my hands as well. With the lady's help I picked up the bike.

'You poor thing! Come home with me and we'll get you cleaned up,' she said. Then she added, 'Well, it's not actually my house but I'm living here at the moment.'

She looked so concerned that I felt it would be rude to tell her that it would have been quicker for me to go home to the schoolhouse. Accepting her offer I managed to turn the bike round and we began to walk back towards Gate Foot. Wheeling the bike was almost as hard as riding it as it was taller than I was. The lady put a frail hand on one of the handlebars and we walked awkwardly along together, the bike prodding me as we went. I told her who I was and where I was staying and she said that was a coincidence as she was an evacuee as well, that she came from Manchester and that she was staying with an elderly lady like herself. I hadn't met an adult evacuee before, apart from Miss Dixon, but as she was here as a teacher that was different.

'It's beautiful here, don't you think? We are both so lucky! I can't walk very far but I do like to get out as much as I can. Now, let me just see that Miss Spriggs doesn't mind ...' We had stopped outside a cottage and my new friend went inside for a minute before coming back out and waving me in. 'Leave the bike against the wall,' she said.

The cottage was tiny compared to the schoolhouse. The room I walked into smelled of woodsmoke. It had a low ceiling and seemed to be a kitchen, living room and dining room all in one.

'This is my hostess, Miss Spriggs,' said my new friend. 'And did I even tell you my name? How rude of me! I'm Elizabeth Castle.'

Miss Spriggs, who had already filled a bowl of water, sat me down and dabbed at my scratched hands and legs. Her chin carried on into her neck in soft folds of flesh, but she had a kindly face. She told me that everyone in the village knew Mr and Mrs Thornton and that they were a fine couple. She was an Anglican and a parishioner at St Patrick's, but even some of the congregation there, she admitted, said that Mr Thornton was an inspirational preacher.

'And we all have the same God, after all,' declared Elizabeth Castle, who was filling a kettle and making sympathetic faces as she watched the operation.

Miss Spriggs's family had farmed in the valley for a very long time. 'When I went to school it was in Bampton Grange where St Patrick's Hall is now. Did you know that?'

I thought someone might have already told me, but tried to look interested.

'The school used to be notable for turning out men of letters. We have a saying here that the lads drove their ploughs in Latin and swore in Greek. Have you heard it? Sorry, am I hurting you?'

'No. I'm fine, thank you.'

As she cleaned my wounds and talked about bishops and judges and lawyers, and Miss Castle made us all tea, I looked around me. There were paintings everywhere. A stack of them leaned against a table leg while the walls were covered in dozens more. They had clearly all been done by the same person, and I recognised some as local scenes. Miss Spriggs saw me looking.

'That's my passion you know. If I could have my time all over again I would have gone to art school, but it wasn't really done in my day, at least not for girls like me. I remember at school one day we had an art lesson and our master sat us all on the banks of the Lowther and asked us to draw the river. And we all drew the water in blue – every single one of us. He asked us to look at it again, and sure enough, when we looked properly we saw that the water was lots of different colours, in fact it was changing all the time as the light fell on it. That stayed in my mind and when I started to paint properly a few years ago, I tried to look at things more closely. I haven't managed it yet, but one day I will get the water just right.'

'They're very nice,' I said politely.

'She's good, isn't she?' said Elizabeth Castle. 'I would love to do the same but I'm afraid my eyesight isn't up to it these days. I seem to be failing in general. Don't get old, Gwenda, it's too much trouble!'

The ladies began to talk between themselves about their ailments and soon after that I saw the clock and realised that it was dinner time. I thanked them very much and said goodbye. They said they hoped they would see me again one day.

By the time I had struggled back with the bike, everyone was sitting at the table. Aunty gasped when she saw me. 'What happened to you?'

'I fell off the bike,' I said, glancing at Doug and John. They both looked the other way, guiltily. 'I couldn't stop it.'

'Which bike? John's? That's far too big for you, Gwenda,' said Aunty. 'You mustn't play on that unless the boys are with you.'

'They were supposed to help me get off,' I said, starting to feel sorry for myself.

'John? Douglas? What happened?' asked Aunty.

'Sorry, Gwenda,' said John good-naturedly. 'We thought you must have met someone when you took so long. One of the farm cats had kittens and we went to have a look. We can show you later, if you like.'

That cheered me up. 'I met two nice old ladies,' I said, and told the others about my new friends.

'Miss Spriggs sometimes goes out with her easel,' said John. 'The last time I saw her she went on for ages about how we never look at the water properly when we draw it. I thought I was going to be there all day.'

'She said that to me as well,' I said, pleased to have something in common with John.

Aunty said we should all be more understanding of the elderly as we would be old ourselves one day.

*

Sometimes Doug and John didn't mind me playing with them, especially if I could perform a useful role. It was handy to have an extra person to run after balls or be goalkeeper, or someone easy to catch when we played chasey. But I got fed up when they ran so much faster than me, got too rough, or turned their noses up at the games I suggested.

I was glad when Uncle, Doug and John went fishing for the day and I had Aunty all to myself. She announced that the others' absence was the ideal opportunity for us to tidy the table by the kitchen window, now piled even higher than it had been on the day of our arrival. I had been looking forward to this job as I loved fiddling with things I wasn't usually allowed to touch.

Aunty said we should have special piles and every single thing had to go onto one of them. There was a pile for Uncle and one for Aunty, a pile each for Hugh and John, and even one for me and Doug. There was also one for rubbish and one for things we really couldn't make up our minds about, though we had to try to keep that pile very small.

It was fun at first. I collected all the leaflets and bits of paper, most of which were for Aunty or Uncle. Some of the leaflets were interesting and I started to read about the duties of an air-raid warden in a guide to civil defence measures. I wondered which of them Dad had performed yet. But the novelty of the task began to wear off as I had to ask Aunty what to do with most things.

I was glad when we heard someone at the door and I could rush off to open it. It was Miss Dixon. She had come to say goodbye as she was going to stay with relatives in Newcastle for a short holiday. She said that she was keen to do some fell-walking on her return. Not long after she had left, Mrs Hutchinson, Ada's mother, came round and she and Aunty sat and talked about chapel folk and an impending dance in the church hall to raise money to buy wool for all the knitting everyone was doing for the troops. And as usual, Ada and her antics came up in conversation; Mrs Hutchinson said – would Aunty believe it! – she had cycled all the way to Shap just the day before.

There was a book on the table called *Great Expectations*. I didn't know what it meant but it had a picture of a child on the cover, which was promising. Aunty told me that it belonged on the shelves in the sitting room and that it would be very helpful if I could go and put it back. I left the ladies to their chatter and went into the silent room. There was a pleasant coolness in the air here. I was tempted by the piano, but instead sat down on one of the armchairs, opened the book and started to read. The boggy marshland described on the first page could not have been further away from the pretty green valley where I was living, but as I read about a churchyard and patches of nettles and cattle, I pictured it as if it were here in Bampton.

Aunty came looking for me when Mrs Hutchinson had left and said she had been calling me for ages and wondered where I had got to. I hadn't heard her. Though I didn't understand every word, and some of the sentences were so long I had forgotten how they started when I got to the end of them, I was desperate to know what happened to poor Pip, and was grateful that Aunty was nothing like his terrifying sister, who was bringing him up 'by hand'.

Chapter eleven

One day about a week into the summer holidays I was digging in the front garden with a small trowel Aunty had found for me when a car pulled up on the road outside and two women got out. The driver, a tall thin woman in a tweed skirt with a turban-like hat on her head, stretched herself, looked at the house and said, quite loudly, 'Well, here we are again. It hasn't changed, has it?' She wasn't a young woman, but as she strode up the path towards me, flapping her arms at her sides, she reminded me of a Boy Scout on an outing. Her companion, who was younger, smoothed down her skirt and patted her hair before joining her.

'Hello, little girl. Is Mr Douglas Thornton in?' asked the driver.

I stood up. 'Yes, I'll just go and get him.' Then I remembered that Uncle had gone to Appleby on business. 'I'll fetch Aunty instead,' I said, dashing inside.

'She's their niece,' I heard her say to the other woman.

When Aunty saw the couple she beamed and held out both of her hands in greeting. They took one each and asked after her and Uncle.

'I can't believe it's been a year!' said Aunty. 'How many are there of you this time?'

The driver, who seemed to be the one in charge, said that there were nine of them and that the others would be arriving later on the Penrith bus. 'Jane got married last September and has had a baby, so we shan't be seeing her this year, and as usual we've got some of our new students, but I think you'll recognise most of the others. A great crop this year and a few classicists amongst them to introduce to Mr Thornton!'

Then I remembered hearing Uncle and Aunty talking about 'the teachers' arriving any day now and that the farmer had dropped off a load of straw for them to sleep on. Doug and I had been having a great time clambering on it and wondering if we might be allowed to sleep in the straw too.

Gwenda and Doug with the teachers who slept in the school every summer

Aunty made tea and we sat outside to drink it. After they had chatted she opened the school for them and they parked the car at the back of the house to unload. It was a Morris Eight with a waterfall grille and a beautiful mascot that appeared to have a large jewel in it. The younger lady laughed when she saw me touching it and said she hadn't realised that little girls liked cars so much and Aunty said that she understood from our mother that Doug and I took after our father. The car was full of rucksacks and sleeping bags and I helped to take some of the lighter items inside. Later that afternoon I heard the sound of voices getting closer, then great cheers went up as a group of noisy young women came marching up the path.

I learnt that our visitors were a group of lecturers and trainee teachers from Durham University who came walking in the Lake District every summer. Jenny Charlton was the driver of the car, the oldest one in the party and the ringleader. I am not sure if her acquaintance with Uncle had begun in Durham, where Uncle had also studied, or at a later date, but for several years now Uncle had allowed Jenny and her gang to sleep in the school free of charge while they holidayed in this part of the Lakes.

I hung around watching them, smiling shyly at their laughter, until Aunty whisked me off with her to make tea for them all. When we came back they were making themselves mattresses with the straw by stuffing it into sewn-up sheets they had brought with them, and I rushed to help.

'Do say if she's a nuisance,' said Aunty, but Jenny Charlton said that they never turned down the offer of a spare pair of hands.

I heard them leave the next morning when I was still in bed

and wished I had got up earlier to see them off. I couldn't wait for them to come back and was sitting on the wall looking out for them when they finally appeared.

'You haven't been sitting there all day, have you?' laughed Jenny, tickling my chin with a blade of grass as she walked past. She wore a skirt and jacket and had a walking stick in her hand, but two of the younger women wore trousers not unlike Uncle's plus-fours. I hadn't seen women dressed like that before and thought them very daring, though their outfits must have been much easier to walk in.

'Oh, my poor feet!' exclaimed one of the women.

'The first day's always the worst,' said another.

'Nonsense, it's the second or third day,' said Jenny briskly.

They were all tired and sunburnt, but whenever I saw them they were laughing about something. They were both grown-up and childish at the same time and I longed to be old enough to be able to be the same. They were my introduction to independent women making their own plans without the need for men. I knew that Jenny Charlton was unmarried and when I thought of all the teachers I knew – people like Miss Nattress, Miss Dixon and Miss Williams – I wondered if perhaps teachers weren't allowed to have husbands.

The next day when they returned from their hike I was furious to see Doug and John walking with them. I hadn't noticed the boys leave as I had been in the kitchen with Aunty and Uncle, half-listening to their conversation with a man called Mr Stacey, who was staying with his family at the Crown and Mitre in Bampton Grange. With his tweeds and his walking cane and his cultured voice, he was very much a gentleman.

'You might know my son, John,' he said to me, for John had apparently started Bampton School on the same day as me and Doug, but it turned out that John was in the class above mine.

'I'm sure they are going to get on famously,' said Aunty with a meaningful smile as I got up to leave, 'and Doug is such a charming boy.' But I had heard sounds from outside and was in too much of a hurry to wonder why she was saying that.

As I greeted the tired walkers, I saw that the youngest member of the group, a student teacher called Rosemary, was lagging behind and holding the arm of one of the others. She smiled feebly as she walked past me.

'I think she's coming down with something,' Jenny confided to Aunty later. 'Let's hope she feels better in the morning. She'll be awfully disappointed if she can't come to Haweswater with us.'

That evening as I played with Neville at the table and the boys played cards, Aunty said she had better go and see how Rosemary was feeling. She came back just a couple of minutes later and said that the poor girl couldn't stay there, she was most unwell, and went upstairs to prepare the spare bedroom.

Rosemary was worse the next day and couldn't accompany the rest of the party. Aunty took frequent drinks to her room, but she slept for most of the day. The doctor diagnosed a severe case of tonsillitis.

Uncle said he would send a telegram to Rosemary's parents asking them to come and collect their daughter, but Aunty said that he couldn't do that, not with everything that was going on right now – her poor parents would get such a shock to see the telegram delivery boy. 'It will be kinder to write a letter.'

I took the letter to Ada at the post office first thing in the

morning. I liked to have an excuse to go there as I was sure
one day the baby would have arrived and I wanted to be able
to break the news to the others. Ronnie Scott, the postman
and father of my friend Marjorie, was there too and asked how
I was enjoying the school holidays. Both he and Ada listened
with concern when I told them about poor Rosemary.

'Mind, she's a kind woman is Mrs Thornton,' said Mr Scott.

'She'd do anything for anyone,' said Ada. 'Do ask her if I
can help at all, Gwenda.'

When Mr Scott had gone I asked Ada if she thought her
baby might come soon.

'If it comes in the holidays I'll have more time to play with
it,' I said.

'The baby will come when it's ready,' laughed Ada. 'I'm sure
you'll be one of the first ones to know.'

That night, Paddy, who was the main joker in the group,
came back limping, though she was still laughing, and when
she took off her boots she had the most enormous blister I had
seen. It covered the whole of the ball of her foot. Aunty gave
her a bowl to bathe her feet in and the group debated whether
it was best to pop the blister or to leave it. I hoped they would
pop it while I was there but they were still discussing it when
I went for my tea.

Though Aunty had told me not to bother them, I loved
being around these people and did my best to melt into the
background when I returned after I had eaten. Sometimes they
asked me questions about my family in Newcastle – to my surprise, one of them knew someone who lived in a neighbouring
road in High Heaton – or my favourite lessons at school or

what my hobbies were. But I liked it best when I could just sit and listen to them.

Molly was quieter than the others and liked to sit in the corner and read at the end of the day. When she saw me watching her she held up her book so that I could see the title. It was a book of poetry by Wordsworth and she asked if I had heard of him. I hadn't. She said that Wordsworth had loved this part of the world and written lots of poems about it. I told her I was reading *Great Expectations* and she was most impressed and started talking about Dickens and suggesting other books that I might enjoy, if only I could have remembered their names.

'If the war's still on, I wonder if they'll come next year,' said John one evening when I reappeared after Doug had gone to fetch me. He was busy doing something disgusting with some insects he had dug up and was going to use as bait when he went fishing the next day.

Uncle was fiddling with his pipe – smoking a pipe looked to be more trouble than it was worth at times. He said he thought it unlikely that the war would be over by then and I think even we children knew it. During that month of August 1940 the Battle of Britain was being waged in our skies as the Luftwaffe targeted our airfields in preparation for a German invasion, and though we were untroubled here in our peaceful valley, I had a vague idea of what was happening thanks to the wireless, newspaper headlines and playground talk. Just a couple of days before, Churchill had given his stirring speech, 'Never in the field of human conflict was so much owed by so many to so few.'

'The government might even be calling up women by then,' Uncle added, after taking a satisfied puff.

'Surely not!' Aunty looked up from her knitting.

'Not to fight, but we might need more hands in the factories or on the land. Volunteering isn't going to be enough.'

'Or it might all be over,' said Aunty. 'Wouldn't that be lovely!'

One afternoon Doug and I accompanied John to Burnbanks, the village that housed the Haweswater dam workers. It had taken on an almost mythical status to me. Tobe, one of the boys at school, told stories about the lodgers who lived with his family. Their house was bigger than most of the others in Burnbanks and had rooms to house the single men who worked there, whom his mother cooked and washed for.

'Big Bob's got silver teeth and he's so tall he sleeps on the floor instead of a bed. But my favourite is Halifax Pete. He walks all over the country from job to job. Everything he's got fits in a duffel bag. He says belongings only tie you down. He used to get himself in trouble for drinking so now he gives all his money to my mam and she doles it out to him, like pocket money. She says he's been much better behaved since she started doing that.' (The thought of an adult having pocket money for good behaviour made me smile.) 'And guess what – he can sing "Rule Britannia" with his belches.'

This had us all in stitches, particularly when Jez Percy tried to imitate this accomplishment and ended up sounding as if he was being sick.

However, it was a peaceful scene that greeted us that afternoon. The prefabricated houses gleamed in the sunshine. There were flowers growing in the gardens and washing blowing on the lines. There were no men to be seen. John said that

these ordinary-looking dwellings were far more modern inside
than most of the houses in Bampton as they all had running
water and indoor bathrooms and electricity.

'In fact, I wouldn't mind living here myself. They've got
tennis courts and a bowling green, and that's the recreation
hall over there. There's a good football team too. Dad's played
them before.'

As if hearing the word football, Jez Percy and his younger
brother Alf appeared with a ball and asked us if we wanted
to play.

'Hello, Gwenda-suspender,' said Alf, who was in my class,
running away before I could land a playful slap.

'Mr Ostle's on our tail again,' said Jez. Mr Ostle was the
security man hired by the corporation whose duties seemed to
include keeping a vigilant eye on the village children. 'He gave
us a telling-off before, but he'll not dare if we're with you.' He
looked at John as he said this. A headmaster for a father gave
John a certain status, even amongst some adults.

But John said we couldn't stay, there was only time to show
me and Doug the dam before going home for tea.

I wondered if we might see Halifax Pete or Big Bob when
we got to the dam, and imagined men paddling at the water's
edge plugging holes with mud and pebbles. Work on it was
nearing completion and I had heard Uncle and some of the
men talking about what would happen to Burnbanks when
it was finished. Some of the dwellings that were no longer
needed had already been dismantled – the material used for
the 'war effort'. It sometimes felt as if nothing could be thrown
away these days but had to be kept for some other purpose. At
home in Newcastle we had helped in the collection of pans and

aluminium items for making Spitfires. Doug said that thinking of the war effort was an effort in itself.

We carried on up a path through the trees to the dam, the Percy boys at our side one minute and disappearing the next. The dam turned out to be a giant concrete wall, the water of the lake lapping against the side, quite a long way down, and not a workman to be seen. It was disappointing not to see the tops of the buildings of the drowned village of Mardale peeking through the ripples, but it was an impressive sight nonetheless.

Jez came up behind us. 'And if the Jerries blow it up, then – swoosh! – we all get washed away,' he said cheerfully.

Aunty continued to care for Rosemary until her father arrived to take her home. She sometimes sent me upstairs with little bits of food to tempt her, but she rarely ate more than a bite or two. Her temperature had dropped but she was still very weak. She usually just nodded or smiled her thanks at me, but as she began to feel better, she started to talk. The day before she left she told me I would make a good nurse when I grew up. I should have been flattered. I had wanted to be a nurse ever since I was very little and Ivy and I had played hospitals together, but I could hardly tell Rosemary that the sight of her in this too-hot bedroom which smelled of musty sheets and uneaten food was making me reconsider my plans.

Rosemary's father arrived and we said goodbye to her. The day after that the teachers moved on. They produced presents for Aunty and Uncle – a pretty handkerchief for Aunty and a tin of tobacco for Uncle.

'I hope we'll see you again next year, Mrs Thornton,' said Jenny, taking her hand then giving her a slightly awkward hug.

'Me too, dear,' said Aunty. 'Let's hope the world is a nicer place by then.'

'I wonder if you'll still be here, Gwenda, or if you'll be home in Newcastle,' said Paddy. 'You're going to miss her when she's gone, Mrs Thornton. You're going to miss the pair of them.'

Aunty looked at me. 'Yes, I will. We've become quite used to having them around. But I'm sure they're missing their parents dreadfully.'

'Are you, Gwenda?' asked Paddy with a wink, and I felt as if she knew the truth, which was that I didn't have much time to think about my parents. At Aunty's insistence, Doug and I sat down at the kitchen table once a week to write to them and my mother wrote back regularly. I loved receiving her letters and Doug and I sometimes fought over who would read them first, but I couldn't say that I really missed her or my father. We continued to pray for them every night and I felt as if I was fulfilling my daughterly duties, as well as helping to keep them safe, by doing so.

'No, I mean, yes . . . I don't know,' I mumbled, and Paddy and Aunty laughed.

Although they had only been with us for a few days I could barely imagine life without the teachers. Next summer seemed an impossibly long time to wait before we saw them again.

They sent us a postcard from Windermere a few days later, and not long after that we said goodbye to John until the next holiday. John had told Doug lots of stories about Appleby Grammar and Uncle had even suggested that if the war carried on, and we were still with them in two years' time, he might be driving Doug to Appleby in September as well. Uncle tutored some of the bright children before the grammar school entrance exams – otherwise they stayed at Bampton School to finish their education – but he said he was sure that Doug would sail through them without any extra help.

'Will I go, too?' I asked.

Uncle said the school was only for boys, but he was sure the war would be over by the time I was that old.

Chapter twelve

'Yan, than, teddera, meddera, pimp,' I chanted.

Pimp! What a funny but satisfying word that was!

'Settera, lettera, hovera, dovera, dick.'

Old Mr Brennan had taught me and Doug the sheep-counting numbers and now I wanted to use them all the time. I felt as if I was party to some secret knowledge. Mr Brennan lived in the house facing the mill, beside the bridge, and he was often to be seen wandering along the lanes, fiddling with his pipe and picking things from the bushes. He seemed to be eternally busy yet to have all the time in the world. It hadn't taken long before we got to know him.

'Yan dick, than dick, teddera dick,' I continued.

I had learnt all the way to twenty and then I had pestered Mr Brennan for what came next.

'Nowt,' he said, 'you start all over again.'

He explained that the shepherd would record how many times he had reached twenty by marking it in some way, for example by putting a stone in his pocket or tying a knot in a rope, and then carry on counting from the beginning again. I had counted all the books in the schoolhouse and tried to count the trees in our little wood, but that got too confusing. Now I was going to count all the sheep in the field on the other side of the lane. I sat on the gate and started, then realising I had nothing to record each new score, I clambered down to pick up some pebbles. I put a pebble onto the gate post each time I reached twenty.

Mr Brennan was popular with us children for other reasons. He always had a supply of hazelnuts in the pocket of his jacket and at this time of year they were fresh and nothing like the bullets my parents attacked with their nutcrackers at Christmas. They came in a papery leaf wrapping which we would discard, and the shell was soft enough to crack in our mouths and spit out. The nuts tasted sweet and pea-like, and once you had eaten one you wanted to keep on eating them. The fact that Mr Brennan also kept his baccy in his pocket and that the nuts came with a distinct tobacco flavour didn't put us off. Now, as soon as I spotted him, I would run to catch up with him and beg him for one of his nuts, sometimes even thrusting my hand straight into his pocket to see if I could find one.

He had taught us other things too. He knew what was safe to eat that grew in the hedgerows or the edges of the fields, which plants you could eat the leaves of and which the roots. He told us never to eat – or even touch – toadstools or mushrooms, but to leave that to the experts. We ate well in the schoolhouse but I still could have eaten all day long if I had the chance and the countryside around us was like an extra larder. I gobbled down dandelion and clover, chickweed and the slim green leaves of wild garlic. The common mallow was practically totally edible – leaves, shoots, flowers, roots. At home we had gone brambling every October and my mother had produced pies and jellies with the fruit, as well as a crab apple jelly from the tree in the garden, but there were other new fruits to be gathered here and Miss Dixon was coming to collect me soon as she wanted me to help her to gather bilberries.

As soon as I heard Aunty call me I got down and returned to the schoolhouse.

'Yan, than, tedderra, meddera,' I was still saying to myself as I went into the kitchen, where Miss Dixon was sitting with Aunty at the table. I felt as if I could cast a spell with those words – not that I would have wanted to cast a spell on Aunty or Miss Dixon, though Doug might have wanted to magic Miss Dixon away on Friday bath nights.

'Listen to this child,' said Aunty. 'She's becoming a little Westmorland girl! I don't know what her parents will say when they see her next. I don't know if they will even understand her!'

Miss Dixon smiled and said that some people had the same problem with the Geordie accent. Then she stood up and said briskly that we should set off straight away as she had met Mr Brennan on the way and he had told her it was going to rain later.

We took the lane south, via Gate Foot, then headed off over the moorland to the eastern shores of Haweswater, where trees like marching armies covered the slopes. Miss Dixon said she had seen a whole hillside covered in late-cropping bilberries on a walk a few days ago but she had had nothing to put them into at the time.

'I'm sure they were just here,' she said, half to herself, as I scrambled along behind her, my much shorter legs finding it an effort to keep up. The ground was spongy in some places, rocky in others, with lots of little tufts that seemed designed to trip me up.

Finally she stopped and pointed. I couldn't see them at first as the whole slope was covered in the short sturdy plants. 'Here we are, and the birds haven't got them yet, though not for much longer, I fear. Let's get to work.'

She took the bags Aunty had lent her from the rucksack she was carrying and passed me one.

'This is one of the awkward things about not being in your own home, Gwenda – having to borrow the most mundane items. I'm not sure I'll ever get used to it. And not being able to do things the way one wants to. I have to bite my tongue half the time with Miss Household.'

I didn't think that Miss Dixon would ever bite her tongue with anyone, but I gave her a small smile in sympathy before I started picking.

'Do you know,' she went on, 'I've watched her pick up a cup from the draining board to dry it when it's quite obviously per-forming a more useful function propping up a saucer. Saucer first, it makes much more sense. I'm sure your mother knows that, she seems such a sensible woman. I've tried to explain it to Miss Household but I know when my advice isn't welcome. Ah well, isn't it a beautiful day? I don't know that I believe we're getting rain. Those clouds look far too friendly to me. Still, best get on with it.'

Miss Dixon's conversation washed gently over me. I had nothing to add to it. I liked Miss Dixon, and Uncle said she was a great asset to the school, but she had rigid ideas about things and I knew I would never want to get into an argument with her.

'Whortleberries. Huckleberries. Whinberries. They're all names for the bilberry, you know. They're rather nice names, aren't they – we ought to write a song about them. In America they eat a lot of a similar fruit they call a blueberry. They even make a cheesecake with them. They say it's delicious, but can you imagine a cake made out of cheese?'

I said that I couldn't.

I was sitting on the ground to pick. Miss Dixon declared that I had the right idea and sat herself down too. The bilberries were delicious – tiny and bursting with sweetness. I was eating as many as I was picking.

Miss Dixon began to tell me about her niece, Daphne, who was the same age as me. 'I'm knitting a jumper for her,' she said. 'If you don't mind I'll bring it to the schoolhouse some time to see if it fits you. I think you're about the same size as Daphne, though one does forget how quickly children grow when one doesn't see them for a while.'

When we had filled most of the bags, Miss Dixon declared that as we had to carry them home, we had probably done enough for one day. We sat for a while looking at the choppy water of the lake below us.

'What happened to all the people?' I asked her.

'What people, Gwenda?'

'Who lived in the drowned village.'

'Ah, Mardale. Well, they all moved to new homes. They knew what was going to happen a long time before it did, though I expect it was still very upsetting for them. I suppose some of them might live in Bampton now.'

The thought that Haweswater had swallowed up a village always made it seem slightly sinister to me. I felt that the waters might be capable of grabbing me or some other hapless passer-by if we got too close and subjecting us to the same fate.

'Shirley says that the bell on Mardale church still rings.'

'Well, that would be very clever considering that the bell was removed and given to another church,' said Miss Dixon sharply. 'A church bell is a work of craftsmanship, and rather expensive too.' She gave me one of her 'teacher' looks. 'I hope you don't believe everything you are told, Gwenda.'

'I don't,' I said, feeling foolish. I wanted to explain that it was the ghost of the bell that Shirley's uncle had heard, not the bell itself, but decided that would only sound sillier.

I still imagined that the village had been drowned in one mighty whoosh of water that swirled around the buildings and rose and rose until even the tallest building had been submerged. It wasn't until I was older that I discovered that the village had been demolished first and that only the foundations had been left – foundations that are visible today whenever the water is very low.

'Of course you don't,' said Miss Dixon. 'You and Douglas are very bright children. Tell me, what do you want to be when you grow up?'

'A nurse, I think.'

'Not a teacher, then?'

'Um, maybe.'

'Well, don't rule it out. It's a fine profession for a woman.'

She pointed at the steep western slopes of the valley. 'Ah! I never get tired of these views. What a beautiful part of the world to be in. And when you think about what is happening in some of our cities right now ...' She tailed off and gave me a thoughtful look, as if to see what I already knew, before carrying on. 'You know what the Germans are doing now, don't you? They think that they can destroy our morale and bomb us into submission. That madman Hitler has bitten off more than he can chew, I can tell you!'

I nodded. I knew from the adults' conversations that the war had taken a new course and that the Germans, having failed to destroy our airbases and factories, had decided to bomb our cities instead. Mam's letters, of course, told us very little about that side of things. She wrote regularly, but there was more news of Aunty Edith and Beryl or the neighbours than anything else. When she did mention air raids it was only to make us laugh by telling us how Mr and Mrs Young were both so deaf they didn't hear the siren and she had to bang on their back door to rouse them before taking cover in the shelter herself.

On our way back to Bampton we saw a familiar figure coming towards us before heading off across the fells. The man waved at us before he disappeared. It was Billy Preston.

'Mr Preston's going rock climbing,' I informed Miss Dixon, knowing from Ada that that was one of his favourite pursuits.

'Such a nice fellow,' said Miss Dixon. 'And such a popular teacher. He'll be making the most of his free time before his baby arrives.'

*

Billy Preston climbing at Mardale

When I came home from school one afternoon Aunty was stirring a pan at the range, Miss Williams was at the table and a serious-looking boy was sitting beside her.

'This is John and he's come to live with us,' said Aunty, as if it was the most normal thing in the world. 'He's an evacuee, just like you.'

John Stacey, it turned out, was the son of the smart gentleman I had met earlier that summer. His family had historic links with Bampton and though he lived in south-east England he spent his holidays here. Now his parents were going back to Kent and wanted a good home for their only child. His father, who had contracted polio after his service in the last war, had asked Uncle if both John and his nanny could stay in the schoolhouse. Although I didn't know this at the time, Uncle's reply had been, 'We will be happy to take John, but not his nanny. The boy will be the laughing stock of the village if he has a nanny with him.'

I don't know what sort of look I had on my face as Aunty introduced us – I am sure it was surprise rather than hostility – but Aunty said sharply, 'Well, aren't you going to say how-do-you-do and make your new playmate feel welcome?'

The boy blinked, then gave me a shy smile as we greeted each other.

'How old are you?' I asked him.

'I was eight in July,' he replied.

I smiled back at him. It would be nice to have someone closer in age to me than Doug.

'You're going to make quite a little team,' said Miss Williams as she got up to catch her bus. 'But gosh, you'll be rather outnumbered, Gwenda, with all these boys, especially when other John comes home again! Still, I'm sure you can hold your own.'

John was installed in the small bedroom at the front of the house that looked out across the fields to Bampton Grange and Knipe Scar. You could read the time on the church clock from his window and Uncle joked that he need never be late

for church, for John was an Anglican, not a Methodist like
we were. He seemed happy to be on his own, in the early
days at least. Once I peeped round his door and saw him
sitting on the floor, a look of concentration on his face, as he
constructed something with a pile of bricks. But they weren't
like the bricks that Doug and I had once played with. These
brown rubber bricks had interlocking parts so that John was
able to build some quite sophisticated contraptions with them.
I would have liked to join him but I could sense that I wouldn't
be welcome. Aunty told us that John wasn't used to sharing
things, having no brothers or sisters of his own, but said that
Doug and I could help by setting a good example. I promptly
showed him a selection of the few toys I had with me – my
tatty comic, my crayons and Neville – and asked if he would
like to play with them, but he politely declined.

John had brought his bike with him and as they grew more
friendly he and Doug would sometimes go cycling together,
leaving me on my own. But with my crockery houses, my
books and Neville to amuse me, I can't remember minding
too much.

Now that we had settled into our new life, I began to get into
trouble more often. The first bad thing I remember doing was
losing the key for the front door. This large wooden door was
rarely locked, not even at night, and its huge key fascinated
me. It was like the key to a castle or a prison. I managed
to wriggle it free of the lock and used it in my games. One
Saturday afternoon Marjorie, Janet and I took it in turns to
free a princess from the dungeon, which could only be done
with the giant key, which we took it in turns to hide. The

John Stacey, Haweswater, 1940

dungeon was the patch of nettles on the other side of the wall that I liked to walk on (I had already managed to fall into the patch once, appearing in front of Aunty with a rash all over my arms and legs). But when one evening Uncle noticed that the key was missing, I realised that we had abandoned the game when Janet's sisters had turned up unexpectedly and the key had been forgotten. Doug and John helped me to look for it, but it had been hidden too well. It was getting dark, so Uncle said I would have to resume the search tomorrow. I looked and looked, but it never did turn up.

The subject of the key would come up in conversation from time to time to remind me what could happen when I was careless. This was one of the main differences between my parents and Aunty and Uncle. At home I might have received a smack for something naughty, then the matter would be forgotten. But here the taunt of 'Remember who lost the key!' would pop up every now and then to shame me. Sometimes I thought I would have preferred the smack!

Chapter thirteen

Aunty switched off the wireless when I walked into the kitchen one afternoon after school. I caught the word 'casualties' but not what the story was about. Later I heard Doug and John talking in John's bedroom and I listened at the door. I learnt that a ship evacuating British children to safety in Canada had been torpedoed in the Atlantic and that many lives had been lost. Even at that age the appalling irony of it was not lost on me – children sailing to a new life and safety losing their lives on the way. It was all wrong.

Doug said to John, 'It might have been me and Gwenda, you know. Our parents were going to send us to Australia.'

'Really?' John sounded interested.

'Yes, we've got relatives there, but Gwenda was too young to go so they changed their minds.'

When I caught Aunty doing the same thing later, I declared, 'I know about the ship and all the children, Aunty.'

Her face dropped and for a horrible second I thought she was going to cry.

'I'm glad we weren't on it. Me and Doug and John. And your John.'

'Oh, Gwenda! It's dreadful, just dreadful,' she said. 'Come and sit on my knee for a minute and we'll get on with that knitting. It's quite upset me, it has.'

We settled in her rocking chair and I leaned back into her. Aunty's lap was soft. Her pinny always smelled of baking and fresh bread.

After many lessons I had now mastered knitting and had insisted on my first solo project being a pair of socks for a soldier. I hated doing purl stitches but I could do socks all in plain knitting. 'In, over, through, off,' I said to myself, as Aunty had taught me. 'In, over, through, off.' I said it with every stitch. It must have driven Aunty mad, though she never said so. She spent a lot of time picking up my dropped stitches.

I was still working on the first sock. It had orange stripes on the cuff and I was very proud of it.

'It's getting quite long now,' said Aunty. 'It's time to turn the heel.'

'My soldier might have long legs,' I said.

'You still need to turn the heel,' said Aunty. 'I haven't seen a sock without a foot before. Come on, I'll show you what to do.'

I often pictured the soldier who would wear my socks and his delight as he received them, though the picture changed from day to day; some days he was Billy Preston, who was an RAF Reservist, and other days he was Hugh, Aunty and Uncle's eldest son, whose photo I had seen in the sitting room.

Or sometimes he was Dad, who on some battlefield in Europe would open the package and say, 'By jingo, I do believe these are the ones our Gwenda knitted!'

It was my seventh birthday in October. Aunty and Uncle gave me a child's Bible and Aunty made me a cake. There were presents to open from home – a jumper from Mam and Dad, which Aunty said would be perfect with winter on its way, and a stocking hat from Mrs Young, which I liked even more.

After school Ada and her mother came round for my birthday tea. Mrs Hutchinson gave me a handkerchief with GB embroidered on it and Ada and Billy, who had gone to Penrith at the weekend to buy some things for the baby, handed me the latest copy of *Enid Blyton's Sunny Stories* which felt like a minor miracle when Mam had told me there were no comics being produced in wartime. I almost wished all my visitors gone so that I could sit down and read it undisturbed.

That same week came the day I had been longing for – the day free from lessons for picking blackberries and rosehips. Uncle said there was no point in him giving the whole school the day off until he was sure that the fruit was good and ready, so every evening after tea, Doug, John and I accompanied him down lanes and into thickets as he checked the berries for ripeness. I crossed my fingers every time, but it always seemed to be, 'Not quite there yet. Look how hard these ones are.' But finally, the time was right.

We all took a packed lunch to school that day which made it feel even more special. Aunty gave the three of us a large buttered teacake each. We were split into several groups, with the older children walking all the way to Haweswater and the rest of us foraging in the hedgerows closer to home. I could see that Doug was pleased to be in Mr Preston's group. The teachers carried sticks and helped us to find the best places to pick.

I knew not to eat raw rosehips, but I was eating almost as many blackberries as I was adding to the baskets. Miss Pickup saw my stained mouth and said, 'Gwenda Brady, I wasn't aware that you were the cause we were all working for.'

It felt as if the whole village was involved in this enterprise. As we filled the baskets at our feet, the older children emptied them into larger containers and took them on wheelbarrows to the church hall where the Women's Institute ladies were waiting to wash and sort them, ready for making their jams and jellies. When we had finished, Marjorie and I had long rough scratches all over our arms and legs and I could feel tiny thorns in the tips of my fingers.

Aunty had a big smile on her face when I got home.

'Ada's had her baby!' she announced. 'It's a little boy. What a surprise for Billy when he gets back!'

'Can I see him?' I begged, but Aunty said that we would have to wait as Billy would want to get acquainted with his new son and Ada would be tired.

'After tea then?'

'No, no, no! But we'll go soon, I promise, if Ada doesn't mind.'

I couldn't wait. My first proper baby! I was already planning the things this child and I would do together when he was older, and if Ada would let me.

When Saturday came Aunty took me, Doug and John to see him. He was asleep, his face a scrunched up ball of red. I wanted to hold him but Ada said that it was best to make the most of the peace and that there would be plenty of time for cuddles later. Mrs Hutchinson was there too, making tea for everyone and peeping into the cot every few minutes.

He was called David.

'He looks like an angry old man,' declared John, and I looked across at Ada, worried that she would be offended, but she only laughed.

Billy came into the room and Doug said to him, 'We can take David on the fells when he's older, Mr Preston.'

I glared at Doug. 'I'm the one who's taking him out. Didn't you say so, Ada?'

It was just a few weeks later, in November, that Billy was called up for active service and had to leave his wife and baby for the RAF.

I remained devoted to Judith and she seemed to be equally devoted to me, though I imagine that the extra food I gave her had something to do with this. Not surprisingly, she grew fatter than the other hens. When I didn't see her one morning, in spite of my initial concern, I didn't dwell on it for long. We had a visitor, Aunty's sister, and an overnight visitor was quite a special occurrence so I didn't want to miss out on what was going on.

Aunty Mary came to stay a few times a year. She was the only one of Aunty's siblings who was not married and, since her sisters' marriages, lived on her own in a small house in Harrington in West Cumberland which she called 'The Result'. It wasn't a proper holiday, as far as I could see, as she spent a lot of time helping Aunty, but she enjoyed her visits and Aunty must have been grateful as there was a constant stream of jobs to do in the large house and garden – even more now that she had three evacuees living with her. And so Aunty Mary cheerfully helped her to chop wood, prepare meals, wash and dust, dig up potatoes and weed the garden. I learnt later that she was a great help to all of her family, not just Aunty, and after the war, in her late fifties, she would marry the sweetheart of her youth after he was widowed, living happily with him until her death.

When a whole day had passed with no sign of Judith I thought about asking Aunty, but she was busy and seemed distracted. The next day she sent me to fetch some potatoes from the sack in the store room out the back and that was where I saw her. I knew it was her. She was hanging on a hook on the back of the door. One of her eyes was looking straight at me. I stood transfixed for a few seconds then I ran out crying.

'You are a silly one,' said Aunty, wiping my tears. 'I told you not to feed her too much. But they're all going to go that way one day. That's just the way it is. She'll make us a lovely dinner on Sunday and we might even get some soup out of her as well. You can help Uncle to pluck her if you like.'

That made me cry even harder. Later I saw Doug and John receiving a lesson in the art of plucking from Uncle in a corner of the garden, feathers blowing around their feet. I even heard them laughing. I told Aunty that they were all cruel and heartless. Aunty said that no one would force me to eat Judith if I didn't want to. Thank goodness – I would rather starve than do that.

On Sunday John set off on his bike to St Patrick's Church in Bampton Grange, where he was also a member of the choir, though he took pride in managing to avoid all their practices. At chapel Ada and Billy were showing off baby David and Aunty said I could walk home with them as she had to get a move on. Ada even let me help to push the pram. I had to step back every time someone stopped us to look inside. When I walked into the schoolhouse a delicious smell was wafting from the kitchen. My mouth started to water straight away. I had already set the table in the dining room for the six of us before leaving for chapel.

Uncle carved the bird and put a mixture of brown and white meat on everyone's plate. Aunty looked at me briefly, as if she was about to say something, but must have changed her mind. I knew that was Judith on my plate, of course I did, but I was hungry. And didn't Aunty often say that in wartime it was more important than ever that we didn't waste anything? Uncle asked me to say grace, which was often my job these days, and as soon as I had finished I tucked straight in before anyone could make me change my mind. The meat was succulent and delicious. It might even have been the best meal I had eaten in Bampton. No one mentioned Judith, and I was relieved. I could even pretend to myself that it wasn't her. And as we ate our blackberry pie and custard after, there was the usual delight in wondering if I would have the dish with the spots. It was one of the great mysteries of my life that whatever we had for pudding – even if it was something that had been made in advance and left to set – I had that dish, although it appeared to be identical to the others in every other way.

'I wonder if I'll be the lucky one today,' Uncle would say as he got to the end of his pudding and I would look across at Aunty who would smile but give nothing away. Then he would feign dismay over his dish being plain on the bottom and ask Doug if he had it. Doug, never one to turn down the chance to tease me, would declare that he did and I would feel a growing sense of alarm until I discovered that I had the dish after all. If its aim was to ensure I ate up every last mouthful, it worked, for I never left anything behind, even if it was rice pudding which was one of my least favourite things.

'Well,' Aunty Mary said after the meal. 'That was delicious. And I don't know what you feed your chickens on, but that was one of the tastiest I've had.'

There was an awkward silence. Aunty looked at me. Doug and John grinned at each other across the table and tried not to laugh. Uncle put on a jolly face and said to his sister-in-law, 'But have you still got the energy for a short walk this afternoon?'

'I knew that was Judith,' I said to everyone, but looking mainly at Doug.

But later, when I was on my own, I wiped away some hot tears. 'I'm so sorry, Judith, wherever you are now. I wouldn't have eaten you if I'd known it was you. Honestly.' But I added, in case God heard my lie, 'I'd have got into trouble if I hadn't eaten my dinner. We all have to eat everything in wartime.'

I made up my mind not to become attached to any animals again.

Memories of those who stayed: 'Blown through the bedroom window'

We lived in Cleveland Gardens, High Heaton, the same road as Gwenda but a bit lower down. I had been evacuated to Spittal near Berwick-on-Tweed but had come home because the lady I was staying with was unwell. I was nine years old and my sister Rita, who was also home at the time, was fifteen. It was the night of 3 September 1940 and I was reading when the siren started. Mum came into the room and told me to go straight to the shelter in the garden, which we shared with our neighbours. My father, who would never go into the shelter, remained in bed. Our neighbour Mr Weatherett was already inside the shelter when I got there, but his wife was with Mum and Rita in the kitchen, bottling the plum jam Mum had made. The next thing I remember was looking out of the shelter and seeing that the roof of our house was vertical. It was eerily quiet. Mr Weatherett was unable to see anything as the sandbags had burst and he was covered in sand. Eventually Mum, Rita and Mrs Weatherett appeared, having crawled through the destruction around them, which included broken glass and sticky jam. We all went to the front of the house where we found my father sitting on the wall. He had been blown out of bed and through the window. He was in hospital for a while and then sent to a convalescent home. But poor Mrs Elliott in Jenifer Grove – the road behind us which received a direct hit – was killed in the attack.

Our house was one of three that had to be demolished. Fortunately for us my aunts lived at the other end of Cleveland

Gardens so we had somewhere to go. I was sent to stay with some friends at Heddon-on-the-Wall but came home after nine months.

Jean Atkinson (née Farnsworth), Newcastle,
July 2015, aged eighty-four

Gwenda bumped into her old neighbour Jean again when they were adults as they have friends in common.

Chapter fourteen

When I look back on my life with Aunty and Uncle, I remember not just how kind they were to me and Doug but how important they were to other people too. Everyone in the village knew Uncle, and though he was always 'Mr Thornton' at school, to many of the locals – and to his card-playing friends – he was 'Dougie'. He was a respected member of the community, one to whom people often went for help or advice, but he was also known to have a good sense of humour. Whenever I was out with Doug or John and got talking to someone, you could be sure they would have a story to tell about their own association with him. Depending on the age of the person, there was a good chance that he had taught them, their parents, their children or their grandchildren as he had been headmaster of the school since 1918 (and would continue to be so until 1953). And though some might have

seen more of his authoritarian side than others, there were few
who disagreed that they had received a good education there.
If they were Methodists they would also know Uncle from
chapel, though he was on good terms too with the Anglican
vicar and the flock of St Patrick's Church in Bampton Grange.
(Indeed, Aunty and Uncle joined the rest of the village in the
vicarage garden when May Day came around and I was one
of the children dancing round the maypole.) Some knew him
from the parish council, of which he would eventually become
one of the longest serving members, with a service lasting from
1934 to 1970. Others might remind you that he was one of
the organisers of Bampton Sports, a highlight of the village
year which took place on the first Saturday of September,
though I don't remember it taking place in wartime. This
had been going on since the previous century, growing out
of Cumberland and Westmorland-style wrestling meetings to
become a far bigger annual event that included fell-racing – to
the top of Knipe Scar and back – hound-trailing, pony races
and athletics.

I didn't know much about his or Aunty's backgrounds at
the time – what child shows an interest in that sort of thing?
Most of us think of the questions we would have liked to ask
when it is too late to do so. But I have discovered a few more
details recently. Uncle was born in Appleby, the county town
of what was then known as Westmorland, in 1892. In the 1901
census, the first on which he appears, he is the middle child of
the seven listed, though I believe that two older siblings had
already left home. His father was a joiner and cabinet maker
who had also been born in the town, but his mother came
from Scotland. Ten years later, at the age of nineteen, he was

a student in Durham at the College of the Venerable Bede, which specialised in teacher training, and his first teaching job was at Appleby Grammar School. During the first war he found himself in the Army where the story goes that he felt he was spending an inordinate amount of time peeling potatoes! Feeling that this was a waste of his talents he wrote to protest and was allowed to leave, reputedly becoming the youngest headmaster in the country when he became head in Bampton.

Aunty was born Eveline Margaret Hewetson in Langwathby, Cumberland, a village a few miles from Penrith, in the same year as Uncle. She was the youngest of the five children of a farmer, two boys and three girls, though one of the boys, Thomas, died as a baby before she was born. Tragically her mother died – probably of influenza – in 1895 and the children were brought up by a series of housekeepers. In the 1901 census, Aunty and her sisters were living with an aunt and uncle, who was a Wesleyan minister. Whether this was a short stay or a more permanent arrangement it is impossible to know, though it seems reasonable to surmise that these relatives were providing a home for a while for a motherless young family and, indeed, the couple were apparently keen at one stage to adopt Eveline and her brother William, though their father would not hear of it. Ten years later, as a nineteen-year-old woman, Eveline was living 'on private means' on William's farm in Langwathby along with her sisters Mary and Esther, who was known as Tess. When William married, the three sisters lived happily together in a house of their own for a while, sharing two bicycles and taking it in turns to go out for a spin.

She and Uncle married in Langwathby Methodist Church

Aunty's siblings Tess, Mary and Willie Hewetson

in 1918, the same year Uncle became headmaster in Bampton. I don't know how they met, though there is surely a strong likelihood that it was through the church. Methodism was the guiding force in their lives. Neither of them drank alcohol and they had little regard for those who did to excess.

Despite his many obligations to school, chapel and the community, Uncle found time for his three evacuees. He took Doug and John fishing and shooting and showed them how to prepare their quarry for the pot. (One of the few domestic jobs I remember him doing – apart from chopping firewood – was wringing the chickens' necks.) His own sons shared this love of country sports and would disappear for the whole day with their rods whenever they were home. I invited myself on these fishing trips on a couple of occasions, but they were never very successful. For a start, I found it hard to remain quiet and was frequently told off for talking and frightening the fish. And when I did catch something it was always just an eel, while the boys pulled sparkling trout from the water. Aunty was always pleased with my haul, though, as she could use eels in the mash she cooked for the hens.

Uncle was also quite the joker: he liked to set us little

puzzles and wouldn't tell us the answers unless we could show him that we had tried to work them out for ourselves first. The one below had me stumped for a long time:

YYUR YYUB ICUR YY4me

Too wise you are, too wise you be, I see you are too wise for me!

Another one was: Pot OOO OOOOO

I remember the feeling of triumph when I realised it stood for 'potatoes' (pot and eight Os!).

He taught us how to remember things using mnemonics, for example 'Richard Of York Gained Battles In Vain' to remember the colours of the rainbow. It's probably how I became obsessed with them later when I did my nurses' training, even making up ones of my own to help me remember some of the endless lists that we needed to reproduce in our exams. I used to hold a little class in my room early in the morning of the day we had our weekly test to help a friend who had left school at the age of fourteen and was finding revision difficult. Uncle's influence must have been rubbing off on me all those years later!

Much as I loved Uncle, I looked forward to Friday evenings when he wheeled the motorbike from the garage and set off to Appleby where he sat on the council, yet another of his duties. As he had family in the town he didn't drive back on the pitch-black country lanes but spent the night there, returning to Bampton the following afternoon. The sound of the bike being revved would bring some of the local boys swarming – the Percy boys would be there first if they were still around, offering to lend a hand but really just angling for a ride. If Uncle wasn't in a hurry he would let them have a turn on the driveway.

The house seemed a more serene place without him. Aunty was more indulgent towards us than Uncle was, and she, too, seemed to relax a little more in his absence. In fact, Aunty quite literally let her hair down when Uncle was away.

'Aunty, you've got long hair!' I cried in surprise when she appeared with dark hair hanging below her shoulders. She normally wore it pinned in a roll at the back of her neck and I must have imagined it fixed like that permanently.

She was happy to sit and do nothing as I brushed it for her, not even picking up her knitting. It must have been the only time I saw her with nothing in her hands.

Aunty let us turn the kitchen chairs onto their sides and throw a rug over them to make a house. Doug and John declared they were too old for this when they saw me sitting with Neville in my den, but they changed their minds when they realised that the house could become a submarine or an army tank if they wanted it to be.

There was another game that Doug, John and I played together, but usually only on a Sunday, the day we used the sitting room. It happened in the afternoon when Uncle and Aunty were both busy – Aunty in the kitchen and Uncle in his study putting the finishing touches to his sermon. I'm not sure who named it, but I think that John or Doug must have read the book as we called it 'Around the World in Eighty Days' and the purpose of the game was to travel from one end of the room to the other without setting foot on the floor. Aunty and Uncle would not have been happy to see us climbing on their furniture, leaping from settee to armchair

Eveline and Douglas Thornton, 1918

to piano stool on our perilous journey, but I don't remember them ever catching us.

With Uncle gone we ate differently too. For supper on a Friday Aunty would put a pan of thinly sliced potatoes and some cabbage or other greens from the vegetable garden onto the fire and leave it until the potato was very crisp and brown. We ate it with bread or a fried egg or perhaps a piece of ham and it was the meal I looked forward to the most all week. (Years later, I told Aunty this and she was surprised and delighted – as far as she had been concerned it was just a make-do meal that she could rustle up quickly.) Saturday lunch was another treat – soup served in a pudding basin and bread straight out of the oven.

*

Too old to be called up for active service this time, Uncle was a staunch member of the Observer Corps (later the Royal Observer Corps) whose headquarters was a wooden hut. He took all three of us evacuees to see the hut, but never at the same time as it was important that we weren't tempted to chatter. The men inside it were always very quiet and serious. Hanging from the ceiling were models of every type of British and German plane and there were silhouette drawings of the planes on the walls. Uncle explained how important the role of this corps was, and how a skilled observer could identify a plane from the briefest glimpse of its outline. Indeed, one of the volunteers had correctly identified a German plane which had later been shot down over Yorkshire.

The summer of 1940 and the twelve months that followed were a busy time for Uncle and his fellow Observers. Although we were not a prime bombing target, the Lake District did not escape enemy bombardment altogether, though most local attacks were probably due to error or planes having to jettison their bombs after failing to identify their proper targets.

On our doorstep was a tank range. Lowther Castle and its parkland, home to the Lowther family since the Middle Ages, had been requisitioned by the Army for tank weapon testing which resulted in a diversion of part of the road between Bampton and Penrith. Sometimes you could hear the sound of gunfire coming from there, or soldiers would pass through Bampton on route marches. We children would shout encouragement at them, but Uncle had to reprimand a group of boys who got too carried away about what they wanted the soldiers to do to the Germans, reminding them – and the rest of us – that most Germans were ordinary people like us.

While we observed the rituals of the war here in Bampton with our blackouts at the window, masked headlights on vehicles, making do and mending, and were as keen as anyone to do our bit to help – all those berries I picked, all that knitting I started, all those prayers I offered up! – we were safely removed from it. But back in my home city the war had come almost to our front door. In early September, just before my father left to join the Royal Engineers, he was one of the first on the scene when a high explosive bomb landed on the street behind ours, killing a woman and causing further casualties. Our neighbour Mr Farnsworth was blown out of his bedroom window and into the front garden. Dozens of houses were damaged or totally destroyed that night. My mother, in the shelter with Mr and Mrs Young, said that she thought her end had come as the earth shook around her and debris rained down on the roof. It was when I heard stories like that that I felt I had missed out on some of the fun by being in Bampton.

Living with Uncle sometimes meant being put forward for things I didn't want to do, thanks to his sense of duty. How many times over the years did I hear, 'Oh, Gwenda will do this!' So when a wealthy man who lived with his young daughter and her governess in a large country house nearby expressed concern that the girl had no playmates of her own age, Uncle immediately suggested that I go for tea one afternoon to keep her company. Perhaps he thought it would be the start of a long friendship.

I was quite intrigued by the idea of a girl who didn't go to school as I thought that such things were confined to some of the books I read. Aunty and Uncle both told me before I went that it was a grand place and I would have to be on my best behaviour. I promised that I would. When Aunty and I arrived there after a two-mile walk, I could see what they meant. It was the biggest house I had ever seen, the long driveway lined with trees that rustled their golden leaves in the autumn sunshine. We pulled a heavy metal rod to ring the door bell and heard it chiming far inside the house. After what felt like a long wait, Aunty rang it again and a man opened the door and apologised for keeping us waiting. He thanked Aunty for bringing me and asked if she would like to come in for a drink, but she politely declined and said she would come back for me at five o'clock. The man showed me into a hallway with a huge staircase at its centre. This swept up to a large landing and then branched out to both the left and the right.

The man, who told me he was the father of my prospective playmate, was dressed formally, as if he was about to attend a business meeting, but he was very friendly and I felt sure that his daughter would be nice as well.

'And now we must find Henrietta,' he said, which I thought was strange when she had been expecting me. 'Her governess tells me that she has been a little difficult this morning. I do hope you will make allowances for her, my dear. It's not often we have visitors.'

After looking inside several rooms on the way, he showed me into a room on the first floor that he called the nursery and asked me to wait. It was a large bright room with post-card-perfect views of the fells from the window. There wasn't a lot of furniture in it – a dining table and chairs in one corner, a trunk, a child's-size table and chairs – but it was full of toys. There was a rocking horse pushed up against a wall that I longed to climb onto, a dolls' house by the window that I would have loved to peek inside, and shelves full of books and games and jigsaw puzzles. It was a paradise for a seven-year-old girl! I had never seen so many toys in one place before and began to envy the girl to whom they all belonged.

After about ten minutes – during which I sat politely as I hadn't been given permission to touch anything – a tall, slim woman came into the room with a hand on the shoulder of a girl whom she introduced as Henrietta. The lady said that she was terribly sorry to have kept me waiting but Henrietta had been out on her pony and had needed a quick wash and change of clothes. She said she would leave us on our own to play, but before she went she asked me if at teatime I would like the crust of the bread. I told her that I would – I loved the crust.

'Henrietta does not eat the crust,' said the lady, looking at Henrietta as she spoke.

Henrietta said, 'Crusts are for feeding the birds. You know quite well I'd rather chew cardboard, Timmins.' I thought this was rather rude but as Timmins was giving me a conspiratorial sort of smile I smiled back.

'Where do you live?' asked Henrietta when Timmins had gone. She showed no sign of recognition when I told her, even though Bampton was the nearest village. I added that I came from Newcastle, which was getting bombed, but she didn't seem interested in that information either.

'Shall we play?' I asked her.

'You can play with whatever you like,' she replied.

I had to stop myself from heading straight for the rocking horse. I knew I was here to play with Henrietta and told her so.

'Oh, very well. I sometimes play this with Timmins, but

she's a dreadful stick-in-the-mud at the minute and won't play any more. I'll be the teacher and you're my pupil. That means you must do exactly as I tell you. So, sit down here – no, not on that chair, that's mine – and open your text book. Today we're going to study French verbs. Now repeat after me, "*Je suis, tu es, il est, elle est*".'

I did this for a while, pleased that I understood and had a reasonable French accent. After we had gone through several verbs I suggested that we swap roles.

Henrietta stood up and put her hands on her hips. 'Really! You must not speak to the teacher like that. Go and stand in the corner.'

'But I just want to—'

'At once!'

I decided to play along with her. It seemed easier that way. I stood in the corner for a few seconds until I was allowed back to my seat where I had to repeat a French rhyme after Henrietta. I knew it from my days at La Sagesse – in fact, I knew it better than she did. I took delight in saying it back to her as accurately as I could and in my best French accent.

'That wasn't what I said.' She frowned at me.

'I know, but it's "*les gens*" – the people – not "*les jeunes*". You see—'

'I thought I was the teacher. Now, say it again.'

She looked even more unhappy when Timmins came back to see if we were ready for tea and said, 'Oh, you're playing so nicely, and what a charming accent you've got, Gwenda! Do you speak French?'

'I'm teaching her,' said Henrietta.

'I went to school in a French convent for a term,' I said.

'You must come again one day and we can all speak French together,' said Timmins, beaming at us both.

I was relieved when a few minutes later she returned – this time wearing an apron – and set the table for tea. When it was all laid out and tea had been poured into our cups, she left us. The teapot was on another table and we were told not to touch it and that she would come to replenish our cups in a short while. There was bread already spread with honey to start and I took the crust, having been told it was specially for me. There were also iced buns on the table and a chocolate cake. I took a bite out of my crust and put it back on my plate as I chewed, the way my mother had taught me. 'Your food's not going anywhere,' she would say sharply if we held on to it while we were eating. But I would have done better to forget my manners today. As soon as I had put the bread down, Henrietta grabbed it, licked off the honey and put it back on to my plate. It happened so quickly and was done with such insouciance, I almost doubted that it was what I had seen. Henrietta was now eating her own bread as if nothing had happened.

I looked at my crust. Yes, the honey had all gone. I could only stare at it in dismay. I didn't know what to do. I couldn't eat it now, but I could hardly leave it like that either. What would Timmins think when she saw it there? How rude she would think I was! And how could I move on to the cakes when I hadn't eaten up my bread? As all these thoughts were racing through my mind the door opened and Timmins came back into the room with a plate of something else in her hand. As she put it onto the table she must have noticed the change in my demeanour as she asked me if anything was the matter. I opened my mouth but no words came out. Then she saw the honeyless crust on my plate. 'Did Henrietta do that?' she asked.

I felt too uncomfortable to reply. I looked at Henrietta to see if she was going to own up but she was looking straight ahead, chewing very solemnly. Without waiting for me to say anything Timmins whisked my plate away from me, cut me another slice of bread, spread it with honey and gave it to me. Then she sat in the corner of the room as we finished our tea in silence.

The incident took away my appetite and though Timmins offered me an iced bun after I had eaten my bread, I did not enjoy it as much as I might have done. I felt miserable and longed to go home to play with Doug and John.

Timmins cleared away the tea things and Henrietta became a bit more pleasant when she had gone, telling me that I could play with the dolls' house if I liked.

It was beautiful. Each room was wallpapered and carpeted; there were even tiny lights on the walls which switched on. But I felt uncomfortable here with this rude girl. I didn't feel truly happy until I heard the doorbell chime, followed soon after by the sound of footsteps coming to fetch me.

'We could play Snakes and Ladders if you like,' Henrietta said, just before Timmins put her head round the door. 'Timmins gets bored with it.' She was arranging her dolls in rows now, clearly deciding that they made more obedient pupils than I did.

I was sorry to leave the dolls' house but I jumped up eagerly as Timmins told me that Aunty was here.

'I'm sorry, I have to go,' I said to Henrietta, who shrugged and turned back to her dolls.

As we walked back down the driveway Aunty was eager

to hear how I had got on and seeing her smiling, curious face made me fill up with tears. I felt as if I had let her and Uncle down in some way.

'Well!' Aunty was shocked. 'How can someone live in a grand place like that and not know how to behave? No wonder the little madam has no friends.'

I don't think I'd heard Aunty speak like that about anyone before and for some reason it made me cry properly now.

'Of course I blame her father. It's a terrible pity she's got no mother but that's still no excuse. Wait until Uncle hears about this.'

I dreaded telling Uncle but he was as shocked as Aunty when he heard and agreed that I didn't have to go to play there again.

Chapter fifteen

A parcel was waiting for me on the kitchen table when I got back from school. Miss Williams was sitting there having her usual cup of tea before catching her bus home.

'Ooh, that looks interesting! Are you going to open it now so that we can all see what it is?'

I picked it up. It felt soft and fabric-like so I guessed that my mother had been sewing or knitting. I was wrong. The gift was shop-bought. 'Chilprufe', said the label. It was a pair of what we called combinations – a woollen vest and knickers all in one, designed to keep me extra warm in the cold winter months.

I held it up in front of me, then, embarrassed to be displaying underwear in front of a teacher, turned my back to her and Aunty and put it back in the paper. They both laughed.

'It looks lovely and cosy,' said Miss Williams.

'Can I put it on now?' I asked Aunty, and shot off to my bedroom before she had time to reply.

Taking off all my clothes took a while in the winter due to all the layers I wore: jumper, skirt, liberty bodice, vest, knickers, knee-length socks. When that was done I sat down on the edge of my bed and stepped into the combinations. The wool felt scratchy close to my skin. There were four press studs that fastened in the crotch to keep it snug, but they were fiddly and it wasn't easy to match them up. I was almost crying tears of frustration when Doug came into the bedroom.

He laughed when he saw me but softened when he saw what a state I was in. I begged him to help me. He decided that the easiest way to accomplish the task was for me to lie on my bed with my knees raised and legs apart while he fastened the press studs. As he had helped me with delicate matters in the past, he didn't seem to be too embarrassed performing this operation. When the job was done, he went back to John's room to carry on with whatever they had been doing; it got dark early now and we stayed inside in the evenings. I put my clothes back on and, feeling very grown-up, though rather itchy, went to join them. They were in the middle of a board game but didn't object to my sitting on the floor at the foot of the bed looking through John's atlas and deciding all the places I would like to visit one day until Aunty shouted that it was teatime.

I had a habit of getting engrossed in whatever I was doing and delaying going to the lavatory until it was quite urgent. Later that evening I made one of my usual dashes up the stairs, relieved that Uncle wasn't in there with his pipe. Pulling up my skirt I reached for my knickers, then remembering what I was wearing, tried to undo the press studs on the combinations. I fumbled around for ages, managed to click one of them open, but couldn't find the others. Unfortunately, my brain had already decided that I was on the lavatory and ready to go, and of course I had left it far too late anyway. To my horror, my new combinations were suddenly soaking wet and there was a puddle on the floor. I tried to mop up the mess only to make myself wetter. Opening the door slowly and checking that the boys weren't on the landing, I called down the stairs for Aunty.

Aunty blamed the 'silly combinations' and took them away to give them a good soak. We agreed that it would be our little secret and we also agreed that I didn't need to wear them again.

'Best that you just write to your mother and say thank you, and leave it at that,' she said.

One day not long before Christmas I was playing by myself in the yard when a young man whose face looked familiar came out of the back door, grinned at me and swept me up into the air.

'Who's living in my house?' he said as he swung me round, and I knew then that this was Hugh, Aunty and Uncle's eldest son, home on leave from the RAF. I immediately liked his cheeky face, and recognised Uncle's mischievous nature.

Doug and John came bounding out of the house a few seconds later. They had just been introduced to him, too, and didn't want to let him out of their sight.

'We've got an errand to run for my mother. Who's coming?' said Hugh, and we all followed him as enthusiastically as if he was taking us on a trip to the seaside and not just to buy four ounces of fresh yeast for Aunty from Mrs Reed's shop in Bampton Grange.

Brothers John and Hugh
Thornton, 1941

Hugh Thornton on the fells
after the war

It took us a while to get there as we kept bumping into
people who wanted to welcome Hugh home and pat him on
the back. Doug and John kept asking him questions about
the war and he answered good-naturedly but without giving
very much away. We met my friend Marjorie and she wanted
to come too. The four of us followed him down the lane and
over the bridge into Bampton Grange. When we got back,
over an hour later, Aunty said that the next time she needed
something she had a good mind to go herself.

My friend Mavis, whom I had met on my first day at school
here, had often asked if I could visit her at her farm on the
crags. Mavis always went straight home when lessons were
over and didn't come to play in the schoolyard in the evenings
or on Saturdays like some of my other friends did. When Hugh
said he wanted to go for a walk on Saturday after lunch and
offered to drop me off there, I jumped at the chance.

I felt proud to have Hugh to myself for a while. He wasn't
just an older boy, like his brother John, he was an adult, and
adults were a different breed entirely and didn't always have
time for children. Walking beside Hugh wasn't like walking
with Miss Dixon, who could fill the air with her musings and
chatter. He asked me a couple of questions – about what I
wanted for Christmas and when I had last seen my parents –
but on the whole he was happy just to look around him and
we fell into a pleasant, easy pattern of walking without saying
much. It must have been a world away from whatever he had
left behind.

We reached the crags where Doug and I had sat and talked
to Peter, our fellow evacuee, all those months ago, and carried

on up the winding road out of the village. It was a steep climb to Mavis's farm and we were both puffing and panting when we reached it.

Mavis was thrilled to see me and Hugh left me with a cheerful wave, walking away whistling 'We're gonna hang out the washing on the Siegfried line' which he had been trying to teach Doug, John and me earlier.

We played hide-and-seek around the farm. In one of the sheds I saw a sheep all by herself in a pen looking very sorry for herself. I asked Mavis what she was doing there on her own and Mavis said she had hurt her leg and so they were keeping an eye on her. I asked if I could stroke her and Mavis said I could if I wanted to, but that she wasn't a pet. The sheep looked anxious when I started to get close to her so I changed my mind, though I was probably more worried than she was.

'She'll not be happy till she's back with her flock,' said Mavis. 'Herdwicks like to be left alone. They don't usually need a hand, not even when they lamb.'

I was impressed by her knowledge and wondered how I could ever hope to achieve my childhood dream of marrying a farmer when I knew so little. Perhaps, I thought, Mavis could teach me some of the things she knew. One of the dogs came to see who I was. Mavis and I built him an obstacle course and made him do tricks. I had never seen such a clever or obedient dog before and wished that I lived on a farm as well. At least I did until I needed the lavatory and Mavis showed me into a cold dark outhouse. I was in such a hurry to get out of it that I stopped in mid flow and hoped that I could wait till I was home before finishing.

We both had red cheeks from the cold. The sun had long

since disappeared behind High Street and it would soon be
dark. Knowing that I had to be back before then I said goodbye
to my friend. I had to be careful not to go head over heels as
I ran back down the hill towards the village.

On these cold winter days, Doug and I would lay out our
clothes neatly before we went to bed, each item in the order
that we needed it, so that when we got up the next morning
we could get dressed quickly. This had been our routine since
the start of the war when we knew we might be woken at
any time by the sirens and have to rush to the air-raid shelter.
Doug and I had turned it into a race to see who could dress
the quickest and we were still competitive, though I rarely
thought about air raids or sirens these days. Thank goodness
I didn't have to put those combinations on! (Doug did ask me
about them once, in an offhand way, and I told him that Aunty
had decided they didn't fit me properly, which he seemed to
accept.) After our speedy dressing we visited the bathroom
then dashed for the warmth of the kitchen – the one room in
the house that was never cold – where breakfast was either a
boiled egg or toast and marmalade.

Hugh left and his brother John came home for the Christmas
holidays. Mam had warned us in her letters that with the war
on, it wasn't going to be like previous Christmases and that we
shouldn't expect much. We hadn't seen her and Dad since their
visit in the summer as Dad was away on active duty somewhere
and Mam was busy serving her teas at the station as well as
knitting scarves and jumpers for soldiers and evacuees. But all
I wanted was a *Chicks' Own* annual and a baby doll and that
didn't seem too much to ask for.

I don't believe we were ever told in Mam's letters where Dad was stationed but learnt later that he spent most of his war years in the Orkneys. He had been disappointed with this as he had hoped to be sent overseas. He was a patriotic man, desperate to do his bit for king and country, and had enlisted voluntarily as his bank job was considered essential. The Orkneys were not where he had visualised spending his services career.

Mam told us that she had decorated the air-raid shelter with some streamers and holly and stored some snacks there – including a tin of biscuits she had been saving – in case they ended up inside it over the festive period. I almost wished I was there, just for the fun of eating treats while the rest of the world fizzed and banged around us. (I think I pictured an air raid as a sort of overblown Guy Fawkes night.)

Miss Dixon was going to stay with relatives for Christmas, but on her last bath night before leaving she presented Aunty with a jar of her bilberry jelly and Uncle with a tin of tobacco, saying that she knew we were all supposed to be giving to the war effort this year instead of buying gifts, but she couldn't possibly fail to give them a small present each after all their kindnesses towards her. She also asked if she could 'borrow' me for a while.

'I'd just like to see how well Daphne's jumper fits you now that it's finished,' she explained. I had already stood patiently on numerous other occasions while sleeves had been held against my arms and measurements made as Miss Dixon used me as a model for the knitting she was doing for her niece. Today I tried the finished product on and it fitted me perfectly.

Uncle always joked when she had gone that he wouldn't

want to be in poor Daphne's shoes if she had dared to have grown at a different rate from me.

'Fingers crossed for Christmas Day, Gwenda!' said Miss Dixon cheerfully as she put it carefully back into its tissue paper, and I wasn't sure if she was still talking about the jumper or hoping that I got what I wanted, but I agreed with her.

On Christmas morning Doug, the two Johns and I had a stocking each containing an apple, a threepenny bit and some wax crayons. After breakfast I gave Aunty a present I had made for her with Ada's help – a handkerchief case. Ada had done most of the work but I had put in a few stitches and chosen the lace trim. Aunty had finished off and sewn up for me a jumper I had started knitting for Neville when I had got fed up with socks, and wrapped it and placed it under the tree.

There were seven of us that day, as Aunty Mary was with us again, but it was still a quieter Christmas than Doug and I were used to. At home in Newcastle the postman would be the first of the day's many visitors, coaxed inside for a drink by my father who was never happier than when he was pouring a glass of alcohol for someone. The neighbours might drop in for a sherry or a whisky and, as they were leaving, Aunty Edith, Uncle Eddie and Beryl would be arriving, bringing Grandma with them. By the time evening came the men would be slightly the worse for wear for drink and even the women would have had more than they were used to, though being ladies they always knew when to stop.

There was no Christmas tipple in the schoolhouse, but we ate well, as always. I helped Aunty prepare dinner before we went to chapel, while the boys were helping Uncle to fetch wood and lay the fire in the sitting room. Dinner was another of Aunty's chickens. Uncle asked me to say grace and I used a simple one that he had taught me: 'God bless this food to do us good, for Jesus' sake, Amen.' Uncle added an extra one today, praying for all the soldiers who were away from their families this Christmas, and looking at me, Doug and John, he said that we should all say a special prayer for our parents as they would be missing us more than usual at this time of year. Then he added with one of his twinkly smiles that he and Aunty felt very fortunate to have us.

I had helped Aunty to make the Christmas pudding a few weeks earlier. She had whispered to me that she had put some beetroot and turnip into it to make up for the lack of dried fruit this year. 'We'll see if any of those boys notice anything different when they eat it,' she said mischievously. We all had to stir it three times and make a wish. Not wanting to waste mine, I asked Doug what I should wish for. He said that I really ought to know that if you told anyone your wish then it wouldn't come true. I thought about it for ages, until Aunty said she couldn't wait till Christmas and then Doug said in a superior voice that everyone knew that there was only one thing you could wish for at the moment anyway. So that decided it: I wished that the war would be over soon and that Mam and Dad and everyone I knew would be alive at the end of it.

Uncle said that the pudding was the best one yet and Aunty and I shared a secret smile. But when he was halfway through his helping he started to splutter and put his napkin to his mouth. I looked at him, alarmed, thinking he was choking, but then he produced a silver threepenny bit.

'I think I'm the lucky one this year,' he said, making sure we had all seen it before popping it into his pocket.

The boys groaned and his son said, 'Oh, Dad, it's always you!'

After another mouthful he did the same thing again and I thought he really must be choking as I only remembered us adding one coin to the mixture. But he produced a second coin from his napkin.

'I thought you'd stirred the pudding, Gwenda,' said Aunty, pretending to be vexed. 'How has Uncle got all the threepenny bits in his helping?'

'Fortune favours the virtuous,' said Uncle, looking at each of us children with a silly expression on his face.

'Dad, that is not how the saying goes!' said John

When he did it a third and a fourth time, the boys were exploding with laughter and I joined in, but half-heartedly, as I'd been hoping I might get a coin. I thought Uncle must be the luckiest man alive and wondered what he would do with all of his threepences.

When dinner was over and the washing-up done – we all lent a hand today, even Uncle – we received our presents from our parents. There was no *Chicks' Own* annual, but my spirits lifted when I saw that my parcel did indeed look doll-shaped, though a lot smaller than I'd hoped. As I tore off the paper I was imagining how pretty this doll was going to look with her golden curls and big blue eyes and wondering what I was going to call her. When I had finished unwrapping, I couldn't say anything for a few seconds, only gawp in surprise. My doll was an exotic creature with an unsmiling mouth, dark eyes and hair and skinny leather limbs. Doug, who seemed happier with his model aeroplane, peered at her.

'She looks foreign,' he said. 'You should call her Maria.' And the name stuck.

Everyone was in a good mood. Aunty had made some pep-permint creams as a special treat. Uncle played the piano and we sang some carols. He tried to coax Aunty into reciting a poem.

'She used to do it all the time when she was younger, didn't you, Aunty?' he said. (They usually called each other 'Aunty' and 'Uncle' in front of us.)

But Aunty said she was out of practice, and anyway, we children would surely rather play while she got the tea ready.

'Longfellow,' said Uncle. 'He was your speciality, wasn't he, my dear?'

'"The Song of Hiawatha", "Evangeline",' said John Thornton, who was a clever boy. Like his father he could read Latin and he had won several scholarships at Appleby Grammar. Uncle and Aunty were very proud of him, though – in common with my own mother – they were not the sort of people to boast. 'We've studied them in English. He's one of what they call the Fireside Poets. My English master prefers Whittier, though.'

'What about "Barbara Frietchie"?' said Uncle, not about to give up. 'It's a while since you've done that one, Eveline.' He looked at me and Doug and John Stacey, and explained, 'They call them the Fireside Poets because they write poems for everyone to enjoy. Poems to be read aloud. You'll study them when you're a bit older.'

I looked at Aunty as she slipped out to prepare tea and real-ised there were a lot of things I didn't know about her. I knew she had been a little girl, once upon a time, but I had forgotten she must have also had a life as a young woman before she married Uncle and came to Bampton.

The boys and I spent most of the rest of the day playing Ludo and Snakes and Ladders. Uncle encouraged me to play some of the tunes he had taught me on the piano. He had suggested recently that I go for lessons to a lady in the village. But I hadn't been playing long when the boys started to groan and asked me to stop.

Chapter sixteen

I didn't love Maria the way I had loved my Venus pencil case the Christmas before. I wanted to but somehow I just couldn't. Her expression was too knowing, too superior. She didn't look at me adoringly, as a baby doll might have done, but rather as if I was lucky to have her although, really, she would rather I didn't. I had told Aunty one day about the time I had offered my pencil case to God and how God hadn't wanted it. Aunty said that it was very generous of me but that she didn't think God would want to deprive me of anything so useful, especially when He knew what care I took over the letters I wrote home. I had worried that she was going to suggest I hand over Neville instead, or one of my very tatty copies of *Enid Blyton's Sunny Stories*, but to my relief she said that my greatest gift to God was to be kind and helpful to other people. That was easy a lot of the time, as I loved going to Ada's to lend a hand with baby David and helping Aunty in the kitchen. However, there were things I didn't enjoy so much, like being sent by Aunty to visit Mrs Morris, whose house lay hidden behind a screen of creepy fir trees.

Mrs Morris lived in Gate Foot on the way to Burnbanks. She was deaf and had an ear trumpet. I hated having to speak into it and she never understood a word I said anyway. The experience was made worse by the presence of Tommy, her huge black cat, which sat on her lap and objected with deep growling sounds when I got too close. As Mrs Morris always wore a long black skirt I sometimes couldn't see Tommy until I was right up to her and I would step back in alarm when I suddenly found a pair of amber eyes following my every move. After a few minutes of stilted conversation, Mrs Morris would send me into the kitchen to help myself to one of her ginger snaps. These were the most fiery biscuits I had ever tasted and brought tears to my eyes, but provided a welcome break from our awkward attempts to converse. When I had finished my biscuit, I shuffled from one leg to another, wondering how soon I could leave without appearing rude, and why it was me and not Doug or John who was sent on these errands. Then I would run down the path and out onto the road before some creature came out of the trees to grab me.

I looked out of the classroom window one day in early February to see that it was snowing. It snowed steadily all morning. Not long after dinner Uncle sent one of the senior girls to each of the classrooms to announce that he was closing school early that day. The next day the snow had blown into deep drifts that blocked the roads. The boys helped Aunty to shovel the passageway in the yard and to clear some of the ground for the hens before they went to school. The snow came over the tops of my wellingtons as I walked the short distance across the yard to the annexe, and it had blown against the walls into piles deeper than I was tall. Most of the children were late that morning. Marjorie came rushing in a few minutes after the bell had rung and sat down beside me, her face pink, saying, wasn't it lovely, but that her father was cursing as it was murder delivering the post in these conditions. Janet, who lived outside the village, arrived half an hour later. None of the Burnbanks children appeared that day.

The snow showed no sign of melting and attendance continued to be low. One morning I arrived in class to find Miss Pickup shivering and saying that the radiators were stone cold. She went to the classroom next door only to discover that theirs weren't working either. Everyone in the annexe moved into the main school building where the classrooms were heated by coke-burning stoves, and Miss Dixon took her class to St Patrick's Hall to make room for us. She did the same the next day and the other senior classes moved to the Methodist Sunday School.

Icicles hung down like a jagged fringe from the eaves of the schoolhouse. The snow made soft shapes on walls and hedges, and on the tops of fence posts it began to curl outwards like the handles of shepherds' crooks. The caretaker fixed the heating system, but when we had more snow a few days later, coupled with heavy wind that made the roads impassable, Uncle closed school for two days. Doug, John and I had a great time having snowball fights, at which I usually ended up the most battered. One day we found two old toboggans in the shed and pulled them to the top of the steeply sloping field behind the wood.

'Let's have a race to the bottom,' said Doug, as he and I sat on one and John on the other. 'Are you ready, John?'

John, who now wore spectacles after an eye test at school, took them off and put them safely in his pocket before saying that he was.

'On your marks, get set, go!'

Doug had to use his legs at first to get us going, but soon we were hurtling at terrific speed towards the wood. The dazzling world shot by. We were bursting with the thrill of it and none of us had seen the danger waiting for us at the bottom of the slope – a wire fence separating the field from the wood. Doug was first to react and yelled something about steering away, but that wasn't possible. He tried to slow our toboggan down with his legs and then tumbled off into the snow, leaving me and John heading straight towards potential decapitation. Doug continued to shout at us both, but it was a hopeless cry. The wire hit me in the neck. The sledge stopped. I gasped for breath, winded by the impact. When I tried to get up it felt as if my arms and legs had been put on the wrong way round and I sank back down. Doug bounded up to us.

'Eugghh!' he said, backing away slightly. 'You both look as if you've been strung up like one of Aunty's chickens.' Then he asked with more concern, 'Are you all right?'

John had a cut that would later turn into a scar neatly matching one he had acquired during an earlier surgical operation, while I had a vivid gash across the front of my neck.

I'm sure it didn't dawn on any of us at the time how serious the consequences might have been if we had been going more quickly. When Aunty saw us she made us promise to be more careful and Doug got into bigger trouble than he usually did for not behaving more responsibly as the oldest of the three of us. She reminded us that the reason we were here in Bampton was for our own safety and asked how she would explain it to our parents if we were badly injured while we were in her care.

'We know it's all our fault,' said John. 'Our parents wouldn't blame you, Aunty, and if they did I would tell them not to.'

Aunty managed a smile and ruffled his hair, but said that our parents might not see it that way and that we would understand when we had children of our own.

The snow lasted for the whole of February and when it melted we faced another problem. Bampton lies on the flood plain of the River Lowther and when the water rushes down from the fells in such quantity it becomes trapped in the valley. Some of our roads turned into rivers, the fields became lakes and animals had to be taken to higher ground. Seeing this watery world from my bedroom window I thought that we would be stranded in the schoolhouse, but in fact the locals are used to this occurrence. Many of the lanes are lined with a low wall for pedestrians to use when they are flooded (this was what I had walked on when Aunty took us home to the schoolhouse on our very first day), garden gates have a ledge to stand on, while planks make impromptu bridges to houses that would otherwise be cut off. And so we carried on as normal, the water rushing past us as we went to the shop or to chapel. We sailed boats in newly formed lakes. Even the Burnbanks children turned up for school every day, draping their dripping coats on fireguards round the classroom stoves or radiators and filling the rooms with fuggy steam.

I saw Mr Brennan in the village and he told me he was on his way home to get his fishing rod.

'I can catch a trout for my tea from my own doorstep,' he said.

I didn't know if he was joking, but it wouldn't have surprised me if he wasn't.

Aunty said she would be glad when spring came this year, and that the three of us could consider ourselves proper villagers now as we had experienced the best and the worst of living here.

If our main enemy was the weather, we knew that other parts of the country were suffering in far worse ways. Not very far from Bampton, the peninsular town of Barrow in Furness was one of these places. Barrow had large shipyards and a steelworks which at one time had been the biggest in the world, so it was an obvious target for the German bombers. A mass evacuation of two and a half thousand children took place in May 1941 and thirty of them came to Bampton School. Uncle told John, Doug and me that many of them came from poor households and that we must be kind to them and share whatever we had. I was quite happy to do this, but as I didn't have many toys here, I wasn't sure that I could be much help. I wondered what John would say if Uncle asked him to share his bricks, but even I could see that some things were just too special to share with strangers.

One of the new girls in my class was called Joan and I couldn't help feeling sorry for her. On her first day with us, just after dinner, she suddenly slumped forwards and fell asleep on her desk. The pupils who had noticed nudged their neighbours and whispered to each other, then looked at Miss Pickup, wondering what she would say. To our surprise she told us to let her sleep and reminded us that we didn't know what sort of experiences she had been through.

In one of our lessons, Miss Pickup asked us all to draw a picture of someone or something that was special to us. I had so many ideas I didn't know where to start, but finally settled on a picture of the Birdman. I wondered if he was still in the Dene every day, or if he had had to go away to fight. I couldn't imagine the Birdman being happy anywhere apart from the Dene, unless he was put in charge of pigeons which I knew were used to carry messages in times of war. I hoped that was the case. As I drew I was aware that Joan, who was sitting beside me, was staring miserably at her piece of paper.

'What are you going to draw, Joan?' asked Miss Pickup kindly. 'It can be anything at all. A person. A favourite toy.'

Joan didn't reply. She was clutching her crayon as if it was going to run away. Finally she said in a tiny voice. 'I've got nothing, Miss. Our house was bombed.'

Miss Pickup said that she was very sorry to hear that and she hoped that Joan would feel safe in Bampton. She said that perhaps Joan could draw something that she would like to have when the war was over. Joan stared at her paper for a bit longer, then she began to draw a doll and, as I sneaked a look at it, a plan formulated in my mind. The next day was Friday and, after getting Aunty's approval, I brought Maria to school after dinner and told Joan that she could take her home for the weekend. I'd actually told Aunty that I wanted to give her Maria to keep, but Aunty was unsure what my mother would think of this when Maria had been a gift, so suggested a loan instead. Aunty and Uncle both said what a kind girl I was, but I knew deep down that it wasn't a terrible hardship for me as I wasn't attached to Maria, though the chair where she sat beside Neville did look rather empty without her while she was away. Joan returned the doll to me on Monday and she did seem more cheerful after that. One day some knitted toys that had been made by Women's Voluntary Service ladies arrived at the school for the new evacuees and Joan told me that she didn't need to borrow Maria any more, but I knew that she was more attached to her than I was so we carried on with our little arrangement.

Despite the bombings in Newcastle, more than half of the Newcastle evacuees had returned home by Christmas 1940, and by the summer of 1941 only eight of us would remain. A handful hadn't even lasted beyond the first few weeks. Being younger than the rest of the party, I don't know the individual reasons for all the departures, though I believe that there were some who felt that they were being used as cheap labour on the farms, or who found country life too hard when they were used to warm houses and indoor bathrooms. Sometimes it was the hosts who were unhappy; one woman I sometimes bumped into when I was with Aunty was always moaning about how much soap she was using to get her young evacuee's clothes clean. 'She wears white blouses! White! Can you imagine the amount of soap I'm going through – and when it's on ration, too! I seem to spend all my time scrubbing these days!' But one child who like us had settled happily into his new life was Peter, the boy we had met by the crags on our first day. Peter was turning into a proper little country boy. He had learnt how to shoot rabbits and often went out with Mr Butler, the man he was living with, to lend a hand on some of the farms. He even sometimes got paid for his assistance.

We met him at the crags again one afternoon. The floods had gone and the fields were bright green and fringed with flowers. He was wearing clogs, like many of the local children, and I decided there and then that I was going to write to Mam and ask if I could have a pair. She would want to know what was wrong with a good pair of Startrite shoes, of course, but as mine were almost worn through from all the slipping and sliding and climbing I did, perhaps I could persuade her.

Peter said that he didn't want to go home – ever – and that he was going to ask his mam if they could move here when the war was over.

'Do you think she'll say yes?' asked Doug.

Peter shrugged. 'I dunno. My sister works in a shop in Newcastle and she'll not want to shift.' Then he brightened. 'Maybe she'll get herself married and get her own place.'

'Has she got a young man?' asked Doug.

'No, I don't think so. But she's that sort of age when they go all lovey dovey.' Then he added defiantly, 'I'm staying here, anyway. What can they do if I refuse to go back?'

'They can't make you,' said Doug, but I thought he sounded unsure.

'I'll run away if they do. I know lots of good places to hide. Hey, I haven't showed you this!' Peter fumbled around for something in his pocket and brought out a twisted piece of metal.

'What is it?' we both asked together.

'Shrapnel,' he said. 'There was a bomb not that far from here and one of the farm lads cycled up to have a look and brought me this back. I'm going with him next time.'

'A bomb near here?' Doug backed away from the item now that he knew what it was.

'Was anyone killed?' I asked.

'Nah, they missed their target. Stupid Germans. We'll win the war easy.'

When Doug and I walked back to the schoolhouse I asked him if he thought Mam and Dad would ever want to come and live here.

'Don't be daft,' he said.

'Why not?

'Where would Dad go to work?'

'He could be a farmer,' I said. 'He likes farms – and the countryside. So there!'

'He might like farms, but that doesn't mean he can be a farmer. And Mam would miss Aunty Kitty and Aunty Nan.'

And Aunty Edith, I thought. And the tennis club. Perhaps we would just come for our holidays instead.

Not long after my good deed with Maria I managed to disgrace myself, this time with John Stacey as my unlikely ally. Marjorie had sneaked a packet of Woodbines belonging to her father out of the house and she and I ran up the hill to a spot where we were just out of sight to smoke them. She put a cigarette between her lips and lit it.

'Have you had one before?' I asked, thinking that she looked as if she knew what she was doing.

'No, have you?'

I shook my head. My father smoked the odd cigarette, though, like Uncle, he was more of a pipe smoker. Marjorie passed me the cigarette and I put it cautiously into my mouth. It tasted dirty, of the smell of men's jackets and unwashed skin and my fingers when they came out of Mr Brennan's pockets. But I wanted to like it. I remembered what the tennis club ladies looked like when they lit a cigarette at teatime and wondered if I could emulate their glamour. I had another puff then started to cough.

'You blow the smoke out of your mouth, not swallow it,' said Marjorie.

'I did. But I can still taste it.'

'Do you like it, then?'

'Not really.' I handed the cigarette back to her. 'I think I'm going to give up smoking.'

'So am I. But you're glad you tried, aren't you?'

'Oh yes.'

'I'd better put these back before Dad notices.'

At the bottom of the hill, as we were climbing over the gate, we met John walking into the village. Marjorie said goodbye and carried on home. I wondered if John could tell what I had been doing – I could taste that cigarette in my mouth – but if he could he didn't say anything. We sat on the gate for a while then went back into the field. The land on that side of the road rose very steeply, starting from the very back of the cottages on the lane, so that their low-hanging roofs were only a few feet above the ground. It looked like a challenge waiting to be taken – I decided to climb onto the roof of Well Cottage. With John's help I managed to pull myself up, both of us laughing so much I don't know how no one heard and came to chase us away there and then. Once on the roof I scrambled up it on all fours to the top. John stayed on the ground as he said he didn't like heights. Now that I was up there I needed something to do and the answer was staring me in the face in the form of a chimney pot. John went to fetch some sticks as ammunition, passed them up to me, and I posted each one down the chimney.

Mission accomplished, we both ran off, laughing at our cleverness, before anyone could see us.

That night John and I were summoned to Uncle's study. He had his headmaster's face on, not our jolly Uncle's. The people who lived in the cottage had heard me on the roof, he said, and had seen us running away. To make matters worse, the chimney we had bombarded was in a bedroom that had just been decorated and the sticks had brought a fall of soot down with them and made a terrible mess. We were sent to apologise and offer to help to clean up. The offer was declined. After that I was so ashamed at what I had done that for a long time I couldn't bear to walk past the cottage, even though it was just up the road from us and on our route into Bampton. Instead I took a long way round which involved crossing through the fields just after the schoolhouse, climbing the hill and entering the village beside the mill. It took ages, but at least I didn't run the risk of bumping into the angry people from Well Cottage.

Memories of those who stayed:
'Harry's death saved the rest of us.'

I was twelve years old and lived with my family in North
Shields, close to the River Tyne. Our family regularly used
the shelter in the basement of the W A Wilkinson's Lemonade
factory as we didn't have one of our own. It had room for over
two hundred people. We went there nearly every evening as it
felt like the safest place to be. It had a stone floor and benches
round the wall and I remember it always being cold. But it had
a good atmosphere and there was usually music and singing.
My friends and I used to wait outside the sweetshop opposite
the factory for it to open, then dash across the road and into
the shelter through a heavy metal door. An interior light
would go off when the door was opened and come on again
when it was closed. My aunt, Mrs Ellen Lee, was warden of
the shelter. She was a big, warm-hearted person, who took
her duties seriously.

I think that the tragic loss of my older brother, Harry, earlier
in the war saved the rest of us from possible death when the
shelter was bombed. We had arrived at the shelter one night
in October 1940 to be told by my aunt that we had better go
home as there was a telegram waiting. We all hurried back to
discover that Harry had been lost in the sinking of the ship
Empire Brigade. From that moment on my mother said there
was no point in us using the shelter – with Harry gone, we
might as well just take our chance. So on the night of 3 May
1941, when there was a direct hit on the factory that sent
the floor above and its heavy machinery crashing onto those

sheltering below, we were at home. One hundred and nine people were killed.

My mother and I went to the site the next day. We were worried that my father might have been there as he was an ARP warden, but fortunately he had been on duty at the harbour. My aunt was still there, working away – she rescued dozens of people that night, despite being injured herself. I can still see her face, etched with soot and grime.

Emily Meek (née Brooks), North Shields,
July 2015, aged eighty-seven

Chapter seventeen

When spring was finally on its way – though it could change dramatically from day to day – Uncle set some of the older boys the task of digging up part of the school playing field to plant vegetables. We had all been told as a nation to 'Dig for Victory', and he and Aunty already grew vegetables in the schoolhouse garden and had dug up their lawns to grow more, but this was on a far larger scale and for the benefit of the whole village. We were the grateful recipients of a box of vegetable seeds donated from America, as certain seeds, including onions, leeks and runner beans, were becoming scarce. Uncle even insisted on cutting seed potatoes in half to make them go further. We had been introduced – via Government literature – to the characters Potato Pete and Doctor Carrot, who advised us to eat plenty of these common vegetables, and we all knew that carrots – of which there was always a steady supply – would help us to see in the blackout and had helped our pilots to win the Battle of Britain. Aunty sometimes used mashed carrot as a sweetener, for example by adding it to jam when she sandwiched a cake. She always said there was no need for us to let the others know – she and I were the cooks and if Uncle and the boys hadn't asked us what went into our recipes before the war, there was no need to suddenly tell them now.

The boys at school enjoyed helping on the allotment as they were allowed to miss lessons. The Percy brothers never played truant if they knew it was going to be a gardening day. Sometimes they stayed to help after school and got sixpence from Uncle for their efforts. Later, when there were crops to harvest, Uncle let them buy some of the vegetables cheaply and take them back to Burnbanks to sell, making themselves some extra pocket money. He always had a soft spot for that pair. But most profits, if there were any, went to the Red Cross, one of whose most popular causes was helping our prisoners of war overseas.

It was May 1941, and after ten months of living in Bampton I no longer felt like a newcomer. My days as a child of the suburbs – of shopping in Newcastle, of car trips to Aunty Edith's at the coast, of helping Mam at the tennis club teas – felt as if they belonged to another girl, one I used to know a long time ago. Occasionally Aunty and I went shopping to Penrith, where we sometimes had a cup of tea and a cake in Birkett's tearoom, and I would be taken aback by the number of people, by the shops and the traffic and the busy market square. One day we stopped to watch two women set up a stall in the square and begin to demonstrate easy nourishing meals to make on rations.

'Now, ladies, I am going to tell you all a bedtime story,' said one of them, by way of introduction. 'Once upon a time there were five housewives. Their names were Lady Peel-Potatoes, the Hon Mrs Waste-Fuel, Miss Pour-The-Vegetable-Water-Down-The-Sink, Mrs Don't-Like-Uncooked-Vegetables and Mrs Won't-Eat-Carrots.' Her head moved from side to side as she scanned all of our faces. I felt as if she already knew who was guilty of which crime. Then she waved her wooden spoon at us all and said with a mischievous smile, 'Don't let any one of them put a nose in your kitchen.'

I spent the journey back to Bampton trying to remember the names of the five wasteful ladies and to think up more. Aunty was getting quite tired of the game.

'Let's play "No one says anything until they see Bampton",' she suggested and thankfully for her peace of mind I agreed.

It always made my heart soar when I got my first glimpse of the schoolhouse through the trees.

After having to postpone an earlier trip due to the weather, my mother came to visit us on the bus one Saturday, the first time we had seen her since the previous summer. As a surprise for me she brought my friend Barbie with her. It felt funny to see her again after such a long time. We sat politely beside each other in the kitchen while Aunty served us all tea and chattered away to Mam. I was dying for Barbie to finish her drink and for the grown-ups to stop talking so that I could ask if we could be excused and I could show Barbie round the schoolhouse and the village.

At last I had my chance. Aunty was getting up to refill

the teapot and she and Mam had temporarily run out of conversation.

'Art thou coomin' t'play?' I asked my friend. At least that is how it must have sounded to Barbie and my mother.

Mam, who was just starting to say something to Aunty, stopped abruptly and snapped her head round to look at me instead, while I noticed that Barbie, too, was gazing at me in a startled way.

Perhaps aware that it might come across as a slight to Aunty if she made a comment about my new accent, Mam gave a small false-sounding laugh and carried on with her conversation. But a few minutes later, as Barbie and I went upstairs so that I could show her my room, Barbie nudged me and said, 'You talk funny now.'

On our way back down we caught sight of John in his room. He was playing with his bricks. Barbie stopped and stared. Like me and Doug, she hadn't seen any bricks like these ones before.

'They're called Minibrix,' I said, and added when we were out of earshot, 'John comes from a very important family.' I had heard a story about his father carrying one of the standards in a parade in front of King George V after the last war.

Barbie seemed impressed. 'Does he let you play with them?'

'Sometimes,' I lied. Actually, it wasn't a total lie, but I had only been allowed to play with a few bricks at a time, unlike Doug, who as a boy and John's senior was granted special privileges.

'I can teach you the sheep-counting numbers,' I said as we reached the through-place on our way to the wood, hoping to impress her further.

'What are they?'

'It's how the shepherds count. Yan than teddera meddera pimp.'

Barbie giggled. 'What's the point of that? Why not just count "one, two, three"?'

'Well,' I began. 'If you're counting sheep . . . um, it stops you forgetting what number you're at when . . . ' I tailed off, not exactly sure of the point of it myself now that I was trying to explain it. 'Anyway, I'll show you the hens now and if there's time we can go to the mill, but you mustn't tell Aunty.'

In spite of Aunty's warning, Doug and I had not been able to resist the lure of the mill wheel. But we knew to give ourselves a good dusting down before we went home so that Aunty wouldn't know we'd been playing in it. Depending on what the miller was grinding, we would end up covered in either flour or sawdust.

Over lunch Mam gave me and Doug all the news from home, which was simply that everyone there was 'keeping well' or that she hadn't seen whoever we asked about 'for a while'. Later she got out her knitting, as she had done on her earlier visit, but at least it wasn't Sunday this time so I didn't need to feel uncomfortable about it. She said that if it was safe, Doug and I could come home for a few days in the summer holidays.

'Well, you could try to look pleased about it,' she said, pretending to be cross when neither Doug nor I said anything. She shook her head in mock exasperation at Aunty. 'I think you're looking after them a bit too well, Mrs Thornton.'

Aunty asked Barbie how she was enjoying living with her aunt and uncle in Ponteland and Barbie told us about the two-bedroom cottage where her grandparents and her uncle's elderly mother were also guests. She slept on a camp bed in her aunt and uncle's room and above her head was a rickety card table holding their tea-making machine.

'It wakes me up with a start every morning when the water starts to gurgle,' she said. 'Then it swooshes into the teapot and an alarm rings.'

Mam and Aunty tittered over this.

'Is it quiet, Barbie, with just you and the adults?' asked Mam, looking up from her knitting towards Doug and John who were playing a noisy card game in the corner.

Barbie shrugged and said there were lots of books to read and there was a big girl next door who took her to school every day.

'I expect they enjoy making a fuss of you,' said Aunty smiling at her.

'Did I tell you about the outfit my aunty knitted me?' Barbie asked, looking at me but telling everyone. 'It's got a blue skirt, a scarlet pullover and a white jumper.'

'How kind of your aunt,' said Mam. 'You must feel very special when you wear that.'

Aunty also thought it sounded lovely. 'It's hard to think that I didn't want a little girl here,' she said with an apologetic shrug. 'This time last year I didn't know what I would do with a girl, but it's hard to imagine not having Gwenda here now. Of course it's a shame she gets left out sometimes when the boys play, but she's very good at amusing herself.'

I smiled at her, grateful that she found it easy to see the best side of me. Mam might have agreed but would rarely voice such an opinion. I believe she thought that too much praise did us no good. She did say, though, that she was glad to hear I wasn't being too much of a scallywag.

*

Spring was turning into summer and Whit Sunday came at last. I had been looking forward to this festival since my first day at Sunday School last year. Aunty had saved a dress my mother had made me, along with a matching ribbon for my hair, to wear for the first time today. But before prize-giving we had the morning service to sit through and a preacher who was getting worked up about the Holy Spirit descending on the disciples. The service went on longer than usual as the tradition was for the children present at the service – me, Doug and three or four others – to recite a poem. Except that Uncle – with his lofty ambitions for us both – had decreed that Doug and I learn two, one of which was a composition of his own. We had been practising all week. The poem that Uncle had penned for Doug was a funny one about him being an evacuee from Newcastle and the congregation chuckled when they heard it. I don't remember the one he wrote for me, but I remember the second one clearly. It was written by Elizabeth Gardner Reynolds and was called 'The Little Black Dog'.

> *I wonder if Christ had a little black dog*
> *All curly and woolly like mine;*
> *With two silky ears, and a nose round and wet,*
> *And eyes brown and tender that shine.*
>
> *I'm afraid that He hadn't, because I have read*
> *How He prayed in the garden alone,*
> *For all of His friends and disciples had fled,*
> *Even Peter, the one called a 'stone'.*

And oh, I am sure that that little black dog,
With a heart so tender and warm,
Would never have left Him to suffer alone,
But, creeping right under His arm,

Would have licked those dear fingers in agony clasped,
And counting all favours but loss,
When they took Him away, would have trotted behind
And followed Him right to the cross!

It had taken a long time for me to get the last verse right and I had stumbled over it as I practised with Aunty, even just before leaving for chapel, mainly as I didn't understand its second line. But I remembered it all when I needed to and there was a general mutter of appreciation around the congregation when I had finished, along with a number of 'Ah's and a few blown noses. I saw Mrs Heatherside dab her eyes and after the service she said to Uncle, 'Dougie Thornton, where do you get them from? You ought to be ashamed of yourself reducing us all to blubbering wrecks.'

At Sunday School that afternoon books were given out for good attendance and there were special prizes for the oldest boy and girl in the class. I was so happy when my name was read out and I trotted up to receive a brand new book. Wanting to savour the anticipation, I didn't open it until Doug and I were walking home across the fields. There was a sticker in the front with a Bible passage printed on it and my name written in italic script underneath. But as I turned the pages I felt the disappointment well up inside me; it was far too easy for me – more like a picture book, with just a couple of sentences on each page. I had finished it by the time we reached the lane.

'What have you got there?' asked Aunty as we came into the kitchen.

Doug showed her his adventure story and I reluctantly produced mine. 'It's a baby book,' I said, feeling even more sorry for myself when I saw her sympathetic face.

Aunty sighed. 'Well, Gwenda, it's not easy buying books for so many children and getting it right every time. They wouldn't expect a girl of your age to be reading such advanced books. Perhaps you can find some more to borrow from Hugh and John's shelves.'

I was tired of reading about treasure and shipwrecks and soldiers. I longed for boarding-school tales and dogs and horses. But I managed to nod and smile at Aunty. I knew it wasn't her fault that there were no books for girls in the house.

Earlier in spring the whole village had been left reeling by some terrible news. Billy Preston, husband of Ada and father of David, our schoolmaster and our friend, had contracted tuberculosis while on active service and been taken to a sanatorium in Meathop, near Grange-over-Sands in the south Lakelands. Billy was so full of life and energy; I couldn't imagine him succumbing to an illness. I remembered the day Miss Dixon and I had seen him when we had been picking bilberries, how he had waved to us before striding off across the fells, and how he liked to climb and play rugby.

'At least when he's better he might not have to go back to fight,' said Doug, who wanted to have his teacher back. 'Isn't that right, Uncle? Might Mr Preston be invalided out?'

Billy Preston and his son David, 1941

Uncle said that was certainly a possibility, but that we had to remember that TB was a very serious illness.

But Doug and I were sure that Mr Preston – as we always called him due to his status as schoolmaster – would get better soon. Once, at Ada's, as I sang 'Clap hands for daddy coming down the waggonway' to David, I stopped suddenly and looked at Ada, worried about the effect the words might be having on her, but she just smiled and started to sing too:

'A pocketful of money and a cart load of hay'.

Chapter eighteen

A couple of days after we had broken up for the summer, Doug and I said goodbye to John and to Aunty and Uncle and squashed onto the bus to Penrith, where we changed to a Wright Bros coach for Newcastle.

The conductress was a large bossy lady who would become a familiar face over the next two years.

'Right, let's have everyone for Newcastle here so that I can count you all,' she said. 'And just remember, I've got eyes in the back of my head.'

There were several Bampton evacuees taking the coach today, including two girls who had so much luggage that I guessed they were going back for good and Peter, who had just a paper bag with his lunch in it.

'I'm coming back for haymaking, whatever Mam says,' he

told us. 'Mr Butler says I can have a go on top of the cart. You've got to be small for that.'

Uncle had told us what a scenic journey we had to look forward to. 'Hartside Pass is magnificent. Have a look out at the top when you're there. The whole of the Eden valley is spread out before you. Then you'll be off zigzagging down the Allen valley. That's what your father enjoyed in his motorbike days and I know exactly why.'

He started telling us to look out for signs of the lead mining that used to take place in the North Pennines, but I wasn't listening any more as Uncle's hand tracing out the twisting roads had filled me with a sense of dread. I was not a good traveller at the best of times and in the past had often had to swap seats with Mam and sit in the front of Dad's car to stop myself from feeling sick.

As we climbed up to Hartside Summit, the driver slowing for each bend then speeding up again, slowing down then speeding up again, in a pattern that seemed to have been designed to churn up my insides, I stared straight ahead, sealing my lips tightly, trying to pretend I was fine.

'You're white as a sheet, hinny,' said the conductress, stopping beside our seat as she walked up and down the aisle with her bucket. 'Make sure you get off for some fresh air when we get to the top.'

I had to look away from the bucket as the very sight of it was almost enough to make me retch.

The cool air at the top of Hartside, where we all got out for a few minutes, felt as welcome as a cold drink on a hot day. I stood beside Doug, breathing it in, as he looked down across the wide valley and wondered if it was possible to spot

Bampton. But back on the bus, as we began our winding descent and the smell of fumes drifted through the open window, I knew I couldn't hold out any longer. I clutched Doug's arm, he called to the conductress and she stuck her bucket under my nose just in time.

Aunty had given us a teacake for lunch and Doug took his from his bag. But as the smell of vomit began to mix with the fumes, he seemed to reconsider and put it away.

'Anyone else for the sick bucket?' asked the conductress, moving deftly from person to person as if she was taking part in an elaborate dance. 'I think I'm going to need two of these and two pairs of hands when I've got you lot again.'

I got off for some fresh air again in Alston, felt better for a while but continued to be sick until we reached Hexham from where it was a straight road home.

'I'm not travelling with her any more,' was the first thing Doug said to Mam as we got off the bus in Newcastle.

We caught another bus to High Heaton. Through the window I saw people going about their business next to bombed-out buildings. Signs pointed the way to public shelters. Shops had notices in their windows informing people of the products they didn't have. Some had long queues outside them stretching all the way down the street. It was as if the photos from the newspapers I sometimes glimpsed had suddenly come to life. I noticed that most people carried their gas masks. I instinctively put my hand on mine. Doug and I had brought ours with us but we rarely carried them around in Bampton. It was July 1941 and the big headlines now were all about Hitler's invasion of the Soviet Union, which had begun a month earlier in June. We were all thankful that he had given up his plan to invade Britain, apart, that is, from some of the boys I knew who insisted they had been looking forward to it and who enjoyed looking for German spies wherever they went.

I read one of the signs on the bus:

Don't start to shop till ten o'clock
Be back again by four
Our workers need to travel
If we mean to win the war

I wondered why anyone would even want to spend six hours shopping when, as my mother so often said, there was nothing much to buy. As we walked up Cleveland Gardens I saw the bombed houses on the other side of the road, shockingly close to ours, and thought of Mr Farnsworth sitting in the garden in his pyjamas wondering where his bed had gone.

'I don't know what the Germans have got against our road,' said Mam, as she saw us both staring.

Walking into our home was rather like entering some stranger's house with its different smell and rather insubstantial feel after the solid schoolhouse. I kept slamming doors without meaning to as they were so much lighter than the ones we had become used to. It felt as if Dad was going to walk through the front door at any minute in his warden's uniform and make us laugh with the story of someone's foolishness. Our father was a quiet man, really, but the house still felt empty without him. A lingering smell of tobacco when we opened the cupboard under the stairs was the main reminder of his presence.

Our bedroom looked neater and the shelves of the bookcase more empty than I remembered. Mam confessed that she had given some of the books and wooden jigsaws that she considered we had grown out of to a family friend who had been in hospital for a serious operation, and others to the WVS shop.

I would have gladly donated some of my books and toys but I felt that she could have asked me first so that I could have told her what I was happy to give away and what I would have liked to keep.

As if reading my mind, Mam said, 'Won't it be lovely when the war's over! We can all be a bit selfish again, but for now it's a crime to have more than we need.'

And I knew that my lips would have to stay sealed.

One of the first things we did was dash out to see the air-raid shelter. Mr Young had grown peas and beans up the side of it and there was a pile of sandbags on either side of the entrance. Mam pushed Mr Young's wheelbarrow out of the way and said, 'That'll be just like it, we'll break our necks getting into it.'

It looked almost homely with its pile of blankets and magazines, a box with food and drink, a lantern and a wireless. The biscuits in the box were a brand I hadn't seen before and Mam said they had come in a food parcel from her brother Walter in Australia, along with some tea and cocoa, tinned meat and fish, and that it was at times like this that she counted her blessings that he was there.

'I wish I could have seen it here at Christmas!' I said, remembering how Mam had decorated the shelter then.

'I'll be happy never to see it again,' she replied. 'The hours I've spent in there over the past year!'

I would have liked to go to the Dene next to see if the Birdman was there but Mam had other plans. We were to go and say hello to Mr and Mrs Young and then to call on some of the other neighbours who had been asking after us. As most of them invited us inside, that took up the rest of the afternoon.

The next day we went to the coast to see relatives. As we set off for the bus stop I said hello to the postman, though he was an older man and not the one I remembered, and I spoke to the lady who lived at the end of the road whose name I'd forgotten but whose dog was called Spot. She seemed pleased that I had remembered Spot's name and began telling us how when he first heard the air-raid siren he had jumped up and fetched his lead, ready for walkies, but now he knew what it was and rounded up the whole family, seeing them all into the shelter before taking his place at the entrance to ward off any intruders. My mother said how clever he was, but we must make a move as we had a bus to catch, but before we had reached the end of the road I waved hello to a lady whose daughter had been in my class at Cragside School and she crossed the road to speak to us. She wanted to know how I was getting on in Bampton and told us that Joyce was quite happy in Tebay once she had moved to a different family as she hadn't seen eye to eye with the daughter in the first house.

When we were finally on our way, Mam glared at me and said, 'What's got into you, talking to all and sundry? If you carry on like this I'm going to pretend you're not with me.'

I told her that in Bampton everyone stopped to chat. Mam didn't reply. I wondered why she had to be in such a hurry all the time.

Doug went to stay with a friend for a few days while Mam and I got the bus to Seahouses for a short holiday. Her good friend Nan came with us. Aunty Nan and Uncle Arnold were the friends my parents played whist with on Sundays in pre-war days and Uncle Arnold, like Dad, was in the forces. We stayed in The Bamburgh Castle, a hotel beside the harbour with views across the North Sea to the Farne Islands. The beaches were out of bounds, some of them littered with anti-tank devices, but we could go for walks and there was a lively atmosphere in the village. I suppose, with the war going on for almost two years now and no end to it in sight, people felt the need to at least try to carry on as they would have done. So there were lots of parties like ours – family groups, minus the men.

The three of us went for long walks and treated ourselves to ice creams. There was no rationing on hotel meals at that stage in the war, so we ate well. One day we walked up the coast to Bamburgh, where the castle was being used as a military head-quarters and men in uniform mingled with holidaymakers.

I made friends with a girl of about my age called Mary Jane who was staying in our hotel with her mother, brother and grandmother. Our mothers exchanged polite conversation. If they had been on their own they might even have become friends too. Mary Jane's family always sat at the table next to ours in the dining room and the adults usually enquired after each other's day between courses. Mary Jane's brother, Derek, was obsessed with aeroplanes and the war in general and was what my mother and Aunty Nan called 'a bit of a know-all'. Aunty Nan giggled and said she was surprised he wasn't running the country as he obviously knew a lot more than Mr Churchill did.

One evening as we were eating our green pea soup, the sound of a plane's engine drowned out our conversations. Derek jumped up and rushed to the window, almost knocking a little boy out of his chair in his effort to catch sight of whatever was passing overhead. Mam and Aunty Nan raised their eyes at each other across the table. Derek and Mary Jane's mother laughed apologetically.

'He gets it from his father. He's in the RAF,' she confided, leaning towards our table.

When Derek came back to the table he was scribbling in his notebook and begging his mother to be allowed to fetch his spotters' cards from his room, but she said that he would have to wait until after dinner. He sulked for the rest of the meal and clattered his knife and fork noisily on his plate to annoy everyone.

'He needs to get something else from his father,' said Mam to Aunty Nan when their party had left the dining room. 'At least his sister has some manners.'

When we went for coffee in the lounge Mary Jane waved me over and we played Ludo. Derek had been reunited with his beloved cards and was explaining to his grandmother what sort of plane it had been and its capacity for wreaking destruction. Mam and Aunty Nan nodded to them all and went to sit at the other end of the room.

The next afternoon Mam and I were in our bedroom when we heard two very loud explosions. We both jumped and Mam put a hand to her heart, then quickly composed herself and said in the manner of someone who was used to such things now, 'Don't worry, it was further away than it sounded.' She went to the window but told me to stay where I was.

'Strewth! They've bombed the lighthouse!' she exclaimed.

When she felt it was safe she allowed me to look. Through the window I saw an eruption of smoke and dust out at sea where the lighthouse was supposed to be.

Someone banged on the door and Aunty Nan came rushing in. 'Did you see? Oh, the poor keepers. I hope they're all right. Oh, dear, it doesn't look good.'

Mam said we should all go downstairs and have a cup of tea and that way we would find out what had happened. Everyone in the lounge was talking about the incident and had their own view on how serious it was. When we heard someone say that a lifeboat had been spotted leaving the island we joined the large group that had gathered at the harbour. There were cheers when a boat containing all three of the lighthouse keepers landed and it was clear that none of them had been injured.

An elderly man, wearing a fisherman-style shirt, told Mam and Aunty Nan that they often saw enemy planes coming across the sea and then turning north when they reached land.

'Aye, we often say, "Poor old Glasgow's getting it later",' he said. 'Eeh, they're beggars, aren't they? Right beggars.' He said it as if he were talking about some minor nuisance – slugs on his lettuces or schoolboys throwing stones. He wasn't the sort to let anything bother him too much.

The attack had damaged the lighthouse's turret and engine room and blown in all the doors and windows. Mam and Aunty Nan said they wondered what young Derek would have to say about it. They said he'd care more about the wing shape and tail type of the plane than the poor old lighthouse keepers.

Their party arrived in the dining room as we were eating our soup.

'Well,' said my mother after we had greeted each other, 'I bet your notebook is chock-a-block after today's shenanigans, young man.'

The boy looked down at the table and his mother leaned over

and said in a stage whisper, 'We had to take my mother to see a friend in Warkworth today and we missed it. He's terribly upset.'

Mam tutted in sympathy. 'Oh! Well, we had quite a view from our bedroom window. I thought we were all goners at first. At least no one's hurt.'

And Derek and Mary Jane's mother agreed that that was the main thing.

Police and newspaper reporters wanted to speak to witnesses to the attack. Most of them had seen three bombs drop from the plane, but only two explosions had been heard, giving rise to fears of a third unexploded bomb. However, none was found and it was believed that it must have exploded at the same time as one of the others.

Not having experienced something like this at such close quarters, I found the whole episode thrilling and could hardly wait to tell Doug about it.

'We'd better get you back to Bampton before anything else happens,' said Mam. 'What will Mrs Thornton think? Your mother takes you for a holiday and you end up in the middle of enemy action!'

On the day we got back to High Heaton I ran to the Dene before Mam had chance to argue. Doug was coming back that evening and we would return to Bampton the next day. I hoped that the Birdman would be there. Things had a habit of changing these days, people disappearing, just when you had got used to them. Why, even my toys couldn't be relied on any more! I crossed my fingers all the way there and as I rounded the bend I hardly dared to look. But there he was, in the same place he had been when I last saw him.

He was talking to a bunch of pigeons at his feet, their heads bobbing up and down as if they were agreeing with whatever he was saying. When he saw me he gave a small nod of acknowledgement. 'You're back,' he said. 'Staying for long?'

I had hoped he might seem more pleased to see me. It had been a whole year, after all. 'Just for a holiday,' I replied. 'I've got to go back tomorrow.'

The pigeons flew off on my approach, their wings crackling.

'You're growing,' said the Birdman. 'Your mam wouldn't know you, would she? And where's Doug? I bet he's a big lad now.'

I told him that Doug was staying with a friend and how Mam and I had been to Seahouses and seen a bomb.

'Aye, I read about that. Well, it's a good job the keepers were safe. That's all that matters. And how's your place in the Lakes? I did see your mam once, a while back now, and she said you'd fallen on your feet, the pair of you.'

'Bampton is grand. I've got a friend called Marjorie, one called Janet and one called Mavis. Mavis lives up on the crags so I don't see her as much. Marjorie's dad is the postman.'

'Well, it sounds as if your mam was right. Mind, I'll not be understanding you if you talk any broader!'

A robin landed on his shoulder. 'I doubt Bobby will either,' he added.

I giggled. 'That's what Mam keeps saying. But my friends there say I sound Geordie. I can do shepherds' counting, you know.'

The Birdman seemed more interested in my counting than Barbie had been and said he was sure it would be very useful.

'There's lots of birds in Bampton,' I added, as we watched a pair of pigeons in their courtly display. 'And Aunty keeps chickens.' I looked at him cautiously, not sure if I should say what I was going to say next and knowing that I wouldn't have done if anyone else had been with me. 'You could come and see us one day, if you want. You can catch Wrights' bus to Penrith.'

The Birdman didn't say anything at first. Bobby hopped from his shoulder to take a piece of cheese from between his fingers. 'That's kind,' he said at last, 'and I know you mean it, as well. But I've a habit of not getting on so well in other places. That's why I'm always here, you see.'

I nodded. I didn't understand really and yet it also made perfect sense.

When the conductress saw me at the bus station she told Mam she was putting me in the front seat, behind the driver, so that she could keep an eye on me.

'She's always been like this,' apologised Mam. 'I'm terribly sorry.'

The conductress said there were usually one or two on every journey and she was used to it now.

It seems strange now to think how easily I said goodbye to my mother as we parted. We had enjoyed our visit home but Doug and I were both happy to be returning. I doubt we spared a thought for what our mother was feeling as she watched her children leave her yet again and went back to an empty house. The bomb so close to our own home had undoubtedly helped to convince her that she had made the correct decision, but I wonder how she really felt every time she let us go.

Before we left, Mam entrusted Doug with some money to buy us both clogs. Clogs! I must have worn her down with my pleading, or perhaps she had come to realise that they were a practical shoe for the countryside, with their metal clinkers on the heel and the toe that could be replaced. How proud I would be when I visited the blacksmith in Bampton Grange when they needed repairing! Mam had given us banana sandwiches for the journey but as I was sick again mine remained in their bag. Doug said I had spoilt them for him as well and that this really was the last time he was getting the bus with me.

Aunty was surprised to see the sandwiches when we were back in the schoolhouse. 'Your mother can still buy bananas?'

The fact that we hadn't seen an actual banana should have made us suspicious of this treat, which Mam would dish up occasionally during the war years. It wasn't until the war was over that she confessed: she made them with mashed potato and banana essence. Doug and I loved them – apart from on bus trips – and neither of us had ever guessed they weren't the real thing.

The schoolteachers arrived the day after we got back, but only six of them. As usual, Jenny Charlton had brought the heavy rucksacks and camping equipment in her car.

'I did wonder if you'd want us this year,' she said to Aunty and Uncle after they'd greeted each other. 'I did wonder if I should even be thinking of a holiday with everything that's going on, so I was delighted to get your letter.'

Uncle said he thought it was important for them to be able to recharge their batteries and that, while he knew he was biased, he couldn't think of a nicer place for them to do it.

'And you've still got a houseful!' said Jenny as Aunty introduced her to John Stacey.

'Hello, Nurse Gwenda!' someone called to me and I didn't recognise the face of the young woman who said it.

'Remember me? I was your patient! I've had my hair cut short since then.'

I could see now that it was Rosemary, the young teacher who had been ill the previous summer.

Paddy, the joker of the group, was with them, but Molly, the one who had liked to talk about poetry and books, wasn't there. I overheard Jenny telling Aunty that Molly had been called up and was working as the driver for someone important, though she was sure they could have found a job that used her brain more.

One day when John Thornton had gone off fishing on his own, Doug and John Stacey set off on their bikes and didn't appear at dinner time. There was a strained atmosphere as Aunty, Uncle and I sat down at midday and started without them. I was making a fuss about a fly that had just got itself trapped on the flypaper above, worrying that it would end up on my plate, and Aunty tutted at my silliness before asking me if I knew where they had gone. I had been playing with Marjorie and hadn't even seen them leave, but had a nagging idea that they might have gone looking for shrapnel following our conversation with Peter. I replied honestly that I didn't know.

The afternoon wore on. I went to see Ada and David and when I came back the teachers had returned from their hike and were tidying up in preparation for leaving the next day. Most of them were going to be volunteering in some way for the remainder of their vacation and there was a lot of laughter about a woman Paddy called 'Mrs H' who ran her mother's local WVS centre and was doing a good job of alienating the rest of her team with her self-importance.

'If we win the war, it'll all be thanks to her!' joked Paddy.

'I'm afraid you'll always discover people like that in this

world,' Jenny Charlton said, picking up a single sock from underneath a mattress and holding it questioningly in the air. 'I'd like to say the war brings out the best in people, but there are one or two exceptions.' She winked at me as she said that.

I helped them for a while then looked up and down the lane for a sign of the boys. I was starting to worry as well and my mind was conjuring up dangerous scenarios. Suppose they had found part of a bomb and it had exploded in their hands! Suppose they ended up cycling back in the dark! The local Home Guard might shout at them to stop, and if they didn't – thinking it best just to pedal faster – they might be shot! I felt quite wobbly just thinking about it all.

They arrived back just as we were sitting down for tea, informing us that they had gone all the way to Penrith and misjudged how long it would take with the diversion due to the tank range at Lowther Park.

'We heard lots of shots!' said John, before Doug shushed him with a frown.

'Didn't you think we would worry?' asked Aunty, looking cross. 'We had no idea where you were.'

'Sorry, Aunty,' said Doug. 'We thought that if John goes fishing for the day it wouldn't matter if we went off as well.'

Aunty reminded them both that her John was older and that he always told her where he was going. The boys promised that they wouldn't do it again.

The next day John took the three of us fishing – no doubt at Aunty's bidding – but I disgraced myself by chattering too much and John told his mother later that it really was the last time. Another day Doug and John Stacey spent hours and hours digging a trench from the stream in the nearby field so that a channel ran through our little wood then back into the stream. We built camps for their toy soldiers in the mud on the banks. While they were re-enacting battles, I dug up and separated some snowdrop bulbs from the waste patch in the garden and planted them along the edge of the channel. Aunty told me I would have to be patient – that snowdrops came up in the winter or early spring – but I couldn't stop myself from looking out for signs of them appearing for the rest of the summer holiday.

On those long fine evenings the sky never seemed to darken and we sat out late and made fires in the wood to bake potatoes or the fish that John had caught.

'We're just like *Swallows and Amazons*,' announced John Thornton as we munched slices of Aunty's parkin by the campfire. 'Have you read it, Doug? Have you, John? I've got a copy somewhere. All we need is a boat!'

The boys decided they were going to build a raft out of all the wood they could find and sail it on Haweswater.

'I know where there are lots of good pieces,' I said jumping up, determined not to be left out of this ambitious plan.

Doug looked helplessly at the older John, who raised his eyes back at him and then said to us all in his I'm-in-charge voice that *anyone* could help to collect wood, but sailing was just for the boys.

'There are girls in *Swallows and Amazons*,' I said crossly. I hadn't read it yet but had picked up the copy John was talking about and even flicked through a few pages before putting it back on the shelf.

We saw the long shadow of Uncle on the edge of the wood as he came to join us with his pipe.

'Don't say anything, Gwenda!' hissed Doug.

'Then you can't leave me out,' I replied, as I skipped off to greet him.

Thankfully the plan never did materialise.

My friends and I had our adventures too that summer. Aunty would give me a teacake for lunch and Marjorie, Janet and I would go exploring.

'If you stay with the beck then you can't get lost,' Aunty would say.

One day we saw crayfish swimming in the water and I made the mistake of telling Doug. The next day he and John Stacey were at our spot when we got there, but as they were better prepared than us we decided to overlook their trespassing as we caught and cooked them on the bank.

On one of these long light-filled days I lost track of the time. Doug found me paddling in the beck about half a mile out of the village, long after my friends had gone home.

'You're in trouble,' he said. 'Where have you been?'

I couldn't believe it when he told me that it was eight o'clock and that everyone was frantic with worry.

I think Aunty was too relieved to be angry when she saw me and even Uncle couldn't stay cross for long. But after that Uncle began to use the school whistle to summon me when it was time to come home. If anyone heard it and saw me they would say, 'Hurry along, Gwenda. Mr Thornton's blown the whistle for you. You don't want to get in his bad books, do you?'

And I would run back, because I didn't.

Chapter nineteen

When summer was on its way out, we gathered fruit and berries again. Aunty bottled and stored her own surplus fruit by using Campden Tablets, pouring a solution over the fruit in their jars until they were needed, when they had to be boiled vigorously to get rid of the preservative. Bampton's Women's Institute had joined the Fruit Preservation Scheme and were taking charge again of jam and jelly production. Like the previous year, we had a day off school for picking and for a few weeks before and after, children would turn up in the morning with bags or pockets stuffed full with whatever they had stumbled across on the journey there.

'I think you've already turned yours into jam, Tobe,' said Miss Pickup to one of the Burnbanks boys as he took a squidgy mess from his pocket. 'What is your mother going to say when she has to wash those trousers yet again? Bring a container with you the next time!'

Everyone wanted to help; everyone wanted to be a part of our country's aim to be as self-sufficient as possible. As with Uncle's vegetables, the jams and jellies that were produced were sold locally or given away to anyone in need, while the rosehips were used to make rosehip syrup, rich in vitamin C, for our troops.

When my friend Barbara from the farm told me that the day had come to kill the pig they had been fattening, she invited us to come and watch. A lot of country people kept animals for slaughter, but in the cities, too, pig clubs were common and when I was home in the summer I had been sent by Mam to put scraps in the pig bin at the end of the road for fattening the neighbourhood pig. Doug refused point blank to witness such a cruel sight so I went on my own. Barbara and I watched as the animal was strung up by its feet and its throat was cut. The poor creature squealed and I closed my eyes until this part was over. An enamel bowl underneath caught the blood which Barbara's mother took to the kitchen to make into black pudding, while the farmer began to cut up the pig, ready for salting and hanging on nails. When we had had enough of this, Barbara and I went to play on the hay bales in one of the barns.

Another regular visitor to the schoolhouse was Aunty Tess, Aunty's other sister, along with her youngest child who was also called John. They lived in Otterburn in Northumberland and had to catch at least three buses to get to Bampton. John Waddell was my age and we paired up quite happily whenever

School portraits of Gwenda and Doug taken in Bampton

he came to stay. We played doctors and nurses when it rained and ran around in the wood and the playground when it was fine. On winter days we spent hours building houses and castles with the coloured bricks that the Thornton boys had played with in their younger days.

John also liked to play board games. He told me that his mother refused to play them with him as they brought back memories of her childhood when she and her sisters had been made to play them by the various housekeepers who had looked after them.

John called Aunty 'Aunt Evie'. I did try it a couple of times as well but it never sounded right. She was just 'Aunty'. Like 'Mam', it didn't need qualifying in any way.

Aunty Tess was warm and smiley, just like Aunty, and

I always looked forward to seeing her. Before the previous war she had cycled to Penrith for classes with the Red Cross, nursing at a hospital in France during hostilities, though she never spoke about that time. She did, though, tell of how her sketching holiday on the continent in the summer of 1914 had been interrupted by the outbreak of war and how she and her companion had rushed to catch the last boat out of France that August bank holiday weekend. Of course to us youngsters these were just stories and I don't suppose that any of us appreciated what the adults around us had lived through in those days.

One thing we grew used to in wartime was people coming and going. The village's young men – like Billy Preston – might suddenly be called up. Sometimes an older one was too. And women could be put to do whatever the government required of them if they were of a certain age and had no dependent children at home. But our friends came and went as well. I was just getting friendly with a girl in my class when she failed to come to school one day, and the day after, and ever again as it turned out. I assume that as she was an evacuee she went home to Barrow, but nobody ever confirmed this. It wasn't uncommon for the Newcastle and Barrow children to go home with little or no warning. One day an irate mother had turned up in the middle of the school day demanding that her daughter be brought to her immediately as they were going 'back to civilisation'. And so it happened in the schoolhouse, too, when John Stacey's parents decided that it was safe for him to return to Kent.

John had been a part of our lives for a year and a half

now – almost all of our stay in Bampton – so we knew we would feel his loss more keenly than that of our disappearing classmates. And yet it also felt almost inevitable that he was leaving us – just another change in our ever-changing world.

'I'll be home for Christmas!' said John, clearly delighted at the thought. We had heard about the large family house in Kent, set in extensive grounds. John lived a different life from most of the people we knew. He added, 'Perhaps you two will as well.'

I knew he was trying to be kind, but the thought of spending a second Christmas here in Bampton was, in fact, just as appealing as the thought of going home. Though Mam said often enough that we would all be together as a family again one day, I wasn't sure if I believed her. It was hard to believe that Doug and I would ever live anywhere except Bampton.

And so one day I came home after playing with Marjorie to find that John had left – and to my dismay, his bricks and his bicycle had gone as well. It would be almost forty years before I saw him again.

Mam wrote that Dad was safe and well, that he wished us a happy Christmas and that as soon as he had some leave they would catch Wrights' bus to see us or we could come home to visit. I hoped that they would do the travelling as the mere thought of making that bus journey again made my stomach flip. She reminded us once again that nobody would be receiving large gifts this year. Doug told me I was wasting my time asking for ice skates and I settled on the more realistic prospect of a *Chicks' Own* annual, especially as it hadn't materialised the year before. However, the parcel which Aunty produced on Christmas Day did not look very book-shaped. I tried to look pleased when I opened a pair of bright green gloves with a matching knitted hat. I was pretty sure that Mam had been knitting them when we had been together in the summer. Doug got a jumper that we could all see was too short when he held it up. We were both more pleased with the tiny toys Aunty put in our stockings that had been made by Mr Brennan – a tank made of old pieces of tin for Doug and a wooden doll for me with a splosh of red dabbed high on each cheek and a pinafore dress made out of an old handkerchief.

With Aunty's help I had made rock cakes for some of my favourite people, including Ada, Mr Brennan and Elizabeth Castle. They had a dollop of jam inside instead of dried fruit, which was now impossible to get hold of.

With John Stacey gone, Doug and John Thornton paired up straight away that Christmas holiday. My parents had agreed to Uncle's suggestion that Doug take the entrance exam for Appleby Grammar in the spring of 1942 for admittance in September and Doug loved to hear about John's life there. He was obviously happy at school and one of those lucky pupils who was not only academic but good at sport as well. When it dawned on me that Doug would be a boarder there, like John, I felt it was most unfair when I was the one who yearned for the joys of dormitory life – for tuck boxes and midnight feasts – after reading about them in my books. Not that I wanted to leave my school and Aunty and Uncle, I just wasn't sure that Doug would appreciate boarding school as much as I would have done.

John had won a book of Tennyson's poetry in the summer and allowed me to borrow it, but when I found a collection of

Wordsworth's poems in Hugh's bookshelves – a prize for an essay he had written while he was at school – I decided I liked the Lakeland poet better. I remembered Molly, the teacher who had been reading Wordsworth the year before, and the poem about a rainbow she had read to me. I couldn't find a poem with a rainbow in the title, so had to go through the book, page by page, until I recognised its opening line:

My heart leaps up when I behold a rainbow in the sky.

Pleased with my discovery I went to tell Aunty. Uncle came into the kitchen as I was reading it, waited until I had finished, then said how apt the phrase was about the child being father of the man. It didn't make much sense to me but I felt pleased to have met his approval.

'You're not leaving poor Gwenda out, are you, boys?' Aunty would ask from time to time, when she saw me sitting reading on my own.

'Gwenda's fine, aren't you, Gwenda?' John would say. 'She's very welcome to play with us if she wants to but I think she'd get a bit bored.'

John had taught me how to play Patience and Clock Patience; if it was a way to keep me from pestering him and Doug then it worked, as I happily played those card games for hours and rarely got tired of my own company when I spent it this way.

One day just before the end of the Christmas holiday it snowed and all three of us rushed out to play together. Our age differences were briefly forgotten as we spent the morning building a snowman in the school yard. Then John told me to stand against the garage door while he and Doug pretended that they were knife throwers in a circus. 'So we shan't be aiming for you, Gwenda,' he explained. 'We'll be trying to miss you.'

I was glad that they were throwing snowballs and not knives or I would have been killed several times over.

'It's been snowing again,' said Aunty one morning in January as she opened our bedroom curtains, and we looked out to see that the snow was still falling thickly. 'Let's hope it doesn't last long. I was going to pop to Penrith this morning.'

'I hope it stays, Aunty!' said Doug, who had leapt out of bed. Aunty laughed and said that she didn't want to sound like an old misery, but adults tended to see the inconvenience of it. 'Though it does look so pretty when it's like this, clean and untouched,' she added.

At breakfast Uncle was in a sombre mood. 'I wonder how many will make it today,' he said. 'The roads look bad. I doubt we'll see any Burnbanks children today.'

'I wish John was still here,' said Doug, looking at how high the snow was in the garden. 'Are they allowed to play in the snow at Appleby Grammar, Aunty?'

It was Uncle who replied. 'As long as they do their lessons, like you do, I'm sure they're allowed to have fun as well.'

As Uncle had suspected, attendance was poor and there were even fewer pupils the day after. I dashed into the kitchen after school to ask Aunty if I could play outside with Marjorie, expecting to see her and Miss Williams chatting at the table, but the room was empty and there was no smell of cooking coming from the range. When I shouted Aunty replied from upstairs, which surprised me as she was never upstairs at this time of day. I found her in our bedroom where she appeared to be packing mine and Doug's clothes into a small suitcase.

I stood in the doorway watching her, wondering what was happening. Surely we weren't going home like this, so suddenly and in this weather. Now that John Stacey had gone, did Aunty and Uncle want rid of us as well? She looked at me and gave a smile, but it wasn't her usual smile, the one that made her eyes smile too.

'Uncle and I have to go away, Gwenda,' she said. She had stopped smiling now and looked more serious than I had ever seen her. Had I done something wrong, something bad? Whatever it was, it was making my heart thump very loudly. 'Uncle and I have heard that John – our son John –' her voice shook a little as she said this, 'that John is very ill and we have to go to Appleby at once to be with him. You and Douglas are going to the Cartwright farm. You know the Cartwrights from chapel. They've very kindly offered to have you and we know you'll be very well behaved for them.'

I gulped. Was it possible that John, whom we had seen just a few weeks earlier, could be so ill that his parents had to leave on a snowy night and go to him? Surely he would be better tomorrow, if only they waited a day. I couldn't think who these Cartwrights were and even if I did know them, I knew that I didn't want to stay with them.

'Can't we come with you instead?' I said at last, in a tiny voice. 'We'll be very good.'

I thought Aunty gave a sob but she turned her back on me as she closed the case and I couldn't be sure. She said she was sorry but we couldn't, not this time.

Half an hour later Aunty kissed us both goodbye. There was no sign of Uncle but Aunty said that she was saying goodbye for him as well. The low sun painted the snow-covered fields orange as we walked down the lane to the Cartwright farm. It couldn't have been a prettier scene but neither of us spoke and we were both nervous and afraid. I liked farms; there was always something going on on a farm and I loved to see the baby animals. The only thing I didn't like was collecting the milk at the weekend from our local farm when the dogs yapped at me. I felt stupid for being frightened of them when they were just little things and wished I could be braver or that the dogs would start to like me. I hoped there would be no dogs like that where we were going.

The tall woman with the angular face who opened the door looked at us in surprise at first before showing us inside. She led the way into a large dimly lit kitchen with little furniture other than the dining table and several wooden chairs. There were a couple of large clippy mats on the floor, but otherwise everything about this room was simple and unadorned.

'The last evacuees we had didn't last five minutes, did they, Albert?' she said as she pointed to the chairs.

I didn't see Albert at first, then something shifted in the corner and I realised there was a man sitting there in an armchair. He nodded and grunted – we didn't know if he was saying hello to us or replying to the lady, or both. It looked as if he was chewing something and chasing it round his mouth as he did so. I wondered if he was the lady's husband or father. The lady held herself very straight, as if she had constantly been told to push back her shoulders, something my mother often said to me. She wore an overall on top of her dress.

'We had two of them from Newcastle first, like the pair of you. Sisters, they were. They were nice enough, though one of the lasses kept saying she was cold. A day like today, now that is cold. But this was the middle of summer. We had the pair of them for a good few months, didn't we, Albert, until they went home to the bombs. Makes no sense at all, if you ask me. And more recently we've had a right one. Ooh, she was too! "My mother this" and "My mother that". Refused to eat her dinner. Was rude to Albert. She never dared be rude to me, though. Not to my face, at least. Anyway, she's gone now, too, and good riddance to her. At least Friedrich appreciates what he gets. Isn't that right, Albert?'

Albert grunted again. I wondered who Frederick was and why Miss Cartwright was pronouncing the name in that funny way. I also wondered if she would ever stop talking. I suddenly felt very tired, as if it was late at night and not just five o'clock. Everything had happened so quickly. I could barely believe that the day had started like a normal day – that I had woken up in our room in the schoolhouse, fed the hens and eaten an egg for breakfast, enjoyed most of my lessons and been told off once for chattering. And now everything had changed.

The woman's tone changed a little. 'But never mind all that, you're welcome with us. It's a sad business, isn't it, and I feel for Mr and Mrs Thornton, I really do. We always like to help someone from chapel, don't we, Albert?'

The lady showed us to our room. The whole house was very bare compared to the schoolhouse, with no carpets – just a few mats made from rags – and no family possessions to be seen. Our room had twin beds, a jug and washstand and a huge wardrobe. There was an outhouse in the yard which had a double-seated

WC. I had used one of these lavatories on the farm where
Barbara lived and my friend and I thought it fun to go to the
lavatory together, but all the time I was here I would sit in terror
of being disturbed by one of the farmhands or Mr Cartwright
and whenever I heard footsteps getting close I would leap up
and pull up my knickers, whether I was ready or not.

We joined the Cartwrights and three farm workers in the
kitchen for tea. Lamps had been lit and the room looked more
cheerful now. Miss Cartwright – we had discovered that our
hosts were an unmarried brother and sister – didn't introduce
us to the others but no one seemed surprised to see new faces
at the table. Two of the farmhands were quite elderly, but
the third was a younger man who spoke only to say please
and thank you, had an unusual accent and smiled a lot at me
and Doug. Tea was thick pieces of ham and pease pudding,
but there was more fat on my meat than lean and I felt as if
I was spending most of my time trying to separate the two.
Everybody else was eating enthusiastically, Albert chewing
even more vigorously than he had been earlier, making loud
chomping noises as he did. I felt embarrassed at the mess I was
making and the pieces of fat that were starting to encircle my
plate when everyone else's looked so clean. Miss Cartwright
made no comment as she served pudding straight onto our
dinner plates. Some of the fat was now floating in my custard
and I had to begin a new operation to fish it out. I got a piece
in my mouth by mistake and after tucking it away in the corner
I finally managed to swallow it. The thought of its slipperiness
made me feel sick even after it had gone. Nobody said much
at the table, apart from the odd grunt of satisfaction coming
from the elderly farmhands and Albert and one very short

conversation about 't'owd yow' who wasn't very well and who Miss Cartwright had some medication for.

When the meal was finished, Friedrich stood up, bowed slightly to us all, and said, 'That was very good! Now I will finish my work. We have a saying in Germany, "He who rests grows rusty". I do not wish that to be me!' He winked at me and Doug.

'A nice man,' said Miss Cartwright to us both when he had left. 'He's a German prisoner of war.'

I felt a shiver of excitement going through me. A German! The enemy! I had heard of a German working on one of the other local farms but hadn't expected to meet one.

'They're hard workers,' she continued. 'Mind, they know they've got their bread buttered being here rather than on some submarine or what have you.'

Doug and I both helped with the dishes, then sat at the kitchen table to do our homework. Later Miss Cartwright gave us a candle each as we paid a last visit to the lavatory before bed.

'Mind the boggle doesn't get you,' said Albert from his chair.

It was the first time I had heard him speak a full sentence. Miss Cartwright told him to shush and said he should have more sense than to try to frighten us. The cold air stung our faces as we made a dash for the outhouse. Inside, I thought I might freeze to death on the seat if I didn't get out of there quickly.

'Wait for me!' I called to Doug on the way back across the yard, looking for boggles in all directions. Miss Cartwright was waiting for us at the farmhouse door with an oil lamp.

'I'll not be doing that every time you want to go, mind,' she said.

'What's a boggle?' I asked Doug as we walked along the passageway to our bedroom. Outside the kitchen the house was so cold that our breath appeared before us. There was ice on the inside of our bedroom window.

'Probably some local bogeyman,' said Doug. 'He was only joking, you know.'

We were shivering as we put on our winter pyjamas. Even in bed I couldn't get warm. I slipped out and got into bed with Doug. He was almost asleep and too drowsy to protest, until I touched his back with my icy hand.

'Go away, you're freezing,' he muttered, but I just lay as still as I could until he had fallen asleep, feeling the warmth radiating from his body. I woke up the next morning curled around him.

Miss Cartwright gave us a hunk of bread and some cheese to take to school as it was more sensible to stay there for dinner rather than come back and forwards in the snow. And so we sat and ate with the other children instead of going back to the schoolhouse for one of Aunty's meals. I hoped that John would get better quickly and that Aunty and Uncle would be home soon.

'Do you think they'll be back tomorrow?' I asked Doug, hopefully, as we trudged back to the farm at the end of the day.

'I don't know,' said Doug. 'I heard some of the teachers talking today. I think it's very serious.'

The snow had been shovelled into piles around the edges of the farmyard leaving a dirty sludge that was now freezing over. We skated on it in our wellingtons before tea and had a quick look round the farm. As I peered over a stable door to see what was inside, a horse's head came shooting out, making me scream and fall backwards onto my bottom.

Doug almost killed himself laughing at me. 'Maybe that's the boggle,' he said.

Friedrich was walking past. 'That's Beauty,' he said. 'She's just a friendly horse. See.' He went up to her and stroked her on the nose. 'You do too.' He nodded at us both and we approached cautiously.

'Ah, she's lovely,' said Doug, and I nervously nodded my agreement.

'It is a good thing to be with animals, I think,' said Friedrich. 'Good for the soul.' And we both nodded again.

The next day the whole school was summoned into the main building. Miss Dixon stood in front of us, looking very serious. She announced that she had some very sad news for us all, for the village and for our headmaster and his family. John Thornton had died of rheumatic fever earlier that day.

Was she really saying that or had I imagined it? I looked at the other people in the room to try to make sense of it. Some of the children began to cry; others just looked shocked, perhaps finding it as difficult as I was to comprehend what they were being told. One or two of the teachers were dabbing their eyes. I looked for Doug but couldn't see him. I felt as if someone had stirred up my insides. John Thornton, that hearty boy who came home for the holidays, who liked to fish and play sports. The boy who had pelted me with snowballs less than a month ago. People like that didn't die. There must be a mistake. But then Miss Dixon read a passage from the Bible and followed that by asking us all to bow our heads while she said a prayer for John and his family. She said that Mr Thornton had spoken to her by phone and asked her to dismiss school early, but that she hoped we would use part of the day to say our own prayers for John, his parents and his brother Hugh.

I couldn't believe that just a few days before Miss Dixon had been at the schoolhouse, taking her bath and measuring me for another jumper she was making for Daphne, and how Uncle had made us all laugh when she had gone by saying that Daphne was going to be mistaken for the Union Jack in those colours. Everyone had been so happy then. I wanted to turn back the clock and for it to be that night again, for none of the bad things to happen.

I found Doug. His face was white. Looking at him made me start to cry. Miss Pickup tried to comfort us both, but in truth I didn't know who I was crying for. For John himself? For Aunty and Uncle? For Doug, who had lost a friend? Or even for myself as a bit of security dropped out of my world.

Back at the farm the Cartwrights were shocked. Albert, on his chair, shook his head and even stopped his chewing for a few minutes. Miss Cartwright said it was a dreadful thing to happen to such a lovely boy and with such fine parents.

That night I fell asleep in my own bed and dropped quickly into a deep sleep. When I woke up the next morning something felt different. My pyjamas were warm and heavy round my tummy and bottom. As I shifted my position it slowly dawned on me that I had wet the bed. I lay there rigid with the horror of it. After a couple of incidents in the schoolhouse many months ago that Aunty had seen to with little fuss, I thought that my bed-wetting days were over. All those prayers I had offered up, for it to happen again here in the home of people I barely knew! I confessed to Doug, who sighed heavily and said he thought that I had grown out of it. I asked him what I should do and he said I had to tell Miss Cartwright as otherwise I would be sleeping in a wet bed when night-time came round. 'And you'll stink,' he added.

It was Saturday so there was no school and I could wait for the right moment, when no one else was around, to confess to Miss Cartwright. She was matter-of-fact about it, as she was about most things, and I saw her later that morning in the scullery, pounding away at the sheets in the sink. When we sat down for dinner at midday I noticed to my embarrassment that my pyjamas and sheets were hanging on the pulley above our heads.

One of the farmhands was late and we waited for him to join us before starting to eat. He arrived, bringing a blast of cold air with him, rubbing his large red hands together. As he took his seat he glanced up at the pulley and said loudly, 'Who peed the bed?'

Miss Cartwright tutted and Albert began to chuckle to himself. 'Who peed the bed?' said Albert, as if it was the catchphrase of a joke that he found particularly funny. 'Who peed the bed?'

'All right, Albert.' Miss Cartwright frowned at him and then at the farmhand, who had picked up his knife and fork and was starting to eat. 'And I haven't said grace yet.'

Doug was squirming in his chair and scowling at me. He was obviously worried that the others might think it was him.

I didn't know if it was a question I was supposed to answer, even if just to protect my brother's reputation, but I was too self-conscious to open my mouth.

''Twas probably a boggle,' said Albert after we had finished praying, and everyone laughed. Friedrich had a hearty laugh and made a funny little hiccupy noise at the end of each burst, which started Doug off and then I laughed too to hide my embarrassment. Even Miss Cartwright relaxed and allowed herself a chuckle.

'I like that word boggle,' said Friedrich. 'You have some fine words in the English language.'

'Is German an easy language to learn?' asked Doug.

One of the farmhands made a humphing noise as if he disapproved of the question. Miss Cartwright regarded Doug with a quizzical expression, then looked at Friedrich as if she was interested in hearing the answer after all.

Friedrich told us that it was not as difficult as people thought. 'We share many words,' he said. 'A lot of your words are Germanic.'

The disapproving farmhand was now muttering something I couldn't hear.

'It is correct,' said Friedrich sternly. 'And you also have words from Latin and Ancient Greek.'

'Listen, Fred,' began one of the workers, 'I hardly think—'

'Eat up, everyone,' said Miss Cartwright, sensing disagreement brewing. 'We can't be sitting chatting all afternoon.'

I wanted to talk about John; I wanted to ask Doug why he had died and what would happen now, but I could tell that I wouldn't get very far with my questions. Doug's face wasn't as pale today but he was more serious than usual and didn't smile much. We spent the afternoon exploring the farm, never quite sure what we were allowed to do but managing to stay out of trouble. Miss Cartwright seemed to be everywhere: in the kitchen, in the scullery, shovelling fresh snow to keep the paths clear, in and out of the barns. Doug followed Friedrich around for a while and I was left to my own devices. When I heard Miss Cartwright's voice coming from one of the sheds I peered inside and saw her milking a goat. 'Come along and I'll show you what to do,' she said. Her fingers moved in an expert way. A steady stream of milk trickled into her can.

'You see, it's not hard. You press your thumb and finger together like this, to trap the milk, then squeeze it out with your other fingers.'

I sat down beside her and with her coaxing and a bit of help managed to extract a thin dribble.

That night I asked Doug if I could come into his bed to warm up for just a few minutes.

'You must be joking,' he said. 'Go to the lavatory in your own bed.'

I pleaded with God not to let me wet the bed again.

In chapel special prayers were said for John and some of the congregation offered words of consolation to me and Doug after the service. School resumed the next day. Miss Dixon said we had to all come together at this difficult time, that we must pray for strength for ourselves and for Mr and Mrs Thornton on their return. The Percy boys and some of their friends, wanting to be helpful, volunteered to turn over the vegetable patch before Uncle came back, but Miss Dixon said that it was rather early for that, with snow still on the ground, but that she was sure Mr Thornton would be most grateful for their offer later.

The week dragged on and nobody mentioned Aunty and Uncle. I wondered if they would ever return. Perhaps they had gone to live with Uncle's family in Appleby. Miss Cartwright was a kind person and looked after us well enough in her brusque way; Albert was quite harmless and even amusing at times. But I longed to be back in Aunty's kitchen, to see the quiet determination on her face as she kneaded her bread or arranged flowers in a vase or put snowfire on her chilblains. I decided that I would never again complain about the yapping farm dogs on a Saturday or having to recite two poems every Whit Sunday, if only I could sit on her lap once more.

One night, fed up with my pleading, Doug relented and allowed me into his bed, but when I was warm he said drowsily, 'Right, out now before you fall asleep.'

I asked Doug if he thought we would ever go back to the schoolhouse. 'If not,' I said, 'I think I'd like to go home.'

Chapter twenty

Extract from Uncle's school log book, preserved today in the village's Tinclar Library.

Jan 20 1942: Severe snowstorm. Forty children present. Registers not marked.

Jan 21: Roads impassable. Thirty-seven children present. Registers not marked. In reply to a telephone message stating that my son John Douglas, at Appleby Grammar School, is dangerously ill with rheumatic fever, I am leaving, if possible, for Appleby to be near him.

Jan 22: Continued snow brought only thirty-eight children. Registers not marked.

Jan 23: Continued wintry conditions caused only forty-five children to be present. Registers not marked.

Since the evening of 21st I stayed at Appleby.

Jan 23: Just after noon today my son John Douglas passed away, his mother and I being present at his death. An inner assurance of his destination gave me the comfort I needed. Everything possible had been done, two doctors and a heart specialist trying in vain to save the life that was wanted Elsewhere. His remains will be interred at Appleby on the 27th inst.

Jan 26: School re-assembled in strength and registers were marked. [Uncle not present]

Jan 27: This afternoon, amid falling snow, we laid John to rest. I record here my appreciation of the kindnesses received by John's mother and me from every direction and make record too of my emotions of deepest gratitude at the presence of so many Bampton friends at the funeral. John was aged fourteen years and two months.

Here are the scholarships held by John:

The County Special Place Scholarship
The Bampton Scholarship
The George Moore Exhibition
The Whitehead Boarders' Scholarship
The Lowther Junior Scholarship

Feb 9: Yesterday, 8 February, our assistant master Mr William D. Preston died at Meathop Sanatorium. He was invalided out of the Army – Air Force – in the late spring of last year – a TB victim, and failed at any time to show signs of recovery. In the passing of Mr Preston, Bampton School has lost a highly esteemed teacher of great promise while the children and I are a valued friend the poorer.

Feb 11: Mr Preston was buried today. Mrs Jameson and Miss Dixon, along with four senior boys and four senior girls, attending to represent the school.

Feb 16: In the afternoon of Wednesday 5 Feb, having been ordered away by Dr Prentice, I left Bampton and went to Otterburn to regain strength and confidence. I returned to full duty today. [Aunty's sister Tess lived in Otterburn, Northumberland, so it seems likely that Uncle went to stay with her.]

Feb 19: Mr Roberts HMI called to collect numbers of children with and in need of wellingtons. He gave me words of sympathy and help.

Feb 24: Mr Dakin, tendering sympathy, and Miss Valentine called to investigate canteen possibilities.

Feb 27: School closed this pm for two days' half term.

Memories of those who stayed:
'Apples and oranges, sweets and chocolate'

Spring 1942

As the oldest grandchild I was very close to my grandparents
and often used to go to their house on a neighbouring street in
Monkseaton for meals. My uncle, Campbell, had enlisted and
was now doing his pilot's training with the RAF in Canada,
and I looked forward to hearing his letters.

'Just listen to this one,' Grandpa said one day, reading from
the letter that had just arrived.

Dear Mother & Father

We are stationed at Moncton just now waiting for our
first school in America. I'm a little scared of this course, as it
is well noted for turning out failures ... and every day there
are more after more rejects coming back to Moncton. Forty
so far this week. Everyone we talk to just pities us, and says,
'Hard luck' ... There's one good thing about it, and that is
a certain job in any of the American airlines after the war
(if you pass) as it is a noted school in America. I can only say
I'll do my best, but failure would break my heart.

The first thing I did when I set foot on Canadian soil
was to buy eight bars of chocolate. Then the first shop
I saw, I went in and bought six apples. Grapes, oranges,
sweets, chocolate etc, you can get in as big a quantity as
you like, so you can imagine how we stuffed ourselves
the first two days. All the streets are lit up, no blackouts at
all. Of course I had to try one of their famous hot-dogs!

My mouth watered at the thought of all those good things to eat. As I was a big fan of American films, I couldn't wait to see Campbell again and hear all about what America was like.

Alder Gofton

Chapter twenty-one

Just when we were wondering if we would ever see Aunty and Uncle again – though in truth it had probably been only two or three weeks – Aunty turned up on the doorstep of the Cartwright farm one Saturday morning. When Doug and I heard her voice, we jumped up at once from our seats in the kitchen, grinning at each other, but sat back down again when we heard her and Miss Cartwright speaking quietly to each other in the passageway. We both held our breath, our initial elation turning to anxiousness. Perhaps Aunty was asking Miss Cartwight if we could stay with her and her brother for the rest of the war. I didn't know what I would say if they walked into the kitchen now and told us that was happening. I would want to be brave about it and not offend Miss Cartwright or make it too difficult for Aunty, but I knew that I wouldn't be able to. Just the thought of it was making me feel tearful. Then they both appeared and Miss Cartwright was giving one of her closed-mouth smiles that pushed up her cheekbones and reminded me of the wooden doll Mr Brennan had made for me. Aunty was beaming at us both and looking as pleased to see us as we were to see her.

'Well, it looks as if you're going home, children,' said Miss Cartwright. 'Can you get your things together quickly and not keep Mrs Thornton waiting?'

We dashed upstairs to pack and a few minutes later were saying goodbye and thank you to our hosts. Albert grunted to us from his chair and nodded at Aunty when she thanked him for having us. Miss Cartwright told Aunty we had been no trouble at all and I felt a sudden rush of gratitude towards her for not mentioning the wet bed. It had only happened once but the memory of it still filled me with shame and I had been terrified of it happening again, almost being afraid to drop off to sleep in case it did.

We walked back to the schoolhouse. Doug was quiet and polite with Aunty and insisted on carrying our case. I chatted away, telling her about the horse, Beauty, and milking the goat and how Albert just sat in his chair chewing and talking about boggles. Doug frowned at me. I think he felt that we should be extra well behaved from now on and that Aunty and Uncle would not be interested in idle chatter any more. The second time he did it I stopped talking in mid sentence and Aunty looked at me, surprised, and then laughed and squeezed my hand and said, 'Oh, I've missed you both! Uncle's in Appleby until this afternoon and I've got us a nice treat for dinner.'

And so we went back to the schoolhouse and life carried on as it did before. Or it did for me and Doug who – though we

Ada Preston, late 1930s

had been deeply saddened by both deaths – were too young to fully appreciate the effect the loss of a child must have on a parent, followed so closely by that of a trusted friend and colleague. When I think about it now, all these years later, I realise how strong Aunty and Uncle were, how strong Ada was and what special people they all were. Aunty and Uncle continued to care for us and to give us a happy home life and Ada continued to welcome me whenever I called – I don't remember her ever feeling sorry for herself.

Our weeks returned to their old pattern. On Thursdays we wrote to our parents. On Saturdays we collected the milk from the farm and tried to avoid the yappy dogs. Sunday, with two or sometimes three visits to chapel – only Uncle went to the evening service in the winter months – was our least favourite day and yet we had grown used to its gentle routine. Uncle had taught me more tunes to play on the piano and, after a few lessons from the old lady in the village, I was good enough to play some duets with him. However, I often ended up too helpless with laughter to carry on when he inserted the names of people we knew into the songs we were singing.

Uncle returned to his council duties in Appleby and on the parish council, while Aunty went back to the Women's Institute. The WI were always busy with some project or other. When it wasn't jam-making time they would be knitting or sewing or holding sales – all with the ultimate motive of helping 'our boys'. If it wasn't a school day I might even accompany Aunty to one of their meetings and that was where I heard 'Jerusalem' for the first time. To everyone's amusement I won the raffle on one of my visits – a packet of paper doilies. The ladies decided that I might prefer something else and Ada came round with a one-shilling savings stamp for me later as a replacement.

Standing on the bridge one day watching the last of the ice melting, Doug laughed suddenly and said that Mr Preston had told him that his elder brother Harry was a daredevil at times and used to pinch clothes props and propel himself down the beck on ice floes. 'But he said we must never even think of doing such a thing.'

I repeated this tale at dinner time, watching Aunty and Uncle closely to see what their reactions would be. To my surprise Uncle nodded his head proudly and said that Harry had been a clever boy who went to grammar school in Penrith and became an aeronautical engineer.

'He's now down south doing some important work for the war,' he said. Then he winked at us both and said, 'I told you that Bampton School produced the best pupils, didn't I?'

But Aunty added, 'That was still a very dangerous thing to do.'

Spring came and we started to spend more time outside again. Gorse was flowering on the fells. 'When gorse is out of bloom, kissing is out of season,' Ada's mother, Mrs Hutchinson, liked to say with a smile and it was true that gorse was nearly always in flower somewhere. The previous autumn I had been invited by Mavis to her fellside home to watch the men burning the gorse to encourage new growth. Mavis said it could only be done when there would be no creatures nesting in it and on a day when weather conditions were just right so that the fire didn't spread and cause damage elsewhere. We watched from a safe distance and heard the gorse spit and crackle as the flames caught it. Men stood with buckets of water in case the wind changed direction and the fire got too close to the farmhouse.

As we walked to chapel across the fields, newly born lambs began to appear. I wanted to stroke them, but whenever I got too close the mothers would kick up their feet, which made a surprisingly heavy thudding on the grass, and scamper away, followed by their brood. Uncle laughed and said he had thought of a good poem for me to read at the next Whit Sunday service.

'Have you heard of "The Lamb" by William Blake? It begins, "Little lamb, who made thee? Dost thou know who made thee?"'

I shook my head.

'It's such a pretty poem, Gwenda,' said Aunty.

'And what do you think the answer is to that question?' asked Uncle, the teacher in him never far away. 'Who created these innocent creatures?'

'Their mothers!' I said triumphantly. But I added, just to be sure, 'And their fathers.'

'God,' said Doug, in a voice that suggested he knew it was the right answer.

Uncle smiled and said that we were both right, but that God was the creator of everything and that was the meaning of the poem.

On the way back from chapel one lamb surprised us all by allowing me to stroke him before trotting off to find his mother.

'Remember what Miss Cartwright said about pet lambs,' Doug reminded me on the way to Sunday School that afternoon, as the lamb – I was sure it was the same one – came running up to me. She had told us how the lambs who had to be bottlefed were 'nobbut a menace' and had a habit of getting themselves into all sorts of trouble. 'I had one lot who went trotting round the farm after Albert as if they owned the place. He didn't know they were there until he heard a racket behind him and found one of them had got his head stuck in a pipe. You may laugh, but that's why we try to pair them with another ewe if they lose their own mother. It's more natural that way.'

But I wasn't going to let Doug or Miss Cartwright spoil this for me. I remembered the cruel fate of my poor hen Judith. I still found it hard not to have a favourite hen but I hadn't named another one since.

I started to go to the field every morning to see my lamb and I was gratified to see how he preferred to be with me rather than his mother. He was the prettiest little thing, white and fluffy-looking – though when I stroked him his wool was quite coarse – with four black knees, a black nose and black freckles on his face. His mother took little notice as he ran up to me. She probably had so many lambs she didn't really care about this one, I thought. My lamb even bleated quite pathetically when I had to leave him. I called him Peterkin and decided that having a lamb of my own would be the nicest thing in the world, at least while I was too young to have a baby.

It was the Easter holidays. Hugh was home for a few days and we had just heard that Doug had passed the entrance exam for Appleby Grammar, so everyone was in high spirits. That morning I went to see Peterkin as usual. When he came lollopping up to me to be cuddled, a thought struck me and once it was there I couldn't get rid of it. I picked him up. He was a bit wriggly and I put him down again, but on another attempt I found that by holding him firmly he stayed still. It wasn't easy going through the gate with a lamb in my arms but as I hadn't fastened it shut I managed to open it using my foot. I walked back up the lane to the schoolhouse. Peterkin was starting to get heavy so I was glad when we reached the field where the hens lived without being noticed. He would be safe here and there was grass to eat and hens to keep him company. Later I would smuggle him some milk. Hopefully he would lap it up from a saucer like a cat. No one need know he was here and as farmers had so many sheep, they wouldn't miss one. Later I might tell Aunty, but not just yet. Peterkin looked a little bemused, then trotted off to explore his new surroundings.

It was lunchtime soon after and we all sat round the kitchen table. When a peculiar noise started up outside, I felt my face go pink, certain that I was about to be discovered.

'Darned rooks!' exclaimed Hugh. 'There are dozens of them nesting in those trees.'

I'm surprised my relief didn't show on my face.

'I thought they were crows,' said Doug.

'Ah, very similar birds but very different as well,' said Hugh, raising a finger and sounding like the teacher he would become one day. 'But nothing makes a noise quite like a colony of rooks. I once climbed a tree in my pyjamas when they started up one night right outside my room. Didn't I, Mother?'

'Did you really?' said Doug, laughing.

'Didn't you get all scratched?' I asked, trying to picture someone up a tree in pyjamas.

'Well, I may have done, but I was desperate. They're restless birds but I was the one not getting any rest that night. They sometimes sound more like wild animals.'

'Lions or tigers, you mean?' said Doug.

'Oh, I think more like angry cats ... or even monkeys.'

'And did you get them to stop?'

Hugh laughed. 'I think I scared them off for a bit, but when they all came back to their nests they started up all over again.'

'Best to let nature take its course,' said Aunty, and Hugh said that she was right, as always, and gave a little bow in her direction making me and Doug laugh.

Everyone was quiet for a while as we finished our bacon turnovers. The rooks had become a pleasant background murmur when I heard Peterkin bleat very loudly. It was definitely him this time. I scraped my plate more noisily than was polite to try to mask the sound. No one took much notice at first, but when the bleating grew more persistent and began to sound a little angry Hugh put down his knife and fork and looked towards the window.

'Talking of noisy animals, didn't that sheep sound very close?' he said.

'They're noisier than usual at this time of year,' said Aunty, tilting her head to one side to listen better. All was quiet, but a few seconds later the bleating started up again.

'I think one of them might be in trouble,' said Hugh, getting up from the table and crossing to the window. Unable to see anything, he said he would have a quick look outside.

'I didn't hear anything,' I said loudly, and Aunty immediately gave me a suspicious stare but just said, 'You've cleared your plate nicely. There's rhubarb for pudding.'

A couple of minutes later Hugh came back into the kitchen.

'Heh heh! I don't believe it! There's a lamb – just a tiny thing – in our garden! How do you think it got there? There's no sign of its mother.'

Aunty knew me too well. She put down her knife and fork. 'Gwenda, does this have anything to do with you?'

Uncle was looking at me now too, but not saying anything. I nodded, hardly daring to meet her eye.

'Gwenda! Did you take it from the field?'

I nodded again.

'Today? This morning?'

'Just before dinner.'

'On its own? Oh, Gwenda! You know that a baby lamb needs its mother! And besides that, it's stealing!'

'I know, but I wasn't . . . ' It had all made sense at the time but my reasons didn't seem so clear now that I wanted to explain them. I hadn't thought of it as stealing, just borrowing Peterkin for a while to care for him more devotedly than his mother ever would. 'I would have given him back when he was big,' I said.

'I'm sure you had the best intentions,' said Uncle. 'The important thing now is that you put things right. If you can get the creature back to its mother quickly the farmer doesn't even need to know.'

'Oh, Douglas, do you think . . . ?' began Aunty.

'No need at all. As long as he's healthy and they haven't missed him yet.'

'He's called Peterkin,' I said. 'He answers when I call him.'

Aunty and Hugh had caught each other's eye and were trying not to laugh. Doug was looking at each of the adults before deciding how to react.

'Peterkin, eh? Well that's a nice name,' said Uncle. 'But I think Peterkin needs to go back to where he belongs. That means now.'

Hugh held out his hand to me. 'Come on, you've finished dinner. Let's get it over with and we'll be back for pudding in a jiffy.'

I left the table, relieved not to be in too much trouble and happy to have Hugh with me. Hugh had been badly affected by his younger brother's death. I had heard Aunty say to Miss Williams that it was doing him good to have some younger company in the house when he came home, and he certainly didn't get left on his own much with me and Doug around. As we walked down the lane to the field, me clutching Peterkin, he told me that he had always enjoyed helping to bottlefeed the motherless lambs when he was a boy.

One of the ewes was standing by herself in the middle of the field making a strange honking noise.

'That's probably mum making that racket,' said Hugh. 'Let's see what happens when you put him down.'

Part of me hoped that Peterkin would stay beside me so that Hugh would see that he really wanted me to be his mother, but he ran straight up to the noisy ewe and after she had sniffed him a few times she allowed him to suckle.

'Well, Peterkin's going to be fine,' said Hugh. 'Let's get back for pudding. I think we've got the first of Mum's rhubarb today. Do you like rhubarb?'

'Yes. I like everything,' I said, which made him laugh. Then I added, 'Everything except fat.'

I was disappointed that Peterkin didn't come to say goodbye as we left.

The three others were waiting for us before starting their next course.

'All is well,' announced Hugh cheerfully. 'Mother and son are reunited and he's even had a good feed.'

'By, I bet he needed it,' said Uncle.

'We weren't spotted,' said Hugh. 'We were planning to hide behind a tree if we saw anyone, weren't we, Gwenda?'

Uncle asked if we had heard the new nursery rhyme.

> *Gwenda had a little lamb*
> *Its fleece was white as snow*
> *And everywhere that Gwenda went*
> *The lamb was sure to go!*

Doug chimed in, 'In the next verse it follows her to school. Can you imagine that, Hugh? Gwenda with Peterkin sitting next to her!'

Everyone was laughing now. I tried to join in but I felt sad to have lost my lamb. I still thought I could have been a mother to him.

I carried on visiting Peterkin every day and, despite his experience, he was always pleased to see me. He even let Marjorie pet him when I took her with me.

'Most sheep aren't like this,' she said, surprised and delighted.

'I know. He's not a normal sheep. He'd much rather live with me than spend his life in a field.'

Then one day the field was empty and though I went looking for him, I never saw him again.

Hugh Thornton and his parents in their garden

We hadn't known each other for long but I missed Peterkin. For a while, whenever I walked past a field full of sheep I would look for him and call his name. I don't think the adults understood that all I wanted was to have something to take care of, something that depended on me the way I depended on Aunty and Uncle.

But life went on without him. Life went on, too, without John. When I walked past his room I sometimes paused, expecting him to come barging out onto the landing, ready to go fishing, or with some idea of a game for him and the boys to play. Once I saw a flicker of him in his shorts and grey pullover through the gap in the door, but when I checked it was Doug, borrowing a book from the shelves. Aunty and Uncle behaved towards us much as they had done before John's death, but I knew that Aunty was often sad. In chapel she would suddenly squeeze my fingers and we would slip out of the service. Outside she let the tears flow, while I watched helplessly, only able to stroke her hand. Then she would dab her eyes, tut at herself to make me smile and we would go back inside.

Chapter twenty-two

If I was on my own, I still took the long route into Bampton to avoid walking past Well Cottage – the house where John Stacey and I had thrown the sticks down the chimney – which meant that I also avoided Jinny the Witch's house. But when I was with others I had no option but to pass them both. I was often sure that Jinny's curtain twitched as if she was standing there, watching us go by. My friends and I would usually break into a run at this point, just to be sure she didn't catch us. However, emboldened by my recent escapades, I told Marjorie and Janet that I wasn't scared any more. After all, how could Jinny's house be any scarier than Mrs Morris's, with its monster-hiding fir trees? I still got sent to visit Mrs Morris and if I could walk down her creepy path and be eyed up by Tommy the cat – now, there was a witch's cat if ever there was one! – I certainly didn't need to run past Jinny's house, which opened straight onto the road.

'In fact,' I told my friends, 'I'm going to knock on Jinny's door!'

'You wouldn't dare!' said Marjorie.

'What will you do if she opens it?' asked Janet.

'I will say, "How do you do? I've come to introduce myself. I'm an evacuee and I live at the schoolhouse. I don't believe we've met yet."' I was putting on my mother's voice when I said this and it made the other two giggle.

And so one afternoon the three of us approached the cottage and while Marjorie and Janet carried on past it and waited for me round the corner, I stopped beside the front door. My confidence disappeared as soon as my friends had gone, but really, what could possibly happen? And I was only being polite.

As I stood there wavering, listening to my friends egging me on, I thought I saw a movement above me. I looked up. Between the gap in the curtains I could see a face framed by long grey hair. Rooted to the spot, I stared for a few seconds, then looked away. When I looked up again the face had vanished. Was Jinny on her way to stir her cauldron? Was she even on her way to open the door to grab me and put me in it? I didn't stay to find out but took to my heels and ran away to join Marjorie and Janet.

'What happened?' they wanted to know.

'I saw her,' I said, breathlessly, 'and she really is a witch.'

As we were giggling together, somebody called my name. It was Elizabeth Castle, walking by with Miss Spriggs who was pushing some of her painting equipment in an old pram.

'You girls are enjoying yourselves!' said Elizabeth Castle, leaning on her stick.

'I've just seen Jinny the Witch,' I said, pointing back to the cottage.

'You've seen who?' asked Miss Castle.

'Oh! Good Christian people don't believe in witches!' scolded Miss Spriggs. She waggled her finger at us but she was smiling as she did. 'Don't let Mr Thornton catch you saying that, will you? Now then, Elizabeth, shall we carry on? I don't want to miss this lovely light.'

Elizabeth Castle explained that Miss Spriggs was going to paint the village from the crags and that she was going along as her assistant. 'I'm learning such a lot from my hostess,' she said. 'I might even start painting myself.'

'Did you notice,' said Marjorie when they had left us, 'she didn't deny that Jinny is a witch. She just said that we shouldn't believe in them.'

'Oh, she's definitely a witch,' I said breezily. 'I think she even had a big pointy hat on.'

Never very far from trouble of some kind – one day Doug dared me to walk along the wall of the bridge, and I did, until Mr Brennan saw me and hauled me down – I had another close encounter with an animal that spring. My latest pastime was juggling and having mastered two balls at a time, I moved on to three. I could happily occupy myself for hours on my own, playing two- or three-bally against the kitchen wall and singing various rhymes as I did. Aunty never complained, though she must have been driven mad by the continual thumping noise. One day I was juggling on my way home from somewhere and threw one of my balls very high in the air. It landed in a field in which there was a bull. I knew that you didn't go into a field with a bull and I had heard the story of the poor local farmer who had been killed by a bull only a few years earlier. But the fact was, I wanted my ball back. Furthermore, the bull was at the far end of the field, a big lumbering animal who surely had no chance of catching me when I could retrieve my ball in a few seconds. I climbed onto the wall and sat there assessing the situation before I jumped down. The bull wasn't even looking in my direction. I ran towards my ball and now the bull looked up and met my eye. He must have been frightened of me, I thought, as he began to back away. I carried on and retrieved my ball and then I heard the shouting.

'Get out of there! Quick!'

Two farm workers were standing on the other side of the wall. One was pointing behind me and saying, 'Run! Run!'

I was too scared to turn round. They might have been joking, but something about the looks on their faces told me that they weren't. A rush of energy surged through my body and I found a speed I didn't know I possessed. With the ball safely in my hand I made it back to the wall where the men pulled me over.

'By, lass, you didn't half take a chance,' said one of them.

As I finally dared to look behind me, my heart was beating so fast that I thought it might explode from my chest. I saw that the bull, though no longer running, was now standing where my ball had been, snorting angrily through its nose and tossing its head from side to side.

'You'd have been in that garden over there if he'd tossed a little thing like you,' said the second man, pointing to the other side of the lane.

'I only wanted my ball,' I practically whispered. I could actually hear my heart; it was even making my ears vibrate.

How could I have been so stupid, especially when I had been told about the danger of bulls so many times?

'Well, you think what's worth more the next time it happens, your ball or your life,' said the first man. Then he looked at me more sympathetically. 'You all right?' He ruffled my hair. 'Run along now and don't do it again.'

I was surprised to find that after my Olympic sprint of a few seconds earlier, my legs had now turned to jelly. I hoped that Aunty and Uncle wouldn't hear about this, but in a place the size of Bampton most stories had a habit of spreading. I set off wobbily for home but suddenly remembered my manners and called after them, 'Thank you!' in a very feeble voice.

On Whit Sunday of 1942, I recited 'The Lamb', as Uncle had suggested.

> Little Lamb, who made thee?
> Dost thou know who made thee,
> Gave thee life, & bid thee feed
> By the stream & o'er the mead;
> Gave thee clothing of delight,
> Softest clothing, wooly, bright;
> Gave thee such a tender voice,
> Making all the vales rejoice?
> Little Lamb, who made thee?
> Dost thou know who made thee?
>
> Little Lamb, I'll tell thee;
> Little Lamb, I'll tell thee:
> He is called by thy name,

For he calls himself a Lamb.
He is meek, & he is mild,
He became a little child.
I a child, & thou a lamb,
We are called by his name.
Little Lamb, God bless thee!
Little Lamb, God bless thee!

'Remember,' Uncle had said as he coached me, 'you are asking the lamb a question in the first verse. Then in the next verse you've got the answer and you are proclaiming it with joy! It is your job to share that joy with the whole congregation.'

I put as much joy into it as I could but it couldn't have been enough as when I went back to my seat Mrs Heatherside was wiping her eyes again, as was the man sitting beside her, who might have been Mr Heatherside. Aunty looked tearful too, but Uncle winked at me and looked pleased. It was all rather confusing. Ada and Mrs Hutchinson both came up to me after the service and told me how nicely I had recited it. Walking home, I couldn't help thinking of Peterkin and wondering where he was now.

One Saturday at breakfast, not long before the start of the summer holidays, Uncle read out a letter he had received. It was from Jenny Charlton, who was writing to tell him that due to further restrictions on the use of petrol that were due to come into place, she and the teachers would not be travelling to the Lake District this summer. My face fell. Their visit was as much a part of summer here as the returning swallows. I loved listening to their grown-up yet childish chatter, puzzling over the things they found amusing and wondering when I would be old enough to have conversations like they did.

'When the war is over, things will go back to normal,' said Aunty, comfortingly. 'It's a horrible nuisance, isn't it, this war. But Jenny and the teachers will be back one day.'

'Yes, Jenny will be back with her tribe,' Uncle agreed. 'And I wonder about you two. Do you think you'll keep coming back to Bampton when you've gone home? Will you remember your old aunty and uncle when you're back in the big city?'

'Of course we will!' said Doug. 'We'll come for our holidays.'

'I'm going to bring my children here,' I said.

Uncle laughed. 'And how many children are you going to have, Gwenda?'

'Six, I think. And two dogs. I'm going to marry a farmer. Or a nice prisoner of war like Friedrich.' But then I remembered the promise I had made to Philip Orde on the day we had been evacuated. I could only hope that by now he had found someone he wanted to marry more than me. Try as I might, I couldn't even picture his face any more.

'And what about lambs?' asked Uncle, with one of his mischievous smiles. 'How many lambs will you have?' And Aunty told him not to tease me.

One day in August Doug and I caught Wrights' bus home across the North Pennines. The bus was packed and I had to share the front seat with two other Newcastle girls, one of whom was also a bad traveller. Doug sat in the seat behind with another boy, relieved not to be beside me.

'Douglas, is it true you're not coming back to Bampton after the summer?' asked one of my companions in a rather pitiful voice.

'I'm coming back, but I'm going to a different school so I'll only be around in the holidays,' he replied.

'Oh, Douglas, that's such a pity!' She was a pretty girl with long auburn hair, which she kept twiddling with. She looked older than Doug, but he had a habit of attracting female attention of all ages. Even the big conductress, who always looked so business-like, seemed to lose her brittleness when confronted with his floppy blond hair and sweet smile.

It didn't take long before the conductress was doing the rounds with her sick bucket. I succumbed just before we got to the top of Hartside.

'I thought you wouldn't be long,' she said, as I vomited copiously. The other girl beside me stuck her head in the bucket as soon as I had finished. 'This bucket's going to be full the rate you two are going,' added the conductress, inspecting its contents. Doug had said after our last trip home that she seemed to relish collecting it all. 'I think she must sell it for the war effort,' he had said to Mam, who told him, 'Get away with you!'

The auburn-haired girl turned round to Doug again, holding her nose this time, and said that it was so unfair that she had to sit beside us.

We were surprised and delighted to get home and find that Dad was there too.

'You remember your father, don't you?' joked Mam, and we both grinned at him. It had been a long time since we had seen him.

'By Jove, just look at the pair of you!' he said after he had hugged us.

He had brought an Army pal and the pair had hitchhiked down from the north of Scotland. His friend was called Augie and Doug and I liked him very much, though I could somehow sense my mother's disapproval, or if not disapproval, annoyance that our brief family reunion was being spoiled by a stranger.

Augie seemed oblivious to this. 'It's so good of you to have me, Mrs Brady,' he kept saying. 'Arthur's told me so much about you and what a good cook you are. If you eat like this in wartime, then I'll be back like a shot when the war's over!'

My mother said rather stiffly, 'We grow a lot of vegetables and we're very careful. Some of Arthur's old acquaintances from the bank live on farms and we exchange our wares. I certainly don't have anything I'm not entitled to.'

'No, as if you would! But I think my missus could do with a few lessons from you, Mrs B! She's never been much of a cook. Mind, she'd probably give me what-for if I dared say so!'

Mam gave a thin smile and Doug and I laughed. Augie was good fun and he made a big fuss of us both, sharing his large bar of Army rations chocolate between us and being relentlessly cheerful. Sweets and chocolate had only just started to be rationed though it was such a long time since we had had either that although the chocolate tasted weird, we had almost forgotten how it was supposed to taste and wolfed it down. Augie and Dad had also brought tins of a coffee-flavoured condensed milk. A teaspoon of it stirred into boiling water made a delicious sweet drink. Doug and I drank it one afternoon in the garden with Mam's banana sandwiches and felt as if we were really living it up.

Dad said he hoped we were still carrying our gas masks everywhere. When we told him that we weren't he made us promise not to go out without them, and said hadn't we heard of the mock gas attacks that were being carried out to keep everyone on their toes.

'You'll sharp know about it if you don't have your mask,' he warned.

'But it's safe in Bampton, Dad,' Doug said and I nodded in agreement, but Dad said we shouldn't take anything for granted and that we mustn't start getting into bad habits.

They left two days later, unsure how long it would take them to get back to base when they were relying on the goodness of strangers for transport. Augie said he hoped he would see us again one day and that Mam and Dad should come and stay with him and his missus after the war and they would show them the sights in the south. Mam said that sounded very nice.

After lunch on the same day that Dad and Augie left, there was a knock on the door and Mam said in a teasing voice, 'I wonder who that can be.'

I thought it was Dad coming back and rushed to open it. A smart young woman was standing on the doorstep. There was something familiar about her but I couldn't think where I had seen her.

'Well you haven't half grown, but I'd still recognise you anywhere!' she said, giving me a kiss and then a quick hug. 'And where's that brother of yours?'

'Hello, Ivy,' said Doug, appearing from the kitchen and offering his cheek to her.

Ivy! Was this sophisticated person really Ivy? I had thought a lot about the day I would see her again and now that it was here I didn't know what to say to her. We hadn't seen her since the day we left for Morpeth in September 1939, just as war was breaking out. Almost three years had passed since then and it was a long time since Mam had mentioned her in her letters. She looked like a proper lady now, not the girl she had been then. She wore a neat checked suit, the jacket just skimming her hips, and had a small hat perched on the back of her head. I looked at her shyly. Yes, it really was Ivy, but a new adult Ivy.

She and Mam chatted for a while and then Ivy said that she would take us for a walk and we would leave Mam to put her feet up. We went to Paddy Freeman's where some boys were sailing a large boat on the lake. Doug recognised one of them and stopped to talk, while Ivy and I carried on.

'So, how's this war going for you, Gwenda?' Ivy asked me, which I thought sounded a very serious question. But she carried on, mischievously, 'Your mam says you're very religious these days and going to church all the time!'

'We don't go to church,' I corrected her. 'It's chapel.'

'Same thing isn't it? Or perhaps not. What would I know? Anyway, I'm glad you're in a nice spot. Are you still reading lots?' She nudged me. 'Remember all those books we read together!'

I told her about some of the books I had read, if not always through choice, and how Aunty had taught me to knit and Uncle had taught me to play the piano and knew lots of

brainteasers. 'And Hugh's in the RAF,' I said. 'And John's at—'
but I stopped, remembering.

Ivy said they sounded like lovely people.

'Remember how you used to sing in your bedroom, Ivy!
Do you still sing?'

'Of course I do.' She started to hum to herself, though I
didn't recognise the tune.

'And do you remember the Birdman?'

'How could I ever forget him! Have you seen him recently?'

'Not since I was home last summer. We could see if he's
there now.'

We took one of the steep twisting paths that led from
Paddy's to the bottom of the Dene, where the Ouseburn
flowed. But though we looked in his usual places there was
no sign of him.

'Well, he has to go home some time,' said Ivy.

I'd never thought of the Birdman as having a home, but I
supposed that he must live somewhere.

We collected Doug on the way back.

'Doug's got a girlfriend,' I said to Ivy, stealing a glance at
Doug, who was walking on the other side of her.

'Ooh, tell me about her!' said Ivy. But Doug scowled at me
and blushed and said it wasn't true.

'So who was that on the bus?' I asked him. '"Ooh, Douglas,
we're all going to miss you when you go to Appleby. Boo
hoo!"'

'I'm surprised you heard anything. You spent the whole
time puking.'

'Well, that was why I was sick, listening to her all the time.'

'What – a whole bucket full?'

Ivy laughed. 'Yuk! You never were a good traveller, were you? Anyway, I'm sure all the girls are in love with Doug. I know I'd be. I look forward to getting an invitation to both of your weddings one day.'

'I've already promised one boy I'll marry him,' I said, hoping that Ivy would understand the predicament that Philip had put me in.

When Ivy heard what had happened she said that people changed when they got older and that I didn't need to worry – Philip would meet someone else when the time came to get married. I felt a lot happier to hear that.

The day before we returned to Bampton we finally spent a night in our air-raid shelter.

'Well, you've got what you wanted,' grumbled Mam as the siren woke us and she hurried us out of bed. I saw the lights of the searchlight station criss-crossing the sky and heard the sound of gunfire. Mam saw us inside the shelter before going to bang on the Youngs' back door. It had been a warm day but the shelter felt cool now and the bench was hard and uncomfortable in spite of Mam's cushions. We heard Mr and Mrs Young before we saw them. He was talking very loudly and saying that he'd rather die in his bed and she was shushing him and asking him to hurry. Mam steered them in then put some sandbags in the doorway.

Although they can't have been very comfortable, the Youngs both nodded off in their seats, their heads dropping and lifting, dropping and lifting. Mr Young began to snore loudly. Mam sighed and said now we knew what it was like and to remember that she had spent many nights in here. Some nights, she told us, she had wondered if it was worth the trouble of getting undressed for bed when she might be up again half an hour later. 'Though I never did sit and fret waiting for the siren like some folk did. You can't let it rule your life.'

She picked up her knitting. 'Poor old souls,' she said, glancing at our neighbours. 'It's not right that they should have to go through all this. They said three years, didn't they? Hmmm, not much sign of it ending any day soon. Well, you two can play cards now, or read, but don't moan, whatever you do.'

I heard a distant rumbling.

'What was that?' I asked.

'I've told you. Do something to take your mind off it. I'm not answering questions about every crash and bang. That will just get all of us worked up.'

It must have been quiet for Doug that summer when we were back in Bampton, with neither of the Johns to play with and most of his Newcastle friends having gone home. Once he came to Ada's with me to help to amuse David, but when he saw the photos of Billy he looked so upset that Ada was quite worried about him. I think the end of that holiday couldn't come quickly enough for him.

Meanwhile, Marjorie and I got up to lots of adventures. One day – perhaps hoping to have some peace for a few hours – Aunty wrapped me up a teacake and suggested we climb Knipe Scar. I collected Marjorie at Spruce Cottage and we set off through Bampton Grange to the start of the climb. We had seen men running up it and decided to do the same, but we soon became breathless and changed our minds. The route was dotted with gorse bushes which widened at the top

like giant bunches of flowers. We walked straight up until it
became too steep and we found a path that allowed us to skirt
round the sheer rock face and ascend the last part more gently.
At the summit there was a limestone pavement, like a set of
tables and chairs all laid out for us. We sat down, grateful to
rest our legs. I ate my teacake and Marjorie ate her sandwich.

Looking out across the whole of the valley I felt a huge
sense of pride, not just at the climb we had achieved but also
at seeing my home – for that was how I thought of it now –
laid out so perfectly before us. My own valley! I could name
every place that I could see and even knew the ones that were
just out of sight. Closest was Bampton Grange at the foot of
the fell, with the chapel and the schoolhouse both standing on
their own across the fields beyond. Bampton was on the right
and tiny Butterwick – a clutter of rooftops – further over still.
And in a dark gap at the back lay Haweswater, though we
could only see the fells that enclosed it. The gentle curves of
the High Street range were like a basket of eggs protecting us
from the rest of the world.

'Now we have to wave to Aunty,' I said, raising both arms
in the air.

'How do you know she's looking?' asked Marjorie.

'She told me she would. Let's wave at your house too. We
can find out later if they saw us.'

We both waved frantically for a while, jumped up and
down, shouted 'Yoo hoo!' and greeted everyone we could
think of.

'Now that you've been up Knipe Scar, you're a proper
Bampton girl,' said Uncle that evening as he poked around
in his pipe.

'She already is, dear,' said Aunty.

'There have been many who've tried to put into words what they feel about these parts,' he continued, 'and a fine job they've done. Wordsworth's just one of them. But the fells and the valleys mean something different to every one of us and you will always carry your own in here.' He tapped his heart twice.

I nodded and, as Uncle was starting to sound a bit serious, I said, 'The gorse on the way up reminded me of bunches of flowers, Aunty.'

'Well, I'm glad you didn't pick me any,' said Aunty. 'We'd have both got a right prickling from those thorns.'

'And I waved. Did you see me?'

'Of course I did. I waved back at both of you. And I shouted, "Yoo hoo, Gwenda! Yoo hoo, Marjorie!" Didn't you see me?'

I told her that I had, so as not to disappoint her.

On another day that summer, remembering my lesson from Miss Cartwright, Marjorie and I tried to milk a goat. We had been to see Mavis and found the goat in the quarry at the bottom of the crags on our way back. We looked for something to catch the milk in and found a rusty old can in the stream. The goat was chewing on a branch when we got back to her and so engrossed in what she was doing that she didn't seem to mind our clumsy efforts.

'I thought you knew what to do,' said Marjorie, when I squeezed and nothing came out.

'I do. Sort of. Miss Cartwright showed me. There's a knack to it.' The only thing was, I didn't seem to have it.

'What's Miss Cartwright like?' asked Marjorie, sitting on

the ground beside me. 'Some people say she and her brother are a bit mad.'

'They're both nice really,' I said. 'Except that Albert kept telling us the boggle would get us.'

'And you believed him?'

'No I didn't, but I didn't know what a boggle was then.'

I had learnt since that it was a local word for a ghost or spirit. The goat tossed its head and seemed to look at me disdainfully.

'And what was their POW like? There's one working at Bampton Grange as well. Barbara likes him.'

'Friedrich was nice too. Miss Cartwright said he had better manners than any other man she knew. I wonder why we're fighting them if they're all like that.'

'Well, some of them aren't. Hitler's not.'

I had asked Uncle after chapel one Sunday if God loved Hitler. The preacher had said that God loved everyone, but surely he must have made an exception in Hitler's case. Uncle's reply had been that God did indeed love everyone but that he didn't necessarily love what they did.

I wasn't having very much success with my milking. 'Perhaps she's empty,' I said. 'No, look, here it comes!'

It was only a trickle, but I carried on and in the end we had about an inch in the bottom of the can, enough for a mouthful each. I was glad that my mother couldn't see what we were drinking out of; she would have made one of her comments about catching 'hydrophobia' which was what she said when something wasn't very clean, like a tea towel or an eating utensil. The milk had a strong taste compared to cows' milk and I wasn't sure if I liked it, but I felt a sense of achievement at having produced it. I liked the idea of being a little country girl who could look after herself. If I was ever lost in the wild I could milk a goat, cook crayfish on the fire and find plants and berries that were safe to eat. And Aunty had taught me how to make nettle soup. I might suggest to Mam when the war was over that we all go camping. I wondered what she would think of that.

I heard the sound of Uncle's whistle calling me home for tea and we left the quarry and headed back to the road.

Memories of those who stayed:
'Flying is the life for me!'

Late 1942

Whitley Bay and Monkseaton did not escape the bombs that fell on the North East and we spent many nights in our shelter. After one particularly heavy night of bombing, we got home to find all the windows in our house had blown out and our budgie dead in the bottom of his cage.

Meanwhile, Campbell had gone from his base in Canada to Albany, Georgia, and then to a place called Lakeland in Florida to complete his training. He said he felt sorry for the chaps who hung around the post office for letters that didn't arrive. 'Is there any mail yet?' were the words on everyone's lips. 'Flying is certainly the life for me,' he wrote, and he prayed every night that he would get his wings. Though I knew my grandparents worried about him, they were proud too and happy that he had finally found something he really wanted to do.

'I'm having a magnificent time out here,' he wrote, 'but I would give it all up to be back again. This is the only trouble with having parents you love so much, you can't bear to be parted. As long as I know you are safe and in good health, and you know I am safe and having a good time, we will manage the months I think.'

It would be a year before we saw him again.

Alder Gofton

Chapter twenty-three

As we said our prayers on our last night before he left for Appleby, Doug said to me, 'You won't forget to say them when I'm gone, will you? To ask God to keep Mam and Dad safe. They've worked so far.'

I told him I would remember; after all, they were part of our bedtime ritual. 'And I suppose I'll have to start to pray for you as well,' I said. 'What shall I pray? To make you the fastest runner at Appleby Grammar? Or the best at maths?'

'I don't think prayers work like that,' said Doug, throwing a dirty sock at me. But he added, 'Maybe you could pray that I make friends quickly?'

And so the next day, Uncle took the Austin Seven out of the garage and Aunty and I said goodbye to Doug and another boy from the village who was in the year above and whom Uncle was taking too. He looked unsure all of a sudden, but I think we all knew that Doug was the sort of boy who would settle in quickly. He and Mam had done some shopping when we were home in the summer and Aunty had passed on some of John's old clothes and sports equipment, saying that there was no point in hanging on to these things and that John would have wanted Doug to have them.

I missed Doug when he had gone. The times when it felt strangest were mealtimes, when it was just me and Aunty and Uncle at the table – three of us, when in times gone by it had been four, five or even six! – and always my turn to say grace; or at bedtime, with no one to chatter to before dropping off to sleep, though at least it also meant no one jumping on me pretending to be a boggle. And some of the games we had always played together weren't the same on my own, especially 'Around the World in Eighty Days' which, in fact, had been most successful played with John Stacey, too, when knowing what trouble the three of us would be in if Uncle suddenly appeared in the doorway and saw us clambering on his furniture only added to the thrill. But though life was quieter, I was contented enough. I had my special friends. I knew lots of people in the village. And I was devoted to Aunty and Uncle who, I suppose, thought of me more like a daughter now rather than their evacuee.

One day in October, Marjorie and I set off to pick bilberries. I was going to try to find the patch on Haweswater where Miss Dixon and I had gone picking them two years earlier. As we walked through Burnbanks I saw that it wasn't the lively community it had once been. The dam was finished and most of the workers had gone to war. One summer day the year before I had accompanied Uncle to a special ceremony to mark the end of the building works. There had been games for the children, speeches and a concert in the recreation hall, though Uncle and I had left before the evening festivities began. That hall had gone now – dismantled so that the material could be used more usefully elsewhere – and so had some of the houses.

'Gwenda-suspender and Marjorie Daw!' someone called, and it wasn't a surprise to find the Percy boys running up behind us.

'Where are you going? We need to get away. Mr Ostle's after us. If he catches us again he'll tell our dad and we'll get a right leathering,' said Jez.

'What have you been doing this time?' asked Marjorie.

'Nowt!' said Alf. 'But if anything happens here we always get the blame.'

As we left the village, Jez pointed to the trees ahead and said that there was an opening where bilberries were growing like weeds. 'Race you!' he called to his brother. 'Last one there's a Nazi!'

When we reached them they were tumbling on the ground together, laughing and pummelling each other at the same time. We picked quietly for a while, apart from the odd exchange between the brothers as they wondered which of them was picking the fastest. I knew Aunty was going to be pleased with all these berries. She would make a pie for pudding and she might make jam if she had enough sugar.

'Did you know we're moving to a place on the fells?' Jez said out of the blue. 'Our dad can't fight so he's going to have a go at farming.'

'There's no electric on the farm,' said Alf. 'No lights, no lav, no nothing.'

'You get used to it,' I said like an expert, thinking about life with the Cartwrights, though in truth I wasn't sure I would have liked to live like that all the time.

'Mam's gonna hate it. She likes it here with all the mod cons.'

'Is it you who had those funny men living with you?' I asked them. 'Big Bob and—' I couldn't remember the name of the other one.

'Halifax Pete? That were Tobe,' said Jez.

'What happened to them?'

'Didn't you hear? Big Bob died. It were awful. Everyone round here were right upset.'

'What, in the war?' asked Marjorie.

'No, it was where he went to work when he left here. I think he got crushed by machinery.'

'That's awful,' I said.

'Terrible,' agreed Marjorie.

'And no one knows about Halifax Pete,' said Jez. 'He were always on the move anyway. He could be in Timbuctoo by now.'

'Or Tipperary!' exclaimed Alf.

They both began to march like soldiers and sing 'It's a long way to Tipperary'. The Percy boys always made me laugh. They were a couple of scallywags, as my mother would have said. They got into trouble for playing truant and then got into more trouble on the days when they did turn up for school. Though you wouldn't always know it, Uncle was fond of them. They were always first to volunteer for any special jobs – especially if it meant missing lessons – and were the hardest workers on the school allotment.

One day Uncle had regaled us all at teatime with the story of how the lads had sat and watched someone planting out all his young cabbages and when the chap had gone off for his dinner, they had sneaked into his garden and turned them all upside down. Uncle chuckled over this and Aunty said she hoped that Doug, John Stacey and I didn't think he was condoning this behaviour, though she had a smile on her face too. Uncle said they had been thoroughly reprimanded and made to plant them all properly. But he added that he knew deep down that they were good lads and would turn out all right in the end.

Without Doug to help me, it was my job now to collect the milk from the farm on a Saturday by myself. Thanks to those dogs, it was a job I dreaded. Sometimes I tiptoed, hoping that they wouldn't hear me; other times I stamped my clogs, hoping that I sounded like a man. But whatever I did, they always seemed to know it was me. However, since being shown by Jez Percy how you could swing a bucket of water round in the air without spilling it, I had decided to try this with the milk as I walked home with it. I swung the can round and round. It was heavy, but once I had started, the momentum almost kept it going. It was so clever the way the milk stayed in the can, even when it was upside down. I kept it spinning and then let it come to a juddering halt. I hadn't lost a drop. I began to do this every Saturday until I got a little careless and one day the can shot out of my hand and I lost it all. I didn't know what to do. I was afraid of the farmer's wife, who I was sure didn't like me because her dogs certainly didn't, but knowing that I couldn't return to Aunty empty-handed somehow I plucked up the courage to go back.

The farmer's wife was in the scullery and I told her, as apologetically as I could, what I had done. Luckily she seemed to see the funny side and gave me another can, telling me to be more careful. I was relieved: Aunty need never know. But I must have had a guilty look on my face – as well as being a long time on my errand – as Aunty asked me what had happened and I ended up confessing.

It probably didn't help that just a few days earlier I had nibbled almost half of the yeast I had gone to buy for her while walking home with it across the field from the shop in Bampton Grange – this was the quickest route and my preferred one, even though it meant crossing the beck, sometimes having to hold onto a piece of wire attached to the fence when the water was high. Aunty had been about to send me back to the shopkeeper Mrs Reed to complain about the measure when I had admitted my crime. It was surprising how much those little mouthfuls added up to.

'Gwenda, this never happened when you were with Douglas! What a silly thing to do!'

'I'm sorry, Aunty. I've done it lots of times and I've never dropped it before.'

'Well please don't do it again. You'll turn the milk to butter one day if that's what you do with it.' Then, reading my thoughts, she added, 'No, Gwenda! Don't take that as a challenge!'

Wanting to make up for it, I fetched the clean jugs for her to pour the milk into.

'What are you thinking about, Aunty?' I asked her, seeing a dreamy smile cross her face.

'I was remembering when I was little, I was away from

home once, too, and it was my job to collect the milk, just like you. One day some boys threw stones into the can. I was afraid I was going to get into trouble and I started crying and saying I wanted to go home in Ridley's trap.'

'And did you go home, Aunty?' I asked her.

'No, I don't think so. Not straight away. But it was a long time ago.' Then she said, keeping her eye on the milk as she poured it, 'Do you want to go home soon, Gwenda?'

I thought for just a second. 'I want to live here and go to Newcastle for my holidays.'

There was one other job that Doug and I carried out regularly for Aunty that I disliked and that was cleaning out the hen-house. I suppose it was far easier for us to get right inside it than it was for Aunty. We used wire brushes to scrape out all the dirt – which went into the compost – then gave it a good scrub before putting in fresh straw. The smell was terrible but I tried to think of it as being a small sacrifice for our abundant supply of eggs. I had learnt a lot about poultry-keeping from Aunty. If a hen was broody she knew how to put a stop to it. 'Broodiness begets broodiness,' she would say, and would waste no time in putting a box on top of the hen and leaving her without food for a couple of days which usually did the trick. But sometimes a hen would disappear and we would search the wood for her and find her sitting on her eggs. If I was lucky, by the time Aunty found her it would be too late and she would leave her to finish the job.

One day I went into the kitchen carrying a tiny chicken.

'Look, Aunty, isn't she beautiful!'

'Gwenda, how long have you known about this?'

'I just found her when I went to feed the hens. She must have been hiding somewhere.'

'Hmmm. Well, remember, no chickens as pets. We'll give away the ones we don't need so don't get too attached to them.'

'I won't. But this one is called Buttercup and one of her sisters is called Marigold. Buttercup started to follow me when I walked away. I think it's true that chickens think the first thing they see is their mother.'

'Gwenda! I seem to remember hearing something like this before, only it wasn't chickens that time!' Aunty waggled a finger at me. 'Get that chicken back to where it belongs!'

One day when I had been visiting home, my mother and I had seen some girls from the Central Newcastle High School walking by in their uniforms.

'I'd like to go to that school when I'm older,' I told Mam.

'Humph,' said Mam. 'You won't get in there. That's for clever girls.'

I didn't say anything, but I felt a bit hurt. Most people who knew me thought I was quite a bright girl, though my teacher got frustrated with me for chattering too much and often reminded me that I could do so much better if I would only concentrate. Yet I knew my mother didn't mean to be unkind. It was just her way. She believed very strongly that you did not boast about your own children, however brilliant they might be. It was the way she had been brought up. Modesty was the greatest virtue in her book. But I felt a strong desire to prove her wrong and she agreed that I should sit the school's entrance exam when the time came. There was a paper in maths, one in English and a short interview with the headteacher. I found the written papers quite straightforward as I had covered the work in Bampton and I enjoyed chatting with the head and telling her about my life there.

'So, you must be coming back to Newcastle soon,' she said, and I did feel my mouth go dry for a second before I could formulate a reply as, silly as it sounded, I hadn't really thought of that.

Mam told me I had probably just wasted a morning of my life, then we both forgot all about it.

As we came out of chapel one Sunday in the middle of November, there was a new sound coming across the fields from Bampton Grange. The bells on St Patrick's Church were ringing. There had been no church bells rung in the country since the start of the war as they were supposed to be used as a warning of a German invasion. But that threat had passed and today, Uncle told me, Mr Churchill had ordered bells to be rung across the land to celebrate the British victory a few days earlier in the Battle of El Alamein.

'Does that mean the war's nearly over?' I asked Uncle, holding his hand as we walked. I usually held his hand going to and from chapel as it helped to remind me that I shouldn't run and skip on a Sunday. It wasn't that I actually forgot this rule, it was just that it was my natural instinct to do something other than walk sedately.

Uncle seemed to be weighing the thought up in his mind. 'No-o-o,' he said after a pause, 'it's more a case of what Mr Churchill said a few days ago. "This is not the end; this is not even the beginning of the end. But it is perhaps ..."' He gave me the chance to join in.

'"... the end of the beginning,"' I said with him.

I had heard Uncle and Mr Dargue talking about this speech earlier and about Mr Churchill's way with words. Most people I knew, including my parents, were great admirers of our prime minister; they loved to listen to his voice, said that it made them feel stronger just hearing it and certain that all the sacrifices we were making would be worth it in the end.

Uncle looked down at me. 'Does that make sense?'

'Sort of. The war's still on, but ... we're winning!'

To be honest, I felt almost relieved. I wasn't ready for the war to end yet. Of course I didn't want men to carry on dying, for men like Billy Preston to contract TB and never come home again, for men like Big Bob to die in the industries that were keeping the country on its feet. But, with the selfishness of youth, I was happy enough with my life as it was to want it to continue for just a bit longer.

In a sudden surge of patriotism, I said, 'Can I do some more knitting for our men, Aunty?'

I took her hand in my free one as she drew alongside us. We had reached the lane now. Soon the three of us would sit down to Sunday dinner.

'Gwenda, you can knit whatever you like but you have to finish it. A half-knitted sock or a two-inch-long scarf is not going to keep our boys warm this winter.'

'I really will finish it this time.'

'Hmm, I'll believe it when I see it.'

Mam told me in a letter that she had seen horsedrawn cabs in Newcastle, a product of the petrol shortage. But something else had surprised her even more. 'Some children crossed the road right in front of the horse and, when the driver called out to them to watch where they were going, I got the shock of my life: the driver was a lady! She was wearing trousers and a long coat and I dare say I would have taken her for a man if I hadn't heard her speak and taken a closer look. What is the world coming to!'

Doug came home for Christmas and was full of stories about his new school. Uncle and Aunty looked pleased, though I could see the sadness behind Aunty's smile that John wasn't sitting beside him, joining in. I can only guess that Aunty and Uncle must have made a supreme effort that year to make Christmas feel special for me and Doug. The year before, not only had John been with us and in such rude health – teaching me card games, pelting me with snowballs – but he had fallen ill just a few short weeks later. I think that Doug's return made us feel John's absence more and I know that Aunty cried sometimes when she was with her sister Mary, who was our guest for the holidays as usual.

A few weeks later I noticed that my snowdrops had appeared on the banks of the stream that Doug and John Stacey had diverted. I couldn't remember them coming up the previous year but as Doug and I had been living with the Cartwrights and all those sad things had been happening then, I might have missed them. I rushed into the kitchen to tell Aunty. She wiped her floury hands on her apron and came out into the wood with me. She had a funny sort of smile on her face, one that was happy but sad at the same time.

'Do you know what day it is today, Gwenda?'

I shook my head.

'It's exactly a year since John died. These little flowers will help you to remember him.'

'I do remember him the rest of the time as well,' I said to Aunty.

In some ways John was a larger presence in my life now than he had been when he was alive, when he had been just a bit too old to want to spend a lot of time with me. A portrait of him painted by the baron who lived in Beckfoot, a large house just beyond the hamlet of Butterwick, hung in the dining room, where Uncle did his work. The painting showed John doing one of the things he loved the best – fishing on the riverbank. He was sitting with one leg drawn up towards his body, his face half turned towards the viewer, showing a thoughtful, contented expression. Aunty and Uncle were delighted with the result and one day all the pupils were allowed to leave their lessons to file past it. ('Fancy us being allowed in the head-master's house,' I heard someone say later.)

Whenever I clambered onto the big bike – which was still too big for me! – I thought about the day he and Doug had given me a push and set me off on the circuit from Bampton to Gate Foot to Bampton Grange and back to Bampton. That was the day I had almost run over Elizabeth Castle. And I remembered him when I borrowed his books and saw his name written proudly in the front. When I was beside one of the becks I even sometimes heard his voice in my ear, telling me, 'Sshh, you'll disturb the fish.'

I wondered if Aunty really thought I needed the snowdrops to remember John. It was funny the things that adults said sometimes. Like Judith, like Peterkin, like Billy Preston, you didn't forget people or animals just because they weren't there.

Chapter twenty-four

'You know you'll have to come home one day,' Mam had said to me when I last saw her.

'Of course I will, when the war's over,' I replied, though I wasn't quite sure if I meant it.

My poor mother! It barely occurred to me that she might be missing me and Doug far more than we were missing her and that I ought to at least have tried to show some enthusiasm about returning to where I belonged.

Mam sighed. 'Well, the war has gone through different stages. When we were being bombed, you were safest in Bampton and I wouldn't have wanted you anywhere else. Now, I know the war's still going on but we don't have the same threat. And Newcastle is your home after all. Mr and Mrs Thornton have been very kind, but I'm sure they'd like their house back one day.'

'But the bombing might start again and I might get killed! And anyway, they like having me.'

Mam was right. There were still bombing raids, and Newcastle's neighbour Sunderland suffered considerable damage and loss of life in attacks during May 1943. But these days the news seemed to come mainly from places with far-away names like Stalingrad, where in February the Germans suffered their first major defeat. Three months later they were driven out of North Africa. Were people like my parents and Aunty and Uncle feeling more hopeful that the end was in sight? Perhaps.

There were hardly any Newcastle evacuees left in Bampton, but the fact was I didn't really want to come home. For visits, perhaps, but not for ever. I liked my new life. I liked my place at the table in the schoolhouse kitchen and my bowl with the spots on the bottom. I liked collecting warm eggs and placing them carefully in a basket. I liked my crockery houses in the wood. I liked it when the snow came out of the sky in bucket loads and when the roads sloshed with water. And I liked even more the dewy-light days of summer and their gradual shift into blackberry time.

Later that spring, when Mam wrote and told me that I had passed the entrance exam for Central High, I did feel a small thrill at the thought of myself in the brown uniform, taking my place in a new class and making new friends. It was also satisfying to have proved my mother wrong, though later she would tell me that I had probably only been accepted thanks to my father's occupation – bank manager – on the application form!

Uncle said he was delighted because it proved that Bampton

School was carrying on its long tradition of giving all of its pupils a good education. And he reminded me of the local saying about the school, the one that Miss Williams had baffled me with on my very first day – 'They drove the plough in Latin'. It always caused a picture to pop into my head of men toiling in the village fields wearing togas and with olive wreaths on their heads.

I told Ada one morning that I might be going home soon. I had gone to play with David, who was now two and a half. A photograph of him being held by his father when he was just a few weeks old was on the wall.

'But I'd much rather stay here,' I said, thinking she might be pleased to hear this.

Ada spoke to me more sharply than she had done before. 'Well, Gwenda, we can't always do what we want. You're a lucky girl really because now you've got two homes. You know that Eveline and Dougie are always going to care about you, but your parents sent you here because they love you and you can't punish them now that it's time to go back.'

David and I were building a tower of bricks, though David didn't let me build it very high before taking great delight in knocking it down. I concentrated on balancing another brick on the teetering pile. I thought that if I replied to Ada my voice might falter.

'We'll all miss you, of course,' Ada went on, more gently. 'But that's just life, Gwenda. We all have people we miss.'

I pretended to be annoyed with David for toppling the bricks to the floor and grabbed his hands so that he couldn't do it again until he laughingly wrestled them free. I glanced at the photo of him and Billy. I knew I was being selfish. Ada had lost her husband yet she was always smiling and cheerful. David would never get to know his father. But I still felt sorry for myself. I felt sorry for us all.

One day I was on my way back from one of my dutiful visits to Mrs Morris, my mouth still tingling from the heat of her ginger snaps, when I heard the sound of people on horseback behind me. I moved closer to the hedge to let them pass but as they drew level with me they slowed down and a man called to me, 'Child, can you tell me the way to the blacksmith?'

I knew Mr McCormick well now as I went there to get the clinkers on my clogs replaced when they wore thin, watching him hammering new shoes into the horses. It always made me feel important to wait my turn there.

'It's in Bampton Grange,' I said. 'Umm . . . ' I was wondering whether it was quicker for him to carry on up through Bampton or to turn around and go the other way.

As I was thinking I looked up at the other rider. It was a girl and there was something familiar about the face under the riding hat. When she caught my eye she held my gaze for a few seconds then looked suddenly away. That was when I realised that it was Henrietta, the spoilt child I had been sent to play with almost two years before, and this man – I recognised him now – was her father, though I could see he had no idea who I was.

'I think it's quicker to go back, then turn left,' I said. 'You see, it's actually over there.' I pointed across the fields. 'And when you get to Bampton Grange you go over the bridge, past the vicarage and it's just before the Crown and Mitre on the left.'

'What good directions you give!' said the man. 'Thank you so much.' He nodded at his daughter who was already turning her horse around.

'You must live here,' he added, turning his attention back to me.

I reddened slightly. I was dreading him asking me who I was and realising that we had already met. I didn't want to have to remember that day and certainly not while in his company.

'Um, yes, just up there.' I pointed ahead of me towards Bampton in a rather vague manner.

'I often think it would be nice for my daughter to meet more of the local children. It's terribly quiet where we are and her governess has joined the Women's Land Army.' He lowered his voice slightly. 'She can seem a bit aloof but she's actually quite shy. Henrietta, will you come back here please!'

Henrietta had started trotting away. I felt as if my stomach had dropped into my clogs as he called to her, but she took no notice and carried on.

'Well, never mind,' he said, letting her go without further protest. 'We'll try to sort something out. We live in Stony Grange, not far from here. Perhaps you could look us up one day. We'd be delighted to have you. And your name is?'

The question I had been dreading. No one forgot a name like Gwenda. Was I going to tell him? I didn't like lying – well, except when I really had to. I swallowed and hoped that God wasn't watching.

'Margaret,' I said, surprising myself at how easily it slipped off my tongue. Later I congratulated myself on what a good answer it was as there were several Margarets at school.

The man raised his arm in farewell. 'Well, goodbye, Margaret!' he called over his shoulder. 'Thank you. We'll meet again, I hope.'

He really was a charming man, unlike his daughter.

I told Aunty and Uncle about my encounter at dinnertime, though didn't admit to my deceit.

'You should have made up some directions and sent them on a wild goose chase,' said Uncle, to my delight.

'Douglas!' said Aunty. 'That's not a very Christian thing to suggest.'

'I wish I'd thought of that,' I said.

'You see, you're giving the child bad thoughts. And the little girl might have improved since then. You were both so much younger.'

'Up Bread and Butter Lane and right into Honey Lick Close,' Uncle continued.

I giggled while Aunty shook her head at his childishness.

'Gwenda knows I'm only joking,' said Uncle. 'And anyway, I suppose it was the horses that were in need of the blacksmith and we've nothing against them, have we? Just their riders . . .'

Aunty tutted as she dished out the carrots.

'Have you decided what you're going to recite this year for Whit Sunday?' Uncle asked, suddenly changing the subject.

I said that I hadn't.

'We'll have a look at some poems together later. And I've been penning one of my own about you – it's all about how a girl from *Newcassell* (here Uncle put on a strong Geordie accent) turns into a little Westmorland girl and even starts to talk like one.'

*

Easter fell late this year, so the greenness of summer was in evidence in every hedgerow and garden when Whit Sunday arrived. I wore a dress that Aunty had found for me at a WI jumble sale, almost as good as new.

Without Doug I was the only child reciting two poems this year. It was so unfair of Uncle to expect me to learn two when no one else did! The poem that he had penned produced lots of laughter and I had also learnt Wordsworth's 'Daffodils'.

'I remember that day when you and young Douglas arrived in Bampton as if it were yesterday!' cried Mrs Heatherside after the service. 'How old are you now?'

'Nine,' I replied.

'You were two poor little waifs from the city who didn't know a daffodil from a dandelion! And just look at you now! Nine, did you say? Oh, there's nothing like country air, is there, Mrs Thornton! Those little evacuees fell on their feet coming to us.'

Uncle winked at me and Aunty said that they did indeed.

The summer holidays were getting close and I was looking forward to Doug coming home. When I was on my own I still built my little houses in the bushes with the broken crockery and I spent hours playing Patience. If Aunty and Uncle were both free, which only really happened in the evening, we sometimes played Sevens round the kitchen table.

Oh, I had so many plans! I wanted to sit round a campfire again, though it wouldn't be quite the same with just me and Doug and neither of the Johns for company. Perhaps Aunty Tess and her John would come to stay. I might even agree to help Doug build camps for his soldiers in the mud by the stream if he would do some of the things that I wanted to do. And Marjorie and I were planning to climb Knipe Scar every week and to see if we could do it faster each time. Aunty thought we should just go up slowly and enjoy it, but reluctantly agreed to be the timekeeper, probably reasoning that we would grow bored with the idea.

Then Aunty and Uncle received a letter from my parents informing them that they would be coming to take me home in a few days' time. It was early July 1943, almost three years to the day after Doug and I had arrived in Bampton. I'm not sure why they set their minds on the day that they did, but I imagine that it was simply because Dad was home on leave and might not be again for some time and besides, I had to be home for September and starting my new school. There was a letter for me, too, in which Mam told me that if I was good, perhaps Mr and Mrs Thornton would allow me to come back to stay some time.

The day before they were due Aunty helped me to pack my things. I had started a new batch of knitting – little pouches which were sent to hospitals for soldiers to put their keepsakes into. They were more manageable for me than scarves and socks, which I never had the patience or the enthusiasm to finish.

'I'll have to bring this back when I've finished it,' I said, holding up my latest offering.

Aunty patted my hand. 'There'll be somewhere in Newcastle where you can hand it in. There are lots of people helping the war effort there as well, you know.'

'But I won't know where.'

'Your mother will know, silly. What do you think she's been doing all this time? She's been volunteering with the WVS!'

'I haven't even said goodbye to everyone,' I said, sitting pitifully on my bed. The days seemed to have rushed by since the letter arrived.

Aunty was checking the drawers and the wardrobe. 'Well, you said goodbye to some of the people at chapel and you can pop to Ada's now. But why don't I just tell people you'll be back again to visit soon? At least I hope you will.' She widened her eyes at me as if to say, 'You will, won't you?'

'I'm coming back for all my holidays,' I said, feeling brighter all of a sudden. 'And please tell Hugh I promise not to talk next time he takes me fishing. I really want to catch a trout one day like everyone else does.'

Dad had borrowed Uncle Eddie's car, not having one of his own since selling the Vauxhall Ten when he joined the services. He and Mam accepted Aunty's offer of a cup of tea and a slice of parkin, but said they couldn't stay too long as they wanted to get the car back to Uncle Eddie tonight. Mam told Aunty and Uncle that they could never thank them enough and that they were welcome to come and visit us in High Heaton any time.

'And we're so pleased about Douglas, too,' added Mam. 'He's having a super time in Appleby and there's no reason for him not to finish his education there.'

'Our boys loved it too,' said Aunty and we were all silent for a few seconds.

When I hugged them both goodbye, Uncle said, 'Remember, Gwenda, the Lake District will still be here whenever you want it.' He looked at my parents and chuckled. 'Even when we aren't.'

'Oh, we're not doing badly for our ages, any of us,' said my mother. 'This war keeps us fit, if nothing else. And I think the pair of you have been marvellous having our two and young John Stacey descending on you both for all that time. I don't suppose it's been that much quieter with madam on her own.'

Aunty gave me one of her special smiles and said that we had enjoyed the times we had spent together without any of the boys around.

Then we were in the car and we were leaving and I couldn't quite believe it.

'Are you sure you've got everything, Gwenda?' said Mam, turning round to me in the back seat. 'And all of the things that Douglas left behind? We can't just pop back tomorrow and pick them up.'

I wished that we could, but kept my mouth closed.

Later I heard her say to my father, 'Did you see Mrs Thornton's face? She was white as a sheet.'

I always got a shock seeing the bombed houses in our road. Later they would be demolished, but for now they were a reminder of how close the war had come to our front door.

I hadn't been home for several months. Our house felt small and quiet and somehow ordinary.

While Dad was home we went to visit relatives and I saw Aunty Edith and my cousin Beryl again. Beryl had stayed at home in Whitley Bay and wanted to know all about my evacuation. As a special treat to celebrate us all being together again, Aunty Edith had made a chocolate layer cake which she served with ice cream.

'It's from the Cadbury's Red Cross book,' she said, as we all made satisfied noises over it.

'So we're putting on weight for the war effort,' said Mam, patting her stomach. 'Well, I feel it's my duty, don't you, Edith?'

'Can we have another slice, Mum?' pleaded Beryl, but Aunty Edith said that one was sufficient.

'How many eggs did you use?' asked Mam and Aunty Edith said that the recipe didn't require any eggs, not even egg powder, which was one of the reasons she had wanted to try it.

'Aunty doesn't—' I began and then I stopped as Mam and Aunty Edith's eyes both turned to look at me. I had already made the mistake of comparing something my mother had made to Aunty's cooking. I was learning that it was best not to make comparisons.

'Never mind,' I corrected myself. 'It's delicious cake, Aunty Edith, and I can't remember when I last had ice cream. I hope we can get a fridge one day.'

That was a more welcome statement and Aunty Edith nodded her approval at Mam.

Barbie, Nona and Marion were back on my doorstep, inviting me to play.

As we walked to Paddy's together, I asked Nona and Marion where they'd been and how long they'd been back. No one answered and when I looked at them all three were clutching each other as they tried to suppress giggles. Then they succumbed and burst out laughing.

'You talk so funny!' said Nona.

'I told you she did!' said Barbie.

'No I don't. Maybe I think you do.'

'Now don't sulk.' Barbie linked my arm. 'It's quite a nice

Gwenda and her mother, at home in Newcastle

accent. Just say "oop" one more time and we won't laugh any more.'

It was good to see them again and we picked up our friendship readily, but from time to time our different experiences of the previous three years manifested themselves in different ways. My friends sang songs that I had never heard of and were fond of a game in which we had to reel off the names of film stars but, to their utter disbelief, I had never heard of Cary Grant or Bob Hope, or numerous others who had become big names in recent years. They stared in disbelief the time I wore my clogs and I realised with some reluctance that they weren't suitable footwear for the city. I put them to the back of my wardrobe.

I missed Bampton. I missed Aunty and Uncle and all my friends there. I remembered with a stab to my insides that was almost painful that Hugh had promised to take me fishing one more time and the plans that Marjorie and I had made. I thought about Jenny Charlton and her group of teachers and wondered if they might just turn up one day and the stories I would miss hearing by not being there.

Whenever I was told off for doing something naughty, my frequent retort would be, 'I'm going back to live with Aunty and Uncle in Bampton.'

'Tfff, they're welcome to you,' Mam would say. And if Dad happened to be around, he would chuckle behind his paper.

Aunty wrote to tell me how quiet the place was without me and Doug and how she often wondered what we were getting up to.

I wrote back and told her how Doug was home for the summer but that he considered himself too old to play with me any more and that Mam and I had bought my new school uniform. I also told her I had made plans for my next break from school – the half-term holiday in October. 'I'm coming to Bampton,' I wrote. 'I'll see you and Uncle then.'

Memories of those who stayed:
'It's very exciting but hard to explain'

Summer 1943

Campbell had his wings and he was back in Britain. We were all looking forward to seeing him again in July when he wrote to say that his leave had been cancelled. He had been taxiing his plane along the perimeter track on a very dark night and overshot his point. Instead of waiting for an airman to guide him he had turned his plane round and started back, only for his wing tip to clip the nose of a plane coming the other way. He had been given a severe reprimand, which banned his promotion for a year, but to make matters worse, his three weeks' leave had been cancelled and instead he had to take a three-week discipline course. He sounded disillusioned by the severity of the punishment, particularly at losing his leave, but ended his letter cheerfully, reminding my grandmother that he was short of socks, hankies and pyjamas.

Soon after that he was flying raids from Leeming in Yorkshire over Germany. He had a brand new plane that he shared with another pilot. 'It is very exciting but hard to explain on paper,' he wrote. 'Keep smiling.'

We saw him once more and had a get-together in my grandparents' garden. His great pal Harry Brittain, who was also in the RAF, was on leave at the same time and came too. They were both joking and laughing as usual.

One day there was a knock on the door and it was Grandpa, telling us that Cam was missing in action. It was six months before his death was officially confirmed. He had been killed in a raid over Germany on the night of 31 August 1943.

His brother, my Uncle Dick, who always had a way with words, composed an epitaph for his grave, which is in the Reichswald Cemetery in Germany:

> *In proud memory of Cam*
> *The future must be great*
> *To be worth his passing.*

Alder Gofton

Campbell (right) and his friend Harry Brittain, who was also killed while serving in the RAF

Afterword

I wonder if I ever really considered what a wrench it must have been for Aunty and Uncle to let me go after all that time. It was difficult enough for me, but I was a child and highly adaptable. And I had a new school to look forward to, friends to be reunited with and parents who loved me. But I had become the daughter Aunty and Uncle did not have and I know that they missed me very much.

However, I *did* go to Aunty and Uncle's during my next school holiday and it remained my second home for the rest of my childhood. I loved to spend time there, catching up with my old friends and becoming a country girl again.

Aunty and Uncle set up a prize at Appleby Grammar some time after John's death to be awarded to the best all-round pupil and to their delight, Doug won it one year.

I continued to visit Ada, who later bought the old mill

house and converted it to a beautiful home. In 1980 she was awarded the MBE in recognition of her services to the community. As well as spending many years as postmistress and shopkeeper she was also a longstanding member of the WI and the chapel, a parish councillor and a school dinner lady. I also remember going to see Miss Williams, the teacher I had got to know so well from her daily visits to the schoolhouse kitchen. By then she was married and had her own family.

My visits to Bampton grew less frequent when I began my nurses' training in 1952 and later went to nurse in London and America, but I continued to write to Aunty and Uncle while I was away and they to me.

When I met Alder Gofton, my future husband, I naturally took him to meet them. To my amusement – and to Alder's horror – Uncle took Alder into his office to give him a grilling! (I think he must have passed the test, despite not being a Methodist . . .) At our wedding in July 1961 my father gave me away but we asked Uncle to give the speech, something my father was more than happy for him to do.

On Uncle's retirement as headmaster they moved to the old schoolhouse in Bampton Grange and that was where I took my own children to visit them every summer. The older two, Barbara and Sarah, remember how we used to take fishing nets and play by the river just at the foot of the garden. Sometimes Hugh, by then a teacher in Huddersfield, would be there too with his wife Mildred and daughter Hilary. Alder, Barbara and I spent a lovely day with Hilary (now Hilary Horgan) this summer, forty-five years after our previous meeting!

Our visits continued right up until they left Bampton shortly before their deaths in the early 1970s.

Douglas and Eveline with their son
Hugh and his daughter Hilary

Douglas and Eveline with baby
granddaughter Hilary

Hilary Thornton holds Barbara
Fox as a baby, 1962, with
Hilary's mother Mildred and her
grandparents Eveline and Douglas

Gwenda Gofton, Hilary Horgan,
Barbara Fox, summer 2015

Sadly Bampton School closed in 2005 and several centuries of education in the village came to an end. On its closure I attended an open day for past and present students and even had my photo taken for the local paper with the current head-teacher and two other former pupils.

When I began Central High School in September 1943 I met a girl called Daphne. She turned out to be Miss Dixon's niece, the very girl I had modelled jumpers for, and we became good friends. Miss Dixon had a cottage in Redesdale in Northumberland and after the war she invited me and Daphne to stay there in the holidays. We slept in a shed which had bunk beds and it felt like a great adventure.

I stayed friends with the Birdman, even writing to him from America. I wanted to invite him to my wedding – after all, he had known me and Doug since we were very small – but my mother wouldn't hear of it.

In adulthood I bumped into my former neighbour Jean Farnsworth, now Atkinson, whose father was lucky to survive being blown out of bed, as we have some mutual friends. Also through mutual friends (Newcastle feels quite a small place at times!) I met Philip Orde, the boy whose marriage proposal I had accepted as a six-year-old as we prepared to leave Newcastle. After worrying about him for all that time I was a little peeved to find he had no memory of it!

I lost my brother Doug too young – he was only sixty-four when he died in 1995. Not long before his death we had been talking about trying to find out what happened to Ivy, who had disappeared from our lives after the war, but sadly we never got round to it and now it is probably too late.

*

The Lake District has always been one of our family's favourite places and somewhere we have loved to share with visitors from other parts of the UK and overseas. It must be thirty years ago that Alder and I were lucky enough to be offered the chance to stay in the holiday cottage in Butterwick that belonged to friends we made in our parish in Newcastle. Butterwick is just a couple of miles from Bampton, so I was able to return to my childhood haunts once more. We still go to the cottage twice a year, usually with Pat Small – my nursing friend and fellow traveller in the book *Bedpans and Bobby Socks*. It was during one of these stays that I renewed my friendship with John Stacey. John had been a solicitor in London but continued to return

Gwenda Gofton and John Stacey, at Haweswater, October 2015

to Bampton for family holidays, eventually retiring to a house just outside the village with his wife Felicity.

Now we spend an evening with John on every visit, as well as bumping into him in St Patrick's Church in Bampton Grange on Sundays – now that I am also an Anglican! Uncle's beloved chapel was closed some time ago and has been converted to a family home.

Long after I left Bampton, the snowdrops continued to come up every year where I had planted them. Perhaps they still do.

Gwenda Gofton, Ponteland, Newcastle, July 2015

Acknowledgements

How do you write a book about something that happened so long ago? Gwenda's memories about what was such a key part of her childhood are very vivid, but most of the others who could have contributed to the book are, sadly, long gone. While I have used some artistic licence in telling her story, with her help I have done my best to make it as accurate as possible and to ensure that all the characters speak and behave as she remembers them. The intention has been to highlight the truth rather than to mask it. Only a few names and details have been deliberately changed.

I would like to thank all of the people and organisations below, without whom the book could not have been written.

John Stacey, Gwenda's fellow evacuee at the schoolhouse, answered endless questions, supplied photographs and spent time ferreting out information for me in Bampton's Tinclar

Library. (This library, with its wealth of material of local and other interest, dates from the eighteenth century and is open to the public on a monthly basis.) I am particularly grateful for permission to print an extract from Uncle's school logbook, which forms the whole of Chapter twenty.

David Preston, whom I contacted out of the blue, willingly told me more about his parents, Ada and Billy, and allowed me to use some of his family photos.

Hilary Horgan, Aunty and Uncle's granddaughter, shared wonderful memories of her father Hugh and her grandparents as well as providing other information and photographs.

Aunty's nephew John Waddell, who has written his own family history, was a great source of information about Aunty and her family and provided lovely photos.

Jean Atkinson, Barbie Cawthorne, David Cawthorne, Alder Gofton, Emily Meek and Patricia Small all provided fascinating anecdotes about wartime life on Tyneside.

Ploughing in Latin, the book published for the millennium by Bampton and District Local History Society, and the interviews that the Society carried out for its Burnbanks project, allowed me to imagine I was in Bampton even when I was three hundred miles away and to step back in time there.

Peter Bolger's excellent website, North Shields 173, dedicated to the Wilkinson's Lemonade air shelter disaster, alerted me to Emily Meek and her story. Thanks to Peter and Emily herself for permission to retell her account of that night.

The online resource North East Diary 1939–1945 by Roy Ripley and Brian Pears, which chronicles the war day by day as it affected north-east England, was a constant source of reference.

A hand-drawn map of Bampton by my father, Alder Gofton, formed the basis for the version in this book drawn by my husband, Mike Fox. Thanks to them both for putting my vision onto paper.

Thank you for all their hard work to editor Rhiannon Smith at Little, Brown, to copy editor Jayne Booth, production controller Marie Hrynczak, publicist Kirsteen Astor and to designer Bekki Guyatt.

And thank you as always to my editor Hannah Boursnell and my agent Sallyanne Sweeney who both seem to know instinctively which of my ideas are worth pursuing and help to shape the good ones into the books they eventually become.

Barbara Fox